TH FINAL WHISTLE?
Scottish Football:
The Best and Worst of Times

THE FINAL WHISTLE?
Scottish Football:
The Best and Worst of Times

———

HARRY REID

Birlinn

This edition published in 2005 by Birlinn Ltd
West Newington House
10 Newington Road
Edinburgh EH9 1QS

www.birlinn.co.uk
In association with The Saltire Society
Copyright © Harry Reid 2005

ISBN10: 1 84158 362 6
ISBN: 978 1 84158 362 4

British Library Cataloguing-in-Publication Data
A catalogue record for this book is available from the British Library

Typesetting and origination by Initial Typesetting Services, Edinburgh
Printed and bound by Thomson Litho Ltd, East Kilbride

CONTENTS

PREFACE

The faults of this book are mine and mine alone, but for its inception I blame the Saltire Society. This excellent body exists to nurture and promote all that is vigorous and worthwhile in Scottish culture, not just in terms of heritage but also in terms of Scotland's ongoing achievement. The current chairman of the society is an indefatigable enthusiast called Ian Scott, and Ian firmly believes that football is a key component in Scotland's cultural life, in the best and widest sense of that term.

It was at a meeting in the society's premises at Fountain Close, Edinburgh in the late summer of 2004 that this book was born. There was a discussion about a series of small books the society has published on various aspects of Scottish culture. I suggested that football might be an appropriate subject for a future book in the series, and at this point one of those present, the publisher Hugh Andrew, managing director of Birlinn, suddenly became animated. Before we quite knew what was happening Hugh and I had decided to go ahead with a book on Scottish football, but not as part of the Saltire Society series.

Although the Saltire Society is not responsible in any way for the contents of this book, or indeed for its publication, the society's personnel – and in particular Ian Scott himself – have been supportive throughout the project.

The second point to emphasise is that this is a personal book. The first part consists of a wholly subjective account of my experiences as a Scottish football fan, and indeed as a Scottish journalist. But although much in the book is unashamedly individual and idiosyncratic, I've had to remember that football is also about facts and tables and statistics. Indeeed, football is a fertile field for obsessives, statisticians and other anoraks. I have tried hard to be accurate throughout, and checked all facts as scrupulously as I could. In this context I wish to mention a book which was published earlier this year, in May 2005, just as I was finishing this project.

The Roar of the Crowd by David Ross (Argyll Publishing) is largely about attendances at Scottish football matches. This might seem an arcane subject, but I had myself rapidly concluded that the size of crowds over the years was a very important matter. For example, during the brief period of 'New Firm' dominance in the early 1980s, the crowds who watched Aberdeen and Dundee United were for the most part desperately disappointing. David Ross's publisher, Derek Rodger, sent me proofs of his excellent book and I was most interested in the fruits of his researches.

The final point to make is that the pages that follow are essentially about organised, professional league football. They are not about women's football, or the burgeoning five-a-side game, or schools or junior football.

There is at the end a list of the people to whom I am indebted. I wish to dedicate the book to three exceptional footballing men who have not just contributed enormously to Scottish football over the years, but have also given me, in their different ways, many magnificent memories, which I shall cherish till I die. These three men are Sir Alex Ferguson, Willie Miller and Alex 'Faither' Smith.

Harry Reid, 7 June 2005, Edinburgh

INTRODUCTION

Football, the beautiful game, the people's game, has had a bad press in recent years, particularly in England but also right across Europe. Paradoxically, in Scotland, though our world standing has slipped disastrously and our league football has deteriorated alarmingly, we have escaped many of the more noxious problems that have polluted the game elsewhere.

The professional game has been with us for well over a century and for most of this time football's all-embracing and demotic popularity made it a crucial part of the people's culture. Loyalty, dignity, continuity and decency were often qualities associated with the professional game. Clubs related to the communities that spawned them. The essentially mercenary nature of professional football did not overcome its ability to offer many millions of people, whether they themselves could play the game well or not, glimpses of glory and beauty and a more constant if vicarious fulfilment. Identity with a club, its traditions, its fortunes and its vicissitudes gave many ordinary people a sense of personal worth they might not otherwise have had. National teams, particularly in smaller countries such as Scotland, helped to nurture notions of national pride and uniqueness.

Even when the bad times came, with stadium disasters or corruption or vicious hooliganism, the game seemed to be able to regroup – a favourite football word – and move on, renewed and cleansed. Football lived a charmed and apparently progressive existence.

Then, as the game grew yet more popular, a canker began to grow. A few big clubs across Europe consolidated their power. They dominated that money-spinner the Champions League, and they excelled at marketing and began to present themselves as brands first and clubs a poor second. These clubs in some ways became more important than countries; national teams could seem insignificant compared to the behemoths of the club game. And these European superclubs gobbled up the world's best players, including the cream from the two faraway countries that continued to produce the world's most thrilling footballers: Brazil and Argentina.

A parallel, debilitating process occurred. Football, once a noble mani-festation of people's art, became introverted and spiteful in its self-love, its egotism and its overweening distance from ordinary and real lives. The commercialism became consummate. The superclubs reached out to millions worldwide through television and through the high-powered marketing of their franchised goods, but this global business also and ironically brought forth a new parochialism. Football, at the top level, became trapped within its own boorish bubble, and the old notions of decency, restraint, loyalty and continuity started to disappear. One or two of the huge clubs managed to hold on to these old-fashioned qualities more than others, but the overall trend was not ameliorative. The game's princes and generals, its stars and idols, its potentates and pendragons, became super-rich and more and more distant from the loyal footsoldiers, the fans.

A few of the great managers, notably Sir Alex Ferguson and Sir Bobby Robson, had the necessary character and understanding to keep in touch with the older values even as they succeeded as leaders in this new, harsher, dispensation. But for many of those who benefited most from the new, more sullied era, there seemed to be no cord or link stretching back to the past, even the relatively recent past. And so the people's game became wrapped in a clinging gloss of spurious glitzy glamour and at times seemed to nurture a contempt for the real world, and the millions of ordinary folk who ultimately sustained it, believing that no outsiders could teach it anything.

Scotland, happily, was to large extent immune from this process. But at the same time Scottish football was in acute decline and it would be wrong to get too misty-eyed about the couthiness, the quaintness and the sheer commercial incompetence that characterised our lopsided league structure, our often bungling administrative bodies and our floundering club directors.

Further, it must be remembered that a lesser and parallel revolution happened here too. Indeed, the importance of the changes instigated by Graeme Souness and David Murray at Rangers FC in the late 1980s cannot be underestimated. These changes placed enormous pressure on the other member of the Old Firm, Celtic, and the Parkhead club eventually responded, though not before it had come perilously close to bankruptcy.

Despite their strength and their wealth, the two Old Firm clubs had never before realised their commercial potential. They had sold their best and most exciting players to English clubs (notable examples being Jim Baxter from Rangers to Sunderland, Paddy Crerand from Celtic to Manchester United, Alex Scott from Rangers to Everton and Kenny Dalglish from Celtic to Liverpool). But suddenly this changed. These clubs were projecting themselves as brands and were being marketed to a constituency far beyond

Scotland. They created super stadia and a huge season ticket-holding fan base (based on the notion that if you wanted to see the top games, you had to pay for the dire ones too). They were buying in world class players, from England and beyond. Scottish talent seemed almost incidental to their aspirations. And so insidious aspects of the malaise that was bedevilling the game elsewhere became apparent in Scotland too. Megamoney was spent on players who came and went in, it seemed, the blink of an eye. Some hyper-expensive mercenaries hardly kicked a ball.

The two famous Glasgow clubs seemed at last to have completely out-grown the Scottish game, with its three separate administrative bodies and its slightly mothballed, blazer-ridden, old-fashioned governance. The Old Firm had dominated the first hundred years of Scottish league football. Now they seemed set to smother all the other Scottish clubs to the point of total eclipse, and this process looked like lasting indefinitely.

Fans of other Scottish clubs (such as myself) viewed the Old Firm with an unfortunate admixture of disdain and suspicion and resentment. These are not pleasant qualities and I regret them. In the past the Old Firm had nurtured magnificent Scottish players of the calibre of Jim Baxter and Willie Henderson, of Kenny Dalglish and Jimmy Johnstone (though Baxter was purchased by Rangers from Raith Rovers in 1960, when he was 20). No self-respecting Scottish fan, whichever team he supported, could gainsay the genius of such players, who illuminated game after game the length and breadth of Scotland. But when the Old Firm clubs put out teams with at best a couple of Scottish players, this lingering cause of respect vanished.

When I started this book I suspected that it would be better for everybody if the two great Glasgow clubs departed Scottish football for lusher pastures elsewhere. But as I wrote it I was conscious that I was changing my mind. I am now convinced that they should stay. It is in a sense up to the rest of us to make them want to stay.

They have not completely outgrown Scottish football, but we have come close to that position. The Old Firm account for almost seventy per cent of the combined turnover of the twelve SPL clubs. Playing to home crowds of more than 50,000, they accentuate ridiculous crowd disparities that must be the greatest of any league in Europe. They generate a huge amount of cash; according to the Fraser of Allander Institute, the two clubs support more than 3,000 jobs and contribute £118 million annually to the Scottish economy.

But on the playing side, which surely is what ultimately matters most, there has been too facile and timid an acceptance of the myth that the Old Firm are utterly out of reach. In recent years the other leading clubs have not even tried to match them; there has been a degrading poverty of aspiration and a lack of any kind of ambition, even realistic ambition. These other clubs have in effect decided that the real battle, for generations to come, is for third place. This is shameful. It is also, or should be, unacceptable. There are clubs in Scotland that, as I seek to explain in Part Three of this book, could still aspire to a challenge to the Old Firm that could be sustained. Too many people in Scottish football now take it as given that the Old Firm are sublimely installed, untouchable and aloof, in their own separate stratosphere. That need not be the case.

And, to be fair to the two Old Firm clubs, their overall contribution to the Scottish game has been so rich and so vast that it would be sad to see them go to another league. As I suggest above, any Scottish fan who had the privilege of watching the Rangers team of Jim Baxter, Willie Henderson and the young John Greig, or the Celtic team of Bobby Murdoch, Jimmy Johnstone and Billy McNeill saw something that was very special indeed, even in world terms, and therefore must surely have some sense of the awesome contribution of these clubs to the overall Scottish game.

I realise that is a sentimental argument and there is of course danger in sentiment. The wider Scottish game needs realism, patience, vision and ambition and these qualities are difficult enough to find in isolation; to find them added together is a huge ask. There is no longer any room for incompetence or amateurishness in what is after all a professional game. But nor, in Scotland, should we vitiate our game with an arrogant, all-consuming commercialism. We should seek to retain the dignified values of continuity and the socially cohesive values of community links. Somehow we must cling to the best of the past while we embrace the better aspects of the new commercialism.

Scottish football was born out of industry, in the gritty heartlands of Lanarkshire, Ayrshire and Fife, and also, though to a lesser extent, in the cities, particularly Glasgow, Edinburgh and Aberdeen. That fine football historian Bob Crampsey speaks elsewhere in this book of these magnificent breeding grounds, and the Scottish footballer emerging from deprivation. Well, things have changed and our football has to come to terms with a new sociology. Other European countries of Scotland's size have not experienced the heavy, dirty industrialisation that was the hallmark of Scotland, economically and socially, for several generations. So they have not had to confront the brutal and painful loss of industrialisation. Of course there have been huge benefits in that process but it is indubitable that in Scotland there was a link between the shipyards and the coalmines and the factories and a uniquely Scottish style of football.

Now some of these other countries, with a demographically smaller player base, are achieving much more than we are in Scotland in the vital basics: the provision of training facilities, of indoor playing areas and all-weather pitches, and so on. Norway is a classic example. Our game needs practical investment in facilities and the lead for this must come from the top, from the Scottish Parliament.

There is a lot in this book about the era when just about every boy in Scotland played football of some kind. If you didn't, you were aberrant. In Part Two Alan Hansen says simply that if you didn't play, there was something wrong with you. And it's true. In the 1930s, 1940s and 1950s, and into the 1960s, hundreds of thousands of boys played, in these huge, sprawling, anarchic games. They have been called informal games but that is putting it mildly. You played even if you were no good. I was no good, certainly far less good than my more athletic brother, but even I can remember playing till dark and getting rows for coming home late. Games started immediately after school and went on, it seemed, forever. Two or three aside became fourteen or fifteen aside. All you needed was a ball, of whatever kind.

Anyway, my inability to play football with even a modicum of skill or distinction maybe rendered me all the more appreciative of those who do have the skill – and so many Scots did, and still do. I am enormously grateful to all the Scottish professional footballers who have entertained me so richly, occasionally sublimely, over the years.

I'd also like to write in general defence of the Scottish professional footballer, who has not always had a good press; a few of them may have been yobs and hooligans, but they are a small minority. Most of them are very decent people.

When I was researching this book I was waiting to interview a well-known Scottish player. When he hove into view he was intercepted by a club official who told him about a young boy, a fan of his club, who was hospitalised and seriously ill. The boy's parents and the medical team thought that nothing could give him a greater boost than a surprise visit from one of his favourite players. The proposed time was ten the coming Saturday. 'Of course', said the player. 'Give me the details.' Just like that. That is the other side of professional football, and we should never forget it.

Meanwhile, to return to those years, the 1940s, '50s and '60s, the potential player pool then was so immense that genuinely great players emerged with bewildering and thankful frequency.

But in the contemporary world there are many other options for our young people. We live in a more self-centred, consumerist age. There are paradoxes. Alcohol, and to a lesser extent drugs, have never been more readily available for young people; in other ways they are much more protected than they were before.

There is more traffic in the streets, there are (scandalously) fewer football fields, even public parks are sometimes no-go areas, and the emphasis is swinging to individual rather than team sports. The secondary schools, which used to be academies of excellence, no longer regard football as any kind of priority. And the computer is everywhere, not least in the boy's bedroom.

Yet from all I have heard and seen, there are still many, many Scottish boys who do want to play football, and quite a few of them actually do so. A young Rangers fan, John Loughton, quoted at length elsewhere in this book, said to me: 'Some young lads are obsessed with playing football. Probably a smaller number than there used to be; OK. But the youngsters now make this deliberate decision: they either endorse the game or they refuse it. They make a choice. There are so many other cool things to do than just play football. So those who do choose football are committed and enthusiastic.' But he went on to say that far too many of these enthusiastic youngsters were not shown the way to the next stage, not shown that if they worked hard at the game then there was this pathway onto better things.

We need to get more of them started, and more crucially, we then need to help them hone their skills and learn all aspects of the game. The current tragedy is that some of the most able and skilful ones succumb, round about the age of twelve or thirteen, to debilitating peer pressure. They often start drinking, and they lose the desire to practise and to learn.

It is hard to underestimate the ease with which very young Scots can get hold of alcohol. An entire generation is in danger of being wasted. To make it as a footballer you need considerable mental strength but you also need help and support, and at present our wider Scottish society is not doing anything like enough to help our young athletes to counter the insidious and wasting temptations of a booze-ridden youth culture.

I believe that football could become a kind of counter culture. Young footballers need to be nurtured in a culture of commitment, of dedication and discipline. It is not too fanciful to suggest that football could become a means of social regeneration, and could instil hope and purpose into many barren lives. Of course this applies to all sports, but football, with its remaining and peculiarly potent hold on Scotland's national imagination, has a head start.

Finally, there is a lot of nostalgia in this book — that is the prerogative of the football fan through the generations — but I have tried to temper it with realism. Interspersing the reminiscence there is, I trust, the hard business of lessons being learned and conclusions being drawn. There is also much in the book about the Scottish Press. This is partly because for most of my working life I laboured in the vineyard of Scottish journalism, but more importantly it is because the two worlds — that of the football club and the newspaper — used to be almost inextricably intertwined, not always for the best.

And I do remain, as I suspect most proper football fans are, a sentimentalist. As a longstanding Aberdeen fan, my greatest moment must have been when Aberdeen won the European Cup Winner's Cup in 1983, although, as I shall explain, that is not my single fondest memory.

Late on that glorious night in Sweden — indeed sometime early the next morning — I found myself, amid the crescendoing celebrations, aware of a small, lingering sadness. Why on earth was this the case? Slowly, I understood. Aberdeen's opponents, Real Madrid, were managed by the legendary Argentinian Alfredo di Stefano. I had never seen him play, but I'd seen plenty of blurred film footage of his wonderful artistry, and I knew enough about the game to know that he was the most celebrated forward of all time, with the possible exception of Pele.

So in a stupid, irrational kind of way, I did not think that such a titan of the game deserved to lose, even if he was infinitely poorer as a manager than a player, even if his team played with none of the swashbuckling grace that marked his own playing style, and even if that would have meant defeat for my club in their biggest-ever game. Stupid. Even downright crazy. But then most football fans are a little crazy — especially Scottish ones. In Part Three of this book I outline various ways in which the Scottish game can be revived.

That is the great end. Some might accuse me of wishful thinking, even of being crazy, but as I say, football fans are a little crazy, and anyway a lot of useful and important work has already started. We must all, in our different ways, help to see it through. The Scottish psyche is infatuated with football. It is a crucial component of our national life, it is part of our very identity, and we simply cannot, as a nation, allow our football to wither and die.

PART ONE
TRUE TALES FROM ANOTHER CENTURY

The past is a foreign country. They do things differently there.
– L P Hartley

The past is full of life eager to irritate us, provoke and insult us, tempt us to destroy or repaint it.
– Milan Kundera

CHAPTER 1

CHARLIE COOKE

When I started work on this book, I took to applying what I now think of as the Charlie Cooke test. I asked whoever I was interviewing 'Do you remember Charlie Cooke?' or 'Have you heard of Charlie Cooke?'

Charlie was the first footballer who caught my imagination. Gallus, infuriating, impossibly talented, he played for Aberdeen in the early 1960s, moved on briefly to Dundee, was transferred to Chelsea (as the replacement for Terry Venables) where, in the late 1960s, he teamed up with Peter Osgood and gained celebrity status.

He was capped only 16 times for Scotland, a reflection of the abundance of talent that was on tap in the 1960s, perhaps, in retrospect, Scottish football's greatest era. Mind you, that did not appear to be the case as you stood on the dilapidated Pittodrie terraces in the east end of Aberdeen watching dismal fare in crowds of 4,000 or less.

Pittodrie Park (as it was known then; it was renamed Pittodrie Stadium when it became Britain's first all-seated ground in the late 1970s) is the home ground of Aberdeen FC, otherwise known as 'the Dons'. It is situated close to the North Sea and it can be a bitterly cold place. Most football grounds were grim in the 1960s but Pittodrie, though I came to love it, was particularly bleak.

I remember once standing at the side of the Paddock, as it was fancifully named, at the King Street end of the ground. A rotten game had just enough life left in it to die. An old man had seen enough. He shuffled past, enunciated one rasping word: 'Putrid' – and spat viciously. The gobbet was caught in the swirling wind. It described a crazy parabola and splattered spectacularly against the wall. There was more drama in that angry moment than there had been in an hour and a half on the park.

Before Charlie Cooke, there was Graham Leggat. As a schoolboy at the primary department of Aberdeen Grammar School I was no good at football and for the most part uninterested in sport. With a slightly swotty disdain I generally left that kind of thing to my more robust pals and my more athletic brother Hugh. I was therefore amazed at the excitement that my schoolmates evinced one morning sometime in the mid to late 1950s when we were unexpectedly taught PE by a quietly spoken young trainee who looked like a clean-cut rock'n'roll singer (in those days, clean-cut rock'n'roll singer was not a contradiction in terms). He had appeared, without prior warning, in the huts at the back of the school that in these austere post-war years were used as make-do gyms.

His name was Graham Leggat. I'd never heard of him. To most of my mates, he was a celebrity, a superstar, even a god. That particular PE lesson was delayed for about twenty minutes as excited schoolboys scrabbled desperately for paper and pens to get his autograph. Youngsters are connoisseurs of sincerity and I noticed how he scribbled his name and good wishes on grubby scraps of paper with artless modesty and consummate patience.

A few years later, I learned all about Graham Leggat. He was an outstanding, genuinely world-class footballer. He would walk into the England, let alone the Scotland team, of today and could easily earn £50,000 a week or more. When he pitched up as a trainee PE teacher he was also plying his other trade as an inventive, versatile right winger with Aberdeen.

Graham helped Aberdeen to their first league championship in 1955. He also helped the Dons hammer Rangers 6–0 before a six-figure crowd at Hampden in a cup semi-final of 1954. Four years later, he played for Scotland in the World Cup Finals in Sweden. Then he was off to England, signing for Fulham, then a significant force. He formed a devastating partnership with the inside forward Johnny Haynes, England's first £100-a-week (about eight times the then average wage) footballer. Graham scored a hat-trick against Manchester United at Old Trafford, he scored another hat-trick against Ipswich in the space of four minutes, and he was selected for a world eleven.

Graham Leggat was not, however, the most exciting footballer to emerge in Aberdeen in the post-war years. At the same time as he was beginning to dazzle on the right wing at Pittodrie, a skinny bespectacled kid from the Powis area somehow slipped though his home town team's porous local scouting net and started his professional career with Huddersfield Town. His name was Denis Law. In those days, Scottish world class footballers seemed to grow on trees.

It was a few years after my encounter with Graham Leggat, when I was in my early teens, in the early 1960s, that I was introduced to

Pittodrie by my brother Hugh, who was already a committed Dons fan. Like so many other genuine football fans, I do not know why or how I was smitten, but smitten I was. (Aberdeen were then in serious decline after the glory years of the 1950s; it was not as if they were winning regularly or playing spectacular, or even just entertaining, football.) The unlikely talents of Charlie Cooke, rendered even more magical by their dismal and uninspiring context, must have had something to do with it.

Anyway, I learned rapidly about the cruelty of football. I learned about the passionate impotence of the fan on the terraces. Time and again, Charlie would mesmerise the opposition single-handedly, and yet Aberdeen would still lose.

But my loyalty to Aberdeen FC was born. It has been one of the constants in my life for over forty years, and it will be till I die. It is at once pathetic and glorious, this utterly irrational loyalty. My moods on Saturday evenings are to this day dictated by the performance of the Dons. A good result means good spirits for the rest of the weekend.

Charlie Cooke, however, was about more than mere results – that was part of the problem. He made his debut in 1960 and for the next four years he was by far Aberdeen's best player. As such he was always on the verge of being transferred, though I didn't know it at the time. He was almost sold to Leeds United in 1962; in return Aberdeen would have received Billy Bremner, plus a cash adjustment.

Charlie had a special penchant for what the football writers used to call 'mazy dribbles'. He was exquisitely balanced and could beat three or four opponents with gracious, beguiling ease. Football is a team game and the Scots are supposed to have invented the passing game, which is all about teamwork, but archetypal Scottish players like Charlie were at their best as individuals.

The trouble was that there was frequently no end-product to Charlie's pyrotechnics; the tantalising pass at the end of the extravagant dribble petered into no-man's-land, certainly to where none of his colleagues had anticipated. Too often Charlie's cheeky play ended up 'a blin end', as we Scots like to call a cul-de-sac. It was a broad, sunny, expansive blin end, but a blin end nonetheless.

Charlie could, if he wanted, pass the ball beautifully, but more times than not he didn't make allowances for his more limited team-mates. The thought did occur to me, and to some other supporters, that perhaps he mischievously liked to show up his colleagues.

But his effervescent skill and his endless impish improvisation lit up many a dreich afternoon or evening at Pittodrie. And he kept some of his best displays for away games; for some reason, his play was less selfish away from home. At Dens Park on New Year's Day, 1964, I saw him mastermind a wonderful 4–1 victory over a Dundee team, Alan Gilzean *et al*, that had eight months previously marched to the semi-final of the European Cup.

Later that year, I saw him show unlikely grit in a totally lost cause against Hearts, inspired by Willie Wallace, the future Lisbon Lion, at Tynecastle. Aberdeen were 5–1 down at halftime but Charlie inspired a second half fightback, scoring a rare goal himself. The final score was 6–3 but the Dons had rattled Hearts and made a game of it.

A couple of days later Charlie was sold to Dundee for a ludicrously low fee. It seemed the bitterest of betrayals. I was to learn that such betrayals are part and parcel of the life of most Scottish football fans. The next Saturday, a Cooke-less Aberdeen team entertained (ironic word) Clyde at Pittodrie. It was a filthy day and perishing Pittodrie was shrouded in a raw haar. There was a pitiful crowd of less than 3,000 – the meagre ranks of the loyal, or, to look at it another way, the daft residue of the betrayed. The score was Aberdeen 0, Clyde 3. It was the most acrid day of my football-watching career, an early lesson in rancid disenchantment.

I don't know what the management and board of Aberdeen FC were thinking of when they sold Cooke to our nearest rivals for just £40,000. Suffice to note that Dundee sold Charlie on to Chelsea less than eighteen months later for £72,500. That was the day after he had been voted Player of the Year by Dundee's fans. Aberdeen supporters were not the only ones who were betrayed. In these years there was an abundance of playing talent on the pitch and a total lack of everything that mattered off it: vision, investment, competence – you name it. The fans had recourse to only one method of signifying their disgust: withdrawing their support. And of course many of them did. They also relied on the press to articulate their fury, and in Aberdeen a marvellous journalist called Jimmy Forbes, who worked for many years for the *Evening Express*, was excellent at doing just that.

Nowadays, with fanzines, the internet, phone-ins and so on, the fans certainly have plenty of scope for venting their anger. The actions or follies of directors are scrutinised much more closely now. But in the 1960s the fans were regularly let down by anonymous, unknown clowns in the boardrooms, and sometimes the mismanagement beggared belief.

We have here three of the themes that will recur in this book: the chronic inability to retain our best players in Scotland; the besetting sin of financial and business incompetence; and the constant betrayal of the fans.

I don't for one moment blame Charlie personally for going off on his travels, but the other, compensating, thing I remember about these early days of my fanhood was the sheer cussed commitment of so many of the more ordinary players. Few fly-by-night mercenaries infested our game in that era.

A shining exemplar of the wholehearted Scottish journeyman was Ally Shewan, Aberdeen's no-nonsense left back who had little – well, none – of Charlie Cooke's ball-playing skill, but he made up for that with ample physical presence and obvious dedication to the cause. Ally made his debut in 1962 and went on to play more than 350 times for the club, including an utterly amazing run of 313 consecutive appearances. They don't seem to make them like Ally any more. He was a decent, dogged and utterly honest professional of the old school, and the phrase 'club servant' was made for him.

Ally may have been a limited player, but he always gave everything, and he often excelled against the Old Firm. In those days Rangers and Celtic only visited Aberdeen once a season, unless of course there was a cup-tie. Although a huge teeming influx of Glaswegian visitors was welcomed every July, at the time of the Fair Fortnight – apart from anything else they did bring a lot of money into Aberdeen, which was in those days still a holiday resort of some repute – that welcome did not apply to the fans of the Old Firm.

The summer holidaymakers visited the infectious character of their great city on the cold, buttoned-up northern city by the sea and each year for a glorious two weeks Aberdeen became a much more chancy, colourful and cheeky place. Whereas the Celtic and Rangers supporters descended on the city with an arrogance and implicit menace that was heartily resented. There was always enormous pleasure in Aberdeen, even among people without the slightest interest in football, when the Dons beat the Old Firm, and I'm happy to record that they did so surprisingly often. But it wasn't until the greatest manager of them all, Alex Ferguson, a one-time Rangers supporter and a former Rangers player, took over at Pittodrie in 1978 that beating the Old Firm became expected and routine.

In the 1960s, when the Dons were beaten by the Old Firm, they often suffered from dodgy refereeing decisions (yes, I really believe that) or rank bad luck. But occasionally the sheer superiority of the opposition meant that they were fairly and well beaten. One such game that I remember was a League Cup tie when the Dons, playing above themselves as they usually did against Rangers, stormed into a 2–0 lead. Then the magnificent, peerless Jim Baxter took over, utterly eclipsing Charlie Cooke.

Slim Jim strolled around the park, spraying raking, inch-perfect passes out to Willie Henderson on the right and Davie Wilson on the left. These two superb wingers sent in such delicious crosses that Jim Forrest (later to play with distinction for the Dons) and Ralph Brand could hardly fail to score. And they duly got four goals between them. My two abiding recollections of that particular game are of Baxter's imperious, sublime skill and Shewan's stubborn resilience. I said that Ally often raised his game against the Old Firm. Not in this game. Willie Henderson would beat him, and beat him again, and beat him again for fun. Yet Ally never gave up. You remember the greats, of course you do; you should also remember the triers and the journeymen.

One of the larger-than-life characters in Scottish football in the 1960s and '70s was Hal Stewart, who ran Greenock Morton. His talents were essentially those of the publicist and the wheeling dealing impresario and it was he who initiated the influx of Danes – not all of them great, alas – into Scottish football. Other struggling teams followed Morton including Dundee United, and Aberdeen who signed three Danes: Jorgen Ravn, Lief Mortensen and Jens Petersen. Stewart was one of the good guys, a decent and ebullient entrepreneur, but his encouragement of the Danish invasion now seems in retrospect a grisly anticipation of the influx of tenth-rate continental mercenaries who infested Scottish football in the 1990s.

Ravn and Mortensen were forwards, and made little impact, though Mortensen did score a spectacular but flukey equaliser for Aberdeen in the third minute of added time at the end of a game against Dunfermline, then starring Alex Ferguson. The point thus lost was to prevent Dunfermline winning the league that year; football, as I say, is a cruel game. The third Dane, Petersen was the slowest to settle but he became a consistent performer in the midfield and he stayed for six years, till 1970.

The signing of the Scandinavian trio was trumpeted as the start of a much-vaunted new era for the Dons, but, unfortunately, in their second game for the club, against Celtic at Parkhead, they played in a team that was thumped 8–0. These were dismal days for the Dons. They were poorly managed and were sliding fast to mediocrity and worse.

Within a year of that debacle Aberdeen had a new manager, the dour but dedicated Eddie Turnbull. He phased out most of the players he had inherited and introduced many promising newcomers, such as the goalie Bobby Clark, from Queen's Park, who went on to play 17 times for Scotland. Best of all was an extraordinarily gifted inside forward, a Celtic fan from the Barrowfield area of Glasgow called Jimmy Smith.

I can still remember, as if it were yesterday, the night that the 19-year-old Smith made his debut. It was early in 1966 and Aberdeen beat Morton 5–3 before 5,000 or so hardy souls. I was there with my brother and we witnessed the first of many masterclasses in old-fashioned forward play provided by the most beguiling footballer I've ever had the privilege of watching. We had thought that Charlie Cooke was irreplaceable but this gangling youth was, as they used to say, in a different class. He was Charlie Cooke – with the boots of a wizard. Cooke had been very good; Smith was sensational.

Jimmy Smith's arrival in the Aberdeen team towards the end of season 1965–66 was opportune for the club's directors, because it allowed them to sell another Smith, a local lad called Dave Smith, who for a couple of seasons had been impressing as an attacking wing-half.

Dave Smith was sold to Rangers for £55,000 just before the beginning of season 1966–67. At the time I had a holiday job at a transport depot in the West Tullos Industrial Estate and I well remember the fury of my workmates when they heard that Smith had been sold to Rangers.

When we had our tea breaks in the mess the main topic of conversation was football. The men were canny, even philosophical, as they discussed the forthcoming season at Pittodrie. That changed with the departure of Dave Smith. Cautious, slow-spoken men were roused to raw anger.

It was bad enough when our best players were sold to English clubs, but it was especially galling when they were sold to the Old Firm. There was even more anger when a Rangers director announced, a few days after the transfer, that Smith did not seem to be fully fit. We all knew that Eddie Turnbull was a tough taskmaster and an absolute stickler for exemplary fitness.

These absurd comments emanating from Ibrox were given the lie by the fact that Dave Smith excelled in the first game of the season, scoring for

Rangers against Partick. He went on to be an ever-present in the Ibrox team that season. He was to play seven seasons and over three hundred games for Rangers, despite two broken legs towards the end of his career, and he was a consistently accomplished and classy player for them, though he never became a favourite with the Ibrox fans. Perhaps they never forgave him for succeeding the irreplaceable Jim Baxter, who had been sold to Sunderland.

Meanwhile, back in Aberdeen, we consoled ourselves by watching our new hero. Jimmy 'Jinky' Smith had a unique style of playing that managed to be both elegant and awkward at the same time. He would drag the ball past opponents in a languid way that certainly confused his opponents and sometimes confused the spectators. He had the wonderful gift of apparently doing complicated things in slow motion. His perplexing dribbles, his beautifully astute passing and his many goals made him for me the ultimate footballing hero.

Like so many great Scottish inside forwards of that era, Jimmy did not look like an athlete. He was pale, lanky, hunched, almost stooping, and he had a shock of jet-black hair. At times he looked a bit like a skinnier, lugubrious Scottish version of Elvis Presley. He wandered haphazardly round the park looking wasted and lost . . . till he had the ball at his feet.

And he was possessed of genuine physical bravery. He scored more goals than most classic inside forwards of the late sixties and early seventies did. In the penalty box he seemed to gather a shot of additional adrenalin and he fairly crashed the ball into the net. He was a finer header of the ball too, and he scored some spectacular headed goals. Aberdeen sold him to Newcastle United for £100,000 in 1969, at the same time as they sold Tommy Craig, another precociously creative young footballer, to Sheffield Wednesday also for £100,000. More betrayals.

Jimmy Smith starred for the Scottish Under-23 team in 1967 when they annihilated (the word is used advisedly) England by three goals to one. But he gained only four full caps for Scotland, although he was, as I believed then and I believe to this day, a genius.

Although the best football fans tend to be obsessive and thus somewhat parochial in their outlook, only the most myopic are unaware of what is going on in the wider game. For me this process of education about football beyond Pittodrie was aided by the fact that I was packed off to boarding school in Edinburgh. Professional football was regarded by the authorities there as a base and vulgar business but a few of us (including, as it turned out, the headmaster, one Dr McIntosh) would make regular covert trips to Easter Road to watch a Hibs team of almost unlimited though tragically unfulfilled potential being reinvented by the legendary Jock Stein.

Here I saw another member of my Pantheon of heroes, Willie Hamilton, yet another inside forward who did not look the part – he appeared overweight and sluggish – but who had sublime vision and the ability to see passes which no-one else could. When Stein left Hibs after a sadly brief stewardship (another of these betrayals?) to return to Celtic few people anticipated that he was about to build the greatest club side, by far, that Scotland has ever known. What I did personally predict was that Willie Hamilton would quickly follow the big man to Parkhead.

But I hadn't reckoned on Stein's brilliance; he didn't need Hamilton, although he was later to describe him, some people think perversely but I reckon sincerely, as the most talented player he ever worked with. Stein simply moved the Celtic forward Bobby Murdoch, another beefy player with a powerful shot and deceptive subtlety in his range of passes, back into the midfield. Stein did however come back to Edinburgh for another player: Willie Wallace of Hearts.

Each of the players in the Celtic team that won the European Cup two years later was individually outstanding (and famously every single one of them was born within thirty miles of Glasgow) but for me the key member of the team, the matrix, was Bobby Murdoch.

By this time I had moved on to university in England, in Oxford, where for the first time in several years I made one or two futile attempts to play the game at an organised level. Instead I was soon persuaded to become a referee. I knew I had no chance of refereeing games of any significance. Rather I undertook this (almost thankless) task out of genuine altruism, for we were told that amateur football in the Oxford area – and not just in the context of the university – was desperately short of referees. If anyone, however unlikely, could help, well, the people who ran Oxfordshire football were desperate.

And so I attended a long series of classes run by the Oxfordshire Football Association, most of which were absurdly theoretical, dealing with ridiculous scenarios such as what you did if the ball burst the very second it was going over the goal-line into the net (I can't remember the correct answer, though common sense tells me the goal would stand). There was little practical training, but my colleagues and I did some running of the line at quite big amateur games supervised by 'proper' referees.

I eventually received a certificate from the OFA. Despite poor eyesight and poor fitness (my stamina had improved because I was doing hard physical work in the vacations, but this hardly helped my speed) which made me conform to the stock notion of the incompetent referee, I was given quite a few games over a couple of years. I realised that I would not have survived long had I been in a tougher, more industrial environment but I felt I was making some kind of contribution – which, gratifyingly, seemed to be appreciated – in this more rustic context, and I also learned much more about the game.

Luckily most of these refereeing commitments were in midweek so I was able to join a couple of pals on the odd Saturday and take the train to London to watch Chelsea (where Charlie Cooke and Peter Osgood were working their magic for Tommy Docherty) and occasionally Arsenal or Fulham. At that time I instinctively liked Chelsea and Fulham and disliked Arsenal, despite the fact that the Highbury team then included some great Scots like Frank McLintock, Eddie Kelly and George 'Stroller' Graham, who was later to manage the club with distinction.

We didn't go to West Ham or Spurs simply because the grounds were too difficult to reach on whistlestop day trips. I'd love to have seen the Spurs team of Dave Mackay, Alan Gilzean and Jimmy Greaves; I'm not so sorry that I missed the West Ham team that included three of England's World Cup winners.

It was not at all obvious to me that the football on display in the English First Division was superior to what was on offer in the Scottish First Division. Most certainly (as Alf Ramsey used to say) the gulf was nothing like what it is today, and I'm not convinced that there was actually any significant gulf at all. There were differences, of course. The English teams were more physical, somewhat sturdier, and the ball was in the air a lot more.

There seemed more cynicism about the English game but there was also less of the selfish individual self-indulgence I'd seen in Scotland. Charlie Cooke at Chelsea was a man transformed; the lovely ball-playing skills were still there, but he was much more of a team player now. The other point of interest was that many of the best players I saw in London were Scots; I'd actually seen quite few of them expressing themselves more expansively back home in places like Easter Road, Dens Park and of course Pittodrie.

In Oxford itself we sometimes wandered up Headington Hill to see Oxford United (near whose ground lived an old professor called Tolkien who complained about the behaviour of the fans outside his house). The football there was inferior, to put it mildly. Oxford's sole star, if that is the correct term, was one Ron Atkinson, later to gain both celebrity and notoriety as a manager and then as a pundit. Ron, a massive Liverpudlian who in those days was known as 'Tank' was an energetic, bustling player of immense commitment, and thus a stand-out in a mediocre Oxford team, though he wasn't one for connoisseurs of the finer points.

My next move, as I began my journalistic career, was to Newcastle, where by what seemed an amazing and beneficial coincidence, Jimmy 'Jinky' Smith had just arrived from Aberdeen for a £100,000 fee.

Unfortunately the manager who had presided over this purchase, Joe Harvey, did not seem to appreciate the prodigious talents of the player he had just bought. He evidently thought that Jimmy didn't work hard enough. On the other hand, the Newcastle United fans, bless them – probably the most fervent and decent supporters I've ever had the privilege of standing among – took to him immediately. But Harvey preferred unimaginative plodders whose main task was to hoist high balls into the box for the Welsh centre forward Wyn Davies. Like many proficient headers, Davies was not a particularly tall man, but, my goodness, he could leap. (The only forward I saw with an even better spring was Mark Hateley's father, Tony.) Such tactics weren't for the inventive and subtle Smith, and it seemed as if his career in England might be over before it started.

I persuaded my hero to give me an interview, his first in Newcastle. It was arranged with an ease that would not be the case today. He suggested that we meet in the foyer of the main stand at St James's Park and it was there that I conducted my first interview with a professional footballer. (I've done quite a few over the years; contrary to the prevalent prejudice, I've found most footballers to be courteous and thoughtful.)

Smith spoke frankly and the result, my very first piece of by-lined journalism, was displayed with surprising prominence in the next Saturday Sports pink edition of the *Newcastle Evening Chronicle*. The by-line actually read: 'By Harry Reid, a young Aberdeen journalist', which was supposed to suggest that the piece contained special insights into Smith's career at Aberdeen. Certainly the interview was, as I recall, more concerned with Aberdeen than Newcastle, but there were valid reasons for that at the time.

It was probably just a coincidence, but after the piece appeared Harvey did give Smith an extended run in the Newcastle first team. Jinky cemented his role as the darling of the die-hard Geordie fans – among them the very young Steve Bruce, later to excel with Norwich and Manchester United and to become a distinguished manager – and he won plaudits from some of England's best sportswriters, including Brian Glanville, who described him in the *Sunday Times* as an authentic star.

(I was already a considerable fan of Glanville, because he had a well-informed column about European football in, of all places, the *Aberdeen Press & Journal*, thus giving the lie to that paper's alleged parochialism. In my teens I devoured this column avidly, for it opened doors to an exotic world of football that seemed distant and glamorous. These days satellite television coverage has rendered such a column well nigh redundant.)

But despite, or perhaps because of, Smith's success with the fans and the more perceptive journalists, Joe Harvey, whose views unfortunately mattered more than anyone else's, remained unconvinced and before too long Smith was in the reserves again. Indeed he never fully established himself as a fixture in the Newcastle team.

So, partly out of pique, I was soon going to watch Sunderland, a few miles away at Roker Park. Sunderland were fighting a desperate and losing battle against relegation, but were doing so with some style and it seemed to me that they had several players who were well worth watching, and indeed better than anything Newcastle possessed with the exception of the spurned Jinky Smith. I'm thinking of Joe Baker, then in the evening of his career, but a much more cavalier and thrilling centre forward than Wyn Davies; of the immaculate young defender Colin Todd; and of an exciting 18-year-old left winger called Denis Tueart.

At the time I was in Newcastle, incidentally, the results of a major survey of industrial workers on Tyneside was published. Among the findings were that one in ten played sport (mainly football) and one in three watched sport (almost exclusively football).

Before too long I was back in Scotland, working on a variety of jobs for the *Scotsman*. I'd only been back north of the border for a month or so when, for the first time, I saw Aberdeen win a trophy: the Scottish Cup, in April 1970. The score was Aberdeen 3, Celtic 1. My brother and I stood on the great Hampden terrace under the ancient North Stand in a crowd of 108,438. (Thirty-three years earlier another Aberdeen–Celtic final at

Hampden had been watched by 147,365 spectators, still a European record attendance for a club game).

Most of the crowd were Celtic supporters though there were about 25,000 Dons fans present. The supporters mingled amiably; there was no segregation then. For reasons that I don't fully understand, Aberdeen fans have always had slightly better relations with the Celtic half of the Old Firm. My memory is that there was a terrific atmosphere on the terraces; later I heard that there had been more than a hundred arrests in and around the ground, but Hugh and I can recall nothing but good humour and instant friendship in Hampden that day.

The game was refereed by Bobby Davidson, an exceedingly distinguished but persistently controversial official, and I have to admit that the Dons got the breaks (which made a pleasant change). They led at half-time with a penalty scored by Joey Harper. Then with about five minutes to go, the Celtic goalie Evan Williams spilled Jim Forrest's well-struck low shot and Derek McKay, who had arrived in the Dons team apparently from nowhere and was to disappear just as suddenly, pounced to make it 2–0 for Aberdeen.

Glory be! My brother and I embraced in an impulsive act of relief and joy. It was unbelievable: we surely couldn't lose now – we were watching Aberdeen win a major trophy! All those hours of disappointment and frustration on the Pittodrie terraces had been expiated with one swing of an obscure Highlander's boot.

There were twists in the final minutes; Bobby Lennox pulled one back for Celtic and then, deep in added time, McKay scored Aberdeen's third, but it was that second Dons goal that was crucial. Instinctively, Hugh and I both knew the moment it went in that we were no longer losers; we supported a successful team, a team that could actually win a major trophy.

As the Dons fans left the magnificent bowl of the old Hampden we were sportingly congratulated by the Celtic supporters. We replied by wishing them well against Leeds United, whom Celtic were about to play in a European Cup semi-final. (Celtic duly beat Leeds but lost in the final to Feyenoord, a game they should have won easily. Jock Stein's famed tactical nous deserted him, not for the last time.)

My brother returned to Aberdeen on a supporters' train. I stayed in Glasgow. My base that night was just up the hill north of Hampden, in Advie Terrace, the home (ironically a former Church of Scotland manse) of Colm

Brogan, a precociously talented young colleague on the *Scotsman*, who was to die tragically early in 1986.

The Brogans, originally from Donegal, were a high-profile family of academics, teachers and journalists. Colm himself had little interest in football; that night he took me to pubs where he knew there would be few football fans. But later on his home was jam-packed with Celtic supporters, and some benign, teasing truculence was directed towards me, although the general mood was one of bonhomie and fellowship.

Eventually there was loud, defiant, drunken singing of Irish rebel songs intermingled with remarkably passionate and articulate analysis of how Celtic had been 'robbed' by Bobby Davidson. It was also explained to me, at some length and with great passion, that Celtic were a club created by an exiled people, a club born out of affliction and deprivation.

As for Davidson, the fact that he came from Airdrie, which I was now being persuaded was a hotbed of militant Protestantism, was regarded as particularly sinister and damning. There was no doubt that during a key passage of five minutes or so in the first half of the final the Dons had received two vital breaks. First, their penalty, which was a soft but properly technically valid decision – the ball had certainly hit Bobby Murdoch's arm; and secondly a Bobby Lennox 'goal' which was disalowed for a foul on Bobby Clark. I'd have been annoyed about these decisions had I been a Celtic supporter, but I did think that the furious denunciation of Davidson that I was now witnessing spoke of a paranoia beyond rationality.

I was pretty drunk by then, but I was beginning to understand, for the first time, the sheer, relentless, over-riding potency of the Old Firm. This was all about identity, a concept I was only vaguely aware of. Many, possibly most, football fans drift innocently, as I had, into a lifetime of supporting their team. But the fan base of the Old Firm sustains, and is sustained by, an immense burden of social history. I deliberately don't write religious history; for it really has far more to do with race than religion.

That night I received generous hospitality and I was treated with the special kindness and warmth that are unique to Glasgow. But I also witnessed passions that spoke of a tribal intensity hitherto unknown to me. Amid all the inebriated and fervid singing, banter and discussion, it was a seriously educative occasion.

Anyway, I woke at lunchtime after the Brogans' wake/party with one of the worst hangovers I've ever had. I needed to catch a train back to

Edinburgh, for that night I was to work a backshift on the *Scotsman*, but before I left the Brogans' house Colm suggested that I take a short walk with him to look at nearby Cathkin Park, the most forlorn football site in Glasgow.

Cathkin was the home of Third Lanark which had been *the* Glasgow team for those who wanted to make a point of not supporting the Old Firm. That role was also provided by Clyde and Partick Thistle, and to a lesser extent, Queen's Park, the amateur team that played at Hampden, but it was 'Thirds' who were the preferred favourites of the small number of eccentrics who chose to eschew the atavistic certainties of Parkhead or Ibrox.

Always a team with a fine playing pedigree, Third Lanark had finished as high as third (appropriately enough) in the league in 1961. Although at that time they regularly attracted five-figure crowds, they had never been particularly well supported and in the mid-sixties things were clearly going terribly wrong.

The club was bedevilled by something even worse that the customary mis-management and incompetence. There was serious corruption in the board-room. 'Thirds' went out of business in 1967, the year that Celtic won the European Cup in unforgettable style. Thus, in the same year, we witnessed both the apogee and the nadir of modern Scottish football.

As Colm and I wandered round the bereft, derelict amphitheatre that spring Sunday afternoon 35 years ago, he had me laughing with stories of players being paid in coins from slot machines in the club bar, and other such tales. But there was melancholy in the air, as the wind got up and scattered detritus around the weed-ridden terraces. Litter flurried across the pocked remains of the park. It was a rank, sorry place of canker and blight.

Despite my excruciating hangover I was happy because the day before I'd seen my team win a trophy, in a gloriously exciting game watched by more than 100,000 passionate, partisan fans in the national stadium. But here, less than a mile away, were the physical intimations of rottenness and decay, grim harbingers of the failings that were to drive Scottish football ever downwards. Of course there would be rallies, flurries of improvement (not least involving Aberdeen in the early 1980s) and fleeting passages of glory. But the overall trend was ever downwards, to the point where any prospect of meaningful revival can seem just a mirage. And yet: need that gloomy prognosis really apply? There are, at last, two generations on, genuine signs of hope.

In the train back to Edinburgh later that afternoon, my most pressing concern was whether I'd manage to get though my backshift on the *Scotsman*. I'd never before nursed such a persistent hangover. But my brain was also feverishly turning over the events of the last twenty-four hours, and the insidiously complex, sentimental, infuriating, messy mix that comprises Scottish football, this beautiful game that all of us know and so many of us love.

CHAPTER 2

JOHN RAFFERTY

I made it back to Edinburgh in time for my shift on the *Scotsman*. I was working, in these early days, as a news sub-editor. My colleagues were middle-aged to elderly men. They wore stained cardigans and drank bad coffee out of battered flasks. They were pleasant and patient with me as I learned about the exigencies of newspaper production. But there was little liveliness and absolutely no glamour about the sub-editors' section in the *Scotsman* newsroom in 1970. It hardly accorded with the general notion of the excitement of newspaper journalism. The paper was produced in a stately, almost funereal, atmosphere.

Most of these men – there were no women present – were fascinated by football and had strong opinions on the state of the game. A few of them claimed to have played the game with some distinction. But hardly any of them seemed to go to games. This was typical of the period; Scots could see world-class players appearing for various Scottish teams but the attendances for league games were disappointing, to put it mildly. Celtic and Rangers were hard pressed to achieve average gates of 30,000, Aberdeen managed about 16,000 or 17,000 and Hibs and Hearts did well to get into five figures. The conditions for watching the game were woeful, but in all other respects Scottish fans were spoiled, and complacent.

As there was little football on television then, I'm not sure where the sub-editors on the *Scotsman* got their very strong opinions from. It certainly wasn't their own paper, for they had disdain for the *Scotsman*'s sport pages. This surprised me. I sincerely believed that the best writing on the paper was to be found at the back: Norman Mair on rugby and golf, and John Rafferty on football.

Despite my persistent hangover, I got through the shift OK. I was helped by the fact that you could summon a copy boy to get paper cups of coffee from the dirty old machine at the far end of the newsroom. (Summoning a copy boy was about the only thing that accorded with American movies I'd seen featuring newspaper offices). I must have drunk about ten cups of this tepid rubbish, which, while it tasted like mashed cardboard, did keep me going through my shift. And it was better than the hideous liquid that oozed out of the old men's flasks.

At about 10.30 a bundle of first editions of the paper that I had, in a very limited way, helped to produce, appeared in the newsroom. I picked one up and immediately turned to the back, to read John Rafferty's account of the cup final.

I was infuriated. It was a rant, an extended attack on Bobby Davidson's handling of the game. I thought the tone was petty and grudging and devoid of any respect whatsoever for Aberdeen, who the bookies had marked at 6–1 against for the game and who had heroically beaten what was then one of the best two or three club sides in Europe.

Quite forgetting myself, I stormed over to the sports desk, which was presided over by Willie Kemp, an affable sports editor of the old school, and a man who was to become a good friend. With inappropriate and almost insolent fury (I was just about the most junior journalist on the paper) I launched into an attack on Rafferty in particular, and on the paper in general. Willie took this with astonishingly good grace. He told me to calm down, pointed out that the entire editorial floor was listening to me and asked what shift I was on the next day, Monday.

I said that I was to do another back shift. He said that was fine: although John was based in Glasgow, he'd be through in Edinburgh the next day. Willie promised that he'd make sure that John Rafferty made time to see me.

There was irony in the situation. For several years I'd been an avid reader of newspapers and the sports pages in particular. Rafferty was my favourite sportswriter. I was impressed by his stylish and rugged football reporting. Indeed, he was one of the writers who had made me determined to become a journalist.

Willie was as good as his word. I'd never met John Rafferty, but I'd nursed an idea of him. I knew he'd come to sportswriting late, that he had been a teacher in Glasgow, and had been much involved in the city's then flourishing boxing scene. I knew he'd trained the great Jackie Paterson. I also knew that he had succeeded the great Hugh McIlvanney (although he was the older man) as the *Scotsman*'s football writer, and that he wrote in a muscular, Hemingwayesque prose that was unusual, pared and macho. So I was expecting a hard, no-nonsense type. I was nervous.

John Rafferty turned out to be dapper to a degree. He was in his late fifties, though he looked younger. He spoke with a slight lisp and his crinkly back hair was glistening. I caught a whiff of sweet-smelling pomade. He heard me out with courtesy, a twinkle in his eye. Then he asked me to listen to him, without interruption. He gave no ground. He told me of the achievements of Jock Stein and of the unique greatness of the Celtic squad. They'd already beaten Leeds United, then the top team in England, at Elland Road and they were about to do so again in the second leg of their European Cup semi-final. (He was right about that). They would then go on to win the European Cup for the second time in three years. (He was wrong about that).

Aberdeen's cup final win had been a crude interruption of this princely progress; it was a travesty of a result; it was down to disgraceful refereeing and that alone, and it reflected badly on Scottish football. It had made Scottish football a laughing stock just when, thanks to Celtic, everyone was beginning to take us seriously. He conceded no merit, no credit whatsoever, to Aberdeen.

I heard him out, and then argued with him, but to no avail. I now understood that he was a Celtic man through and through. I'd suspected as much, but somehow to have it confirmed with such force, with such devastating clarity, in this long conversation, was salutary. I knew that papers in places like Aberdeen and Newcastle, with their local circulations, were unashamedly partisan in their football coverage; but I'd thought that a national, pan-Scotland newspaper like the *Scotsman* would have pursued a different, more magisterial, possibly even Olympian, approach. Of course the Celtic team of that era were exceptional, and some considerable bias in their favour was understandable, simply because they were so classy, so skilful, so positive, so thrilling to watch. But John's words were mining something deeper.

It was an early and forceful lesson in the nature of sports journalism. Most sportswriters, especially the good ones, had their prejudices, their pre-dilections, their bias and even their demons. I also reflected on what I had witnessed at the gathering at the Brogans' house in Glasgow, two days before, and the sheer weight of the Irish folk history that was informing much of this partisanship. My learning process was continuing.

As the spring of 1970 eased into summer I would finish my backshift on the news section, wander over to the sports desk and help out with the second-edition changes on the sports pages. This was beyond the call of duty and my news colleagues were amused. They told me I was 'slumming'.

In fact the *Scotsman* sportsdesk was undermanned, and very hard working. The pace was much faster than on the news section. Willie Kemp was a great guy who'd worked his way up from the caseroom and who patiently encouraged me. He was a Hearts fan, and a curling fanatic (he helped to pioneer the televised coverage of curling by STV).

I learned that Willie wrote, along with John Fairgrieve (another Hearts fan) of the *Scottish Daily Mail,* an entertaining Scottish football column for the *Sunday Times* under the by-line Angus Brodie. Willie's deputy was Bob Motion, a genial, uncomplicated man who balanced Willie in so far as he was Hibs daft. During the day Bob ran a guesthouse in Newington before arriving for his shift at about 5 p.m. The third member of the team was a young Glaswegian from Dennistoun called David Ross who also showed me great kindness

The Ninth Commonwealth Games were held in Edinburgh that summer at the newly built Meadowbank Stadium, the new Royal Commonwealth Pool and various other venues. It was a wonderfully successful fiesta of sport. Willie Kemp and his small team produced, every night, a broadsheet supplement filled with reports and features. It was widely admired. I was seconded to help to sub-edit it and it was my first real experience of working against the clock.

Each night, when the supplement was complete, we would nip down Fleshmarket Close, through Waverley Station and up the lift to the old NB Hotel (now the Balmoral) where there was a free bar for all the sportswriters covering the games, and their attendant hangers-on. Our supplement was much praised, with sincerity and without condescension.

John Rafferty and Norman Mair wrote marvellously for it, and so did the *Scotsman*'s part-time athletics correspondent, a well-known shot-putter called Sandy Sutherland. But the star of the show turned out to be one of the *Scotsman*'s tiny number of women journalists, a young feature writer called Julie Davidson, who'd never written about sport before but came up with a series of stylish special reports. (I admit I'm biased; she was to become my wife.)

There was headiness in the air that summer. These first Edinburgh Commonwealth Games (not to be confused with the debacle of 1986) were more than a sporting success. They comprised one of the biggest media events, perhaps *the* biggest, ever to have been held in the capital. More than 800 journalists were in town, including some of the most distinguished sportswriters alive. That figure did not include the BBC, who had a huge team of almost 500 covering the Games.

Many of these eminent sportswriters pitched up at the NB in the late evening for their gratis hospitality and they complimented Willie on his supplement. I noted the slightly awestruck pride with which he soaked up the compliments as well as the free booze.

One night towards the end of the Games, as we trudged back from the NB to see to the second-edition changes, I sensed that Willie's mood had darkened. He kept saying, 'This is what it's all about,' or 'This is what it should be all about.' I asked him to explain. We were enjoying a fleeting and glorious involvement with international sport of the best kind, he said. Sportsmen and sportswomen and nations were competing in a friendly, cosmopolitan atmosphere. This was conducive to special, invigorating, refreshing sports journalism. It made you realise that there was so much more to life than Scottish football. The football season wasn't far away, and he was dreading it. Despite Celtic's current greatness, Scottish football was finished – or so he opined.

Something of the same mood pervaded a feature John Rafferty wrote on the last Saturday of the Games. He exulted in a happy international gathering and in the life-enhancing brotherhood of sport, and even he seemed to be suggesting that there was much more to the sporting life than mere football.

On the evening of the last Sunday of that glorious July, we prepared our final coverage of the Games for the Monday *Scotsman*. There was was a splendid picture of the athletes from all over the world celebrating, after the closing ceremony, in a giant conga coiling across Meadowbank Stadium. Willie decided to use the picture really big and demanded a headline to run over it. 'The Games People Play', I suggested; 'Brilliant', said Willie. It was the only time in my journalistic career that I was congratulated on a headline.

As we moved into August and the new football season started, Willie's minor depression continued. This was unlike him; I had not known him for long, but his normal mood was upbeat and sanguine. A darkness was now gnawing away at him. He was becoming obsessed with the incipient decline of Scottish football. 'The danger signs are all there,' he kept telling me. Memories of the freshness, the zest, the innocence of the Commonwealth Games seemed to accentuate his gloom about the tired and petty nature of Scottish football.

In my parochial way, I was unconvinced. For a start, Aberdeen were playing superbly through the autumn and winter of 1970, challenging an outstanding Celtic team all the way. I thought that emerging players like Aberdeen's Martin Buchan and Bobby Clark and their prolific goalscorer Joey Harper, and others like Hibernian's Pat Stanton and Alex Cropley, indicated the brightest of futures for the game – not to mention all the stars playing for the Old Firm (as well as Celtic's established greats like Billy McNeill, Bobby Murdoch and Jimmy Johnstone, exciting new players like Davie Hay and Lou Macari were coming through at Parkhead. And Rangers too had some fine players in that era: John Greig and Willie Johnston, Colin Stein and Sandy Jardine, to name just four).

Altogether this plethora of talent seemed to me to point to a golden international era for the Scottish game, and I hadn't even taken into account the Anglos I rarely saw: players like Denis Law and Billy Bremner. Whereas the Scots athletes who had excelled at the Games, people like wee Lachie Stewart, seemed somewhat ephemeral heroes. But Willie remained unconvinced. The Commonwealth Games had opened new vistas for him; his comments on football were sour.

Then a hideous catastrophe occurred which in a horrid way seemed to reflect Willie's downbeat musings. On the second day of 1971, at the end of the Old Firm game at Ibrox, 66 fans were crushed to death on one of the steep stairways at the Copland end of the ground. The calamity occurred when Rangers fans, leaving slightly early, attempted to turn back when they heard a great roar signifying that their team had scored a last-minute equaliser.

A few months later, early in 1971, Willie Kemp and the *Scotsman's* deputy editor, Eric Mackay, decided to embark on an ambitious series on what had to be done to save Scottish football. It was to be written by John Rafferty, and Willie himself would add a few pieces.

I was not yet a full-time sportswriter but I was covering football for the paper at every opportunity. Eric Mackay told me he would take me off my usual duties so that I could do the research (i.e. the legwork) for John Rafferty. I'd have two weeks off the 'diary'. I was delighted.

I spent a happy fortnight travelling all over Scotland talking to football people about all aspects of the game. Willie Kemp and John Rafferty were great to work for. They gave me the loosest of briefs. John told me to get some background information on various angles, which he'd then write up. 'It's not true till I write it' was one of his catchphrases, sometimes used to explain his disdain for newsgathering and 'exclusives'. He said I could also write one or two pieces under my own name.

As I remember it, our main conclusion was that the structure of the game was lopsided, in favour of the smaller league clubs. We proposed that quite a few of them should be removed from the league. We concentrated on two specific geographic areas: around Brechin, Forfar, Arbroath and Montrose, and perhaps more controversially, around the Falkirk–Stirling axis where there were four Senior clubs – Falkirk, East Stirling, Stenhousemuir and Stirling Albion within eight or nine miles of each other.

I went along with this conclusion (which was hardly revolutionary; as early as 1964 Rangers had proposed a dissolution of the Scottish football league of 37 clubs. They mooted two divisions of 16. Out would go Stenhousemuir, Albion Rovers, Berwick Rangers, Brechin City and Stranraer. As the eminent football historian Bob Crampsey has noted, East Stirling would have been one of the five but for the fact that, extraordinarily, they were at that time in the existing First Division.)

I say that I 'went along' with the conclusion; I felt guilty because, in the course of my researches, I had enjoyed excellent hospitality from the officials of various smaller clubs. I remember being lavishly entertained at the Stenhousemuir social club, and having a full and very enjoyable day with Bob Shaw of East Stirling. It occurred to me then that the smaller the club, the more spontaneous and generous the hospitality. On the other hand, I came to understand that the gregarious folk running these clubs had little football ambition. It was as if they were providing a small-scale social service. They did not see themselves as part of a structure that progressed up to Celtic, then taking part in European Cup Finals. They wanted to keep things going, and that was the limit of their ambitions. They evinced a glorious small-town parochialism.

My recollection is that the *Scotsman* series produced a short and heated period of debate but little long-term impact. Yet we do have too many senior clubs in Scotland; today we have even more league clubs: Four divisions with a total of 42 clubs.

If that *Scotsman* series made scant difference in the long term, it was certainly taken seriously at the time. This was a period when the leading Scottish football journalists, like John Rafferty, were taken more seriously than they are today. This is a pity. I do not wish to be charged with special pleading for sports journalists. As I have indicated, most of them come complete with baggage: interests, prejudices and agendas. Having written that, they are paid to write about and analyse the game and many of them do so more than competently. It would be ingenuous to think that you are going to get pure objectivity from any sportswriter; on the other hand, they are more detached from the game than are the administrators, managers, directors and players who are obviously not disinterested parties.

One reason for the greater authority accorded to certain sportswriters in Scotland 35 years ago was that there was far less television coverage of football. Another, more specific reason, concerns Willie Waddell, the legendary Rangers player who had become manager of Kilmarnock and guided them to league success in 1965. Waddell enjoyed a short but influential period as a full-time football pundit with the *Scottish Daily Express* – then still a very high circulation paper – in the late 1960s.

When Rangers fired their young manager Davie White (not least because of some devastating criticism of him by Willie Waddell in the *Express*) it was Waddell who was appointed in his place. He had a near impossible job, given Jock Stein's mastery of the Scottish club scene, and he was unable to steer Rangers to the league championship he had achieved with Kilmarnock. But he did manage to lead Rangers to European success in the Cup-Winners' Cup in 1972, and the fact that he had eased seamlessly from successful management to high profile journalism and then back into big-time management gave other football writers a reflected authority.

One of Waddell's former colleagues on the *Express*, Jim Rodger, was not the world's greatest writer but he was certainly a consummate football insider, a man who knew most football people well, was trusted and liked by them and was at the heart of many of the big transfers. One example was the sale of Martin Buchan from Aberdeen to Manchester United for £130,000 early in 1972. (For me, yet another of those betrayals). I was by this time, at last, a full-time sportswriter and I remember getting wind that something was afoot and making phone call after phone call. I managed to piece the basics of the story together, from a distance. Little did I know then that the entire cloak-and-dagger transfer was being orchestrated by none other than Jim Rodger, and that the crucial 'meet' took place in a lay-by near Jim's hometown of Shotts.

Martin Buchan did not have great physical presence but he was a calm, organised defender who was to give exceptional service to Manchester United during a difficult period for the club. He always seemed to have time, one of the sure signs of a player of real class. He had been the key, controlling personality in the Aberdeen team that had given Celtic a magnificent run for their money in the league race of season 1970–71. I think I saw more Scottish league games of exceptional quality in that season than any other. Both the Celtic–Aberdeen games were titanic, desperately hard-fought spectacles.

In December 1970 Aberdeen went to Parkhead one point behind Celtic, the league leaders. Hugh and I arrived late at Queen St Station, and we managed to cadge a lift, along with some other Dons fans, in a van that was heading to the East End. We squeezed onto the packed terrace (the crowd was given as 64,000; it seemed much bigger) at the Barrowfield end of the ground, about half an hour late.

But we were to witness an electrifying sixty minutes. In the second half Joey Harper scored with a neat header. This was an affront to the likes of Jimmy Johnstone, Lou Macari and Bobby Murdoch, who then orchestrated wave after wave of glorious, rhythmic attacking football. Johnstone jinked, Macari darted and Murdoch fed them with an inventive mix of perfectly flighted passes. I don't think that I ever saw, before or since, a defence under such sustained pressure. But the Dons' defence was superbly marshalled by Buchan. And one save by Bobby Clark from Macari, right in front of where Hugh and I were standing, was breathtaking; probably the best single piece of goalkeeping I've ever seen. The Dons held out, and moved to the top of the league.

Fast forward five months, to mid-April 1971, and on Easter Sunday I was queuing with thousands of other Dons fans for tickets for the forthcoming Aberdeen–Celtic league decider. A sign of how the times have changed is that there was considerable anger that the club had put the tickets on sale on a Sunday morning. The fact that it was Easter Sunday compounded the offence. *Note*: it was not a question of the game being played – just tickets being placed on sale! Thirty-five years on and professional football contributes as much as anything to the loss of Sunday as a special quiet day. Furthermore, I suspect that today hardly anyone would notice whether it was Easter Sunday or not.

Anyway, the following Saturday the Dons and Celtic fought out a rugged, intense 1–1 draw, before a Pittodrie capacity crowd of almost 40,000. That was the score at half time. In the second half the Dons had a wonderful chance to win the game when their teenage left winger Arthur 'Bumper' Graham broke clear, sprinted forty yards and beat the Celtic goalie Evan

Williams with a lovely lob. But Celtic's centre half Billy McNeill materialised from nowhere to improvise a miraculous goal-line clearance.

McNeill was an authentic 'captain courageous', to employ a phrase much loved of the tabloid writers of that era, a wonderfully consistent and loyal servant of the Parkhead club – and that heroic defensive moment seemed to me to encapsulate all his sterling qualities. I was convinced that had the Dons won that game they'd have gone on to win the league.

As it was, Hugh and I saw them lose their final game at Brockville the next Saturday. It was a tepid anti-climax of a game in which they went down to a penalty scored by Falkirk's George Miller. Celtic thus won the league by two points. Third were St Johnstone, and fourth were Willie Waddell's Rangers. Jardine, Stein, Greig *et al.* Yes: St Johnstone, inspirationally motivated against the odds by their ebullient manager Willie Ormond, were third. That was probably the real story of the league that year.

I saw a sustained standard of league football that season that we'd die for in Scotland nowadays. I'd go so far as to say that the top four teams, Celtic, Aberdeen, St Johnstone and Rangers would easily hold their own in the top half of the current English Premiership.

Each team had several outstanding players and the managers – Stein, Turnbull, Ormond and Waddell – were, in different ways, exceptional football men. The next season Aberdeen again finished second to Celtic in the league, but this time the gap at the end was ten points, not two. Aberdeen were now in serious decline, and it was in a way surprising that they managed to finish well ahead of Rangers, who were to win a European trophy that season.

Before that season started there was a devastating blow for me when Aberdeen's manager, Eddie Turnbull, left Pittodrie for Hibs. I was dumb-founded; I thought that Aberdeen were a bigger club than Hibs. OK, Aberdeen had the disgusting habit of constantly selling their best players, but then so did Hibs (in that era, among those to leave Easter Road were Neil Martin, Willie Hamilton, Peter Cormack, Peter Marinello, Alex Cropley and Pat Stanton). But Turnbull had starred, along with his pal Willie Ormond, in the 'Famous Five' forward line of the early 1950s. People in Edinburgh kept telling me that this was the best forward line Scottish football had ever witnessed, better even than the Lisbon Lions' front five of Johnstone, Wallace, Chalmers, Auld and Lennox. So Turnbull was simply showing a commendable loyalty to the club he loved, and who could decry that?

Aberdeen replaced him with Jimmy Bonthrone, a decent, friendly but somewhat malleable manager.

At this time I was reporting regularly on live football. I particularly liked Wednesday-night games. (Then there were hardly ever games other than on Tuesday and Wednesday nights and Saturday afternoons).

Because the games kicked off at 7.30 and the *Scotsman*'s first-edition deadline for copy was 9.30 at the very latest, you had to phone the copy over in takes. At half time, an account of the first half, which would be the last passage in the actual reprinted report; late in the second half, a brief passage on the early second-half action; and then, just as the game was ending, the score (obviously enough), the intro and assessment, and a brief description of any significant late action. The ultimate nightmare was an exciting climax with a flurry of late goals. What was thrilling about all this was that you were reporting the action that you actually saw taking place before you, often from poorly situated press boxes, surrounded by noisy, baying fans. It got the adrenaline going.

Willie Kemp did not give me too many Dons games to cover (fair enough) but an early one was a League Cup tie against Falkirk at Brockville in September 1971. The Dons needed a point to qualify for a quarter final with Eddie Turnbull's Hibs.

Brockville had one of the better press boxes, but the phones were in a corridor behind the box, so you needed a phonist to get the copy over. (I preferred grounds where you phoned it over yourself). My brother Hugh undertook this task for me that night. Aberdeen led with a Jim Forrest goal at half time but they collapsed in the second half, not least because of two spectacular goals in a five-minute period, both scored by one Alex Ferguson, then in the evening of his playing career. Twice he romped past Martin Buchan and Willie Young, legs pumping, elbows flying, and lashed the ball low past Bobby Clark.

Ferguson was to become a man I revered but I wasn't too pleased with him that night. I thought his fine individual performance had shown up flaws in the Dons' organisation that suggested that worse was to come. And so it proved.

Meanwhile I was learning about the peculiar, incestuous world of Scottish football journalism. In my teens I had been an avid reader of newspapers, mainly the *Press & Journal* and the *Scottish Daily Express*, though I slowly gravitated more to the *Scotsman* and the *Glasgow Herald*. I've already mentioned that the *P&J*, despite its reputation for excessive parochialism, ran in the mid-1960s an excellent column on European football by the distinguished London-based journalist Brian Glanville, and I devoured this eagerly. There was relatively little domestic football on television then, and hardly any European or South American football – so Glanville's column opened up an exotic, exciting and unknown world.

I became fascinated by football writing and noted how the quality varied enormously. I also noted that different papers often carried exactly the same stories, word for word, when it came to English football; I did not then know about agency copy.

When I became involved in sports journalism myself, I was aware of a paradox. Although a few writers were accorded more respect and seemed to carry more authority within the game, football as a whole was far less in thrall to the media. Television was peripheral then, and that is why some pressmen were given a status that they don't have now. Their words were picked over with intense interest by fans, managers and even players. Alex 'Faither' Smith told me that during his playing career with Stirling Albion and Stenhouse-muir and Kilmarnock in the late 1950s and early 1960s, he and his playing pals used to study what their favourite scribes wrote – and then they would discuss and compare match reports and journalistic comments.

Newspaper circulations were much higher then than they are today, and the press had a part in people's lives and indeed in the national culture, which it has, alas, lost. Even into the 1970s, this was the case. When Alex Ferguson arrived as manager at Pittodrie in 1978, his first instruction was that all the morning papers had to be on his desk, first thing.

Up to the end of the 1970s, people used to queue outside newsagents for the Saturday night pink and green football editions (pink in Dundee and Edinburgh, green in Aberdeen – and you had a choice of pink or green in Glasgow). The papers covered the game at all levels with great thoroughness. Sunday papers carried detailed reports of games like Albion Rovers against Stenhousemuir, and the junior game and schools football were also covered assiduously.

Indeed one of the reasons why people were surprised that Aberdeen FC had ignored Denis Law when he was displaying his prodigious goal-scoring talents in schools' football in the city in the 1950s was that the Aberdeen *Evening Express* covered schools' football – including primary-school football – in considerable detail. Law's name appeared frequently in the local paper before he was even at secondary school. Scouts used to scour the papers.

I'm told that scouts started appearing in huge numbers at Recreation Park, Alloa in 1967 to check out a very special forward called Tommy Hutchison because of a couple of ecstatic descriptions of his wing play in reports in the *Sunday Post*. (Hutchison was duly transferred to Blackpool, then captained by the great Jimmy Armfield, and went on to star for Coventry and Manchester City. He played more English league matches – 795 – than any other Anglo-Scot in history. He also won 17 Scotland caps.)

There were some very fine writers for both the tabloids and the broadsheets around in the 1960s and '70s. I'm thinking of men (they were all men) such as Malky Munro (who had memorably chided the young Alex Ferguson for missing a penalty when he was playing for Glasgow schoolboys against London schoolboys), John Mackenzie, Hugh Taylor, Alex Cameron and Ken Gallacher. I'm thinking of Glenn Gibbons (who is still going strong) and Ian Archer and of course John Rafferty. They were all based in Glasgow: John Fairgrieve, Jimmy Forbes and John Mann kept the flag flying in the east.

There was an element of divide-and-rule: most individual pressmen had their specific agendas, their pet contacts, their favourite clubs. I suppose it was always, and will always be, this way; but given the introverted and parochial nature of the Scottish game, it did not always make for the healthiest of atmospheres.

After games then, there were few formal or even semi-formal meets. Rather the journalists hung around in the corridor outside the dressing rooms, or in the lobby or foyer or hall, or in the area of the directors' lounge, and eventually got 'a few words' from often dour and surly managers, or occasionally from players. There was often a tense atmosphere of mutual suspicion.

On the other hand, the directors would occasionally invite you into the boardroom for drinks, especially at the less fashionable clubs. Brockville, Falkirk's old ground, was a place where there was sometimes splendid hospitality. The Hibs board could also be munificent, when the mood took them. One of their directors, an eminent surgeon called Sir John Bruce, was a particularly warm and generous host. I remember one occasion when he invited some of us press boys in to join his colleagues in the Easter Road boardroom and the impromptu drinking session lasted for several hours. (In that era, the Scottish game, at all levels, was awash with drink.)

But there was no consistency in relations with the press. For most of the time, journalists were treated like dirt.

Most of the managers had two or three pals and favourites among the pressmen. As a tyro I had to scrabble for quotes and scraps of information. But some people were a joy to speak to. One such was Hal Stewart of Morton. I remember talking to him after the Greenock club had fought out a valiant 0–0 draw at Ibrox. Willie Waddell was closeted with the pack but I noticed Hal coming down the Ibrox staircase and intercepted him. He chatted away amicably for about fifteen minutes, giving me several good lines. I still remember that with tangible gratitude. Of course, Hal got some decent publicity for Morton – and himself. That was part of the problem; most of the clubs, including the big ones, did not have a clue about even the rudiments of positive media relations.

The facilities for the press were often disgraceful. That has certainly changed. I mentioned the phones; in some press boxes the phones kept disappearing. Also at some grounds the conditions in which you had to phone over your copy verged on the ludicrous. I covered a midweek Texaco Cup game at Broomfield between Airdrie and Derby County. Broomfield was packed that night and there was a fervid, even vicious, Scotland–England edge about the occasion. The weather was wild and wet and the rain lashed into the box, which was not really a box at all, just a long bench at the front of the stand. Immediately behind was a group of particularly noisy and wrathful standites, who bellowed their inventive abuse at the visiting team, and their own, and sometimes the press, with vicious force. Someone had pinched the *Scotsman* phone that night and I had to borrow someone else's when he had finished, and was thus a little late with my takes.

My main memory of that night is of a masterclass on the sodden pitch from Archie Gemmill, then starring for Brian Clough's Derby. It was a typical irony of the times; by far the best player in the resented English team, managed by the man who seemed the ultimate English bigmouth, was a small, sublimely skilled Scot. Some of Gemmill's play that night anticipated an unforgettable moment in a totally different context in Argentina seven years later.

One or two of the managers were boorish and truculent. I had a bad run-in with Eddie Turnbull, a man I'd much admired, albeit from a distance. Bob Motion had suggested that I should do a big interview with Pat Stanton, the Hibs captain. Pat readily agreed. The copy was innocuous enough, but Turnbull took exception to one or two things Pat had said. (Like many of the best managers, Eddie was something of a control freak).

The next game I covered was at Easter Road, as luck would have it. I was phoning over my final take when Eddie came up the short flight of stairs to the press box and loudly inquired if I was present. My craven colleagues pointed in my direction. The irate manager led me downstairs, but not before Stewart Brown of the Edinburgh *Evening News*, who was a good man, whispered to me: 'Let him have his rant. Don't argue with him. It simply ain't worth it.'

When we got to his office Turnbull certainly did rant at me, with foul-mouthed eloquence. I intended to follow Stewart's advice but eventually I could not stop myself arguing back. Funnily enough, Turnbull seemed to respect this. He changed tack, ordered me to get out and then rather incongruously shook my hand.

Later I played over in my head what he had said. I had heard stories of pressmen being bollocked like this but somehow I'd assumed it would never happen to me. What Eddie said wasn't really rational. He accepted that Stanton had been quoted accurately. His complaint was essentially that I'd dared to speak to his captain and canvass his views without him knowing anything about it. He implied that this had undermined him, though Stanton had said nothing critical about him. Turnbull, despite his success, seemed insecure and terribly tense. I suspected that he was under pressure from his chairman, the builder Tom Hart. When Hart was in the mood he too could rant and rave.

My respect for Turnbull was undiminished. I don't think that this eruption was an attempt to bully me or manipulate me; for a start, I wasn't important enough. He was just expressing frustration and raw, genuine anger. I had never seen him play but I'd heard much about his greatness as an inside forward. I well understood that he knew a thousand times more about the game than I ever would. From his early days as coach at Queen's Park he had proved himself an exceptional tactician and motivator and he deserved to win far more than the two trophies he achieved as a manager (the Scottish Cup with Aberdeen, the League Cup with Hibs).

I also knew that despite the surface dourness he had a dry sense of humour. He was given to the occasional quip, as when he famously told Alan Gordon, the fine Hibs striker who was also an accountant, 'The trouble with you, Gordon, your brains are all in your heid'. I used the word striker there, a term that was becoming much in vogue in the early seventies. Turnbull once opined that 'most so-called strikers couldn't strike a match'.

But I suspect he might have been an even better manager – and dare I say, a more effective control freak – had he learned more about media relations. This lack of media guile wasn't necessarily his fault; press personnel then were treated with rotutine disdain by most clubs, despite the fact that the better-known, big by-line sportswriters had more influence than they do now, so it would take an exceptional manager, such as Jock Stein, or later Alex Ferguson, to learn how to manipulate them for their own ends. Fair enough.

CHAPTER 3

WILLIE ORMOND

The main reason I rejected Willie Kemp's growing doom about Scottish football was nothing to do with the state of the club game north of the border. It was rather that I was convinced that we had enough players of world class (many of them playing in England) to make a mark internationally. It had been as far back as 1958 when we had last qualified for the World Cup Finals. I was certain that the national team would do better in the 1970s, and that a bit of World-Cup glory would do the game no end of good at lower levels. I proved to be half right.

The first time I saw Scotland play was against England at Hampden, just a fortnight after Aberdeen had won the Scottish Cup there in April 1970. It was a disappointing goalless draw (the very first in the long and generally eventful history of the Scotland–England fixture). The Scots played with far more passion and flair than the English, whose main concern seemed to be to smother the home team. The major talking point was a bad tackle by England's Brian Labone on Colin Stein inside the box. It was a certain penalty. It was my first lesson in the fact that even so-called top-class international referees could make absurd decisions.

I left Hampden feeling somewhat flat. It was a downbeat introduction to international football, yet I took to watching Scotland regularly. Then, when I became a full-time sportswriter, John Rafferty took me down the Clyde coast to meet the Scottish squad who were preparing for a friendly against Peru (a country that was to inflict on us one our darkest national footballing days. But that was six years later).

As John led me into the Queen's Hotel at Largs, I was amazed. I'd not expected a palace, but I had expected somewhere grander – somewhere with plenty of space and proper recreational facilities, for example. The hotel was like a glorified guesthouse. The staff seemed friendly – but it was a small, cramped place. I found it hard to believe that it could accommodate 19 or 20 footballers.

There was indignation as well as surprise in this reaction. Later, when John was driving me back to Glasgow, I said to him that an international team which was aspiring to greater things, and included some of the most gifted professionals in Europe, should surely be treated with more – well, respect. John, in world-weary mode, found this bizarre.

He told me to remember that it was the SFA who were in ultimate charge of the national team. They thought the Queen's Hotel was just swell. I asked him what he personally thought, but he expressed no concern. I asked him about the lack of training facilities, of swimming pools, practice pitches and the like. There was a putting green, and that seemed about it. John made the valid point that these other facilities, and more, were available at the splendid Inverclyde Sports Complex just a mile or so away at the back of Largs. Even so, my indignation simmered.

When, exactly thirty years later, just before the 2002 World Cup Finals in the Far East, Roy Keane launched his famous attack on Mick McCarthy and the Irish management for the inferior accommodation and facilities in which he and his colleagues were expected to prepare for the most important tournament of them all, I found myself recalling my indignation that day at Largs.

John Rafferty was amused by what he thought was my naïvety. But I did not think that the homely Queen's Hotel signalled in any way that Scotland were striving for the big time. I didn't think the players were being treated like men, or even big boys. The set-up seemed small-time and pretty chaotic, to the point of being unprofessional. John tried to divert me by emphasising how convivial the atmosphere was. He told a few stories about drinking escapades. This surprised me, for, although like most journalists, he liked a drink, he was in his own way quite a puritanical, fastidious man – certainly not a dedicated boozer.

One of the reasons for our trip to Largs was for John to introduce me to Tommy Docherty, who was then managing the Scotland team. (Docherty also managed a remarkable fourteen different club sides, including the Chelsea of Charlie Cooke and Peter Osgood.) 'The Doc' was then in his mid-forties, and in his prime. He was a good pal of John's and they got on famously. John thought it would be useful for me to get to know the national manager. This was one of several kindnesses he showed me after our initial, difficult, meeting.

Scotland won the friendly against Peru easily enough, the only highlight being a beautiful, sweetly-struck goal by Denis Law. It was wonderful that Denis was by then back in the fold, thanks to the Doc, but why on earth was he ever out of it?

The Lawman was not a big or strong player. He was five feet nine, and slimly built. But what he lacked in physique he made up for with his quicksilver, predatory ebullience. He was dynamite in and around the penalty area. He was the most electrifying forward I've ever seen. His pedigree was immaculate. He'd been European Player of the Year in 1964, the only Scot ever to win that special accolade.

Yet he was often spurned by his country. He'd had hardly any caps since 1967, when he had starred in the wonderful team, including Bremner, Greig and Baxter, that had humiliated England, the World champions, 3–2 at Wembley. (Interestingly that team, playing in April 1967, contained only four – Simpson, Gemmell, Wallace and Lennox – of the eleven Lisbon Lions who were to win the European Cup so gloriously for Celtic the very next month.)

Denis was in the international wilderness for five years, between 1967 and 1972, winning only four caps. These were his peak years, between the ages of 26 and 31. He was kept out of the picture partly because of injury and partly because the selectors and the previous managers didn't regard him as a team player, but mainly because of a lingering suspicion of the so-called Anglos (Denis played all his club football outside Scotland).

This was yet another absurdity in the long catalogue of stupidity and pettiness that has besmirched Scottish football. Too often those with power in Scottish football have been small-minded, myopic, pitiful and petty. Here was one of the greatest forwards in the history of world football. Yet his own country pushed him off to Siberia for five of the best years of his enormously distinguished career.

Anyway, when I returned to Largs a few days later to do a piece previewing the home internationals, the players were sprawled all over the small lounge area of the hotel. Denis, who'd seen me park at the front in a *Scotsman* car (a beaten-up Escort; the editorial cars on the *Scotsman* were hand-me-downs from the circulation reps), breezed out and asked if he could borrow it – he had an 'errand' in Largs. (At the bookies?)

I was gobsmacked – this legend, probably the greatest Scotland player of all time, wanted to borrow my crappy car! I handed him the keys and he roared off. My worry was not about my employers' vehicle but about Denis's safety, given my suspicions about the Escort's roadworthiness.

I found the Doc among the players, who were sitting around playing cards and drinking tea. One or two of them were smoking. It was clear that Billy

Bremner was the dominant personality. He eyed me suspiciously, but the Doc was good value. He just got on with his rat-a-tat patter and gave me some great quotes. He was still talking when Denis returned with the car. The Doc was always a controversial character, but as far as I'm concerned he was, and no doubt still is, a real gent.

Shortly afterwards Scotland embarked on a three-game tour of Brazil. The *Scotsman* did not send a reporter with the team, but the Doc had kindly given me the hotel numbers where I could contact him. He said he'd give me a few quotes after each game if I phoned at sensible times. He was as good as his word.

The Doc went off to manage Manchester United and Willie Ormond, who had worked such miracles with St Johnstone, succeeded him as Scotland boss. Willie orchestrated what was the most special international performance I ever saw, in September 1973. Scotland needed to beat Czechoslovakia at Hampden to qualify for the 1974 World Cup Finals.

That night I drove three colleagues from the *Scotsman* over, and was to meet my brother Hugh at Hampden. We hit horrendous traffic on the eastern approaches to Glasgow. Luckily one of the passengers was Alan Hutchison (who'd been brought up in the same street in Cowdenbeath as Jim Baxter) and Alan's wife came from East Kilbride. Alan saved the day by guiding me on a detour round back roads on the outskirts of East Kilbride, through Carmunnock and down towards Hampden from the south. My three colleagues ran off, scared to miss the kick-off, when I was still parking the car. I met up with Hugh, and we took our seats in the main stand, near the Rangers end, just in time. I was breathless, but nothing like what I'd be 90 minutes later.

Although there were six Old Firm players in the Scotland team that glorious night – Jardine from Rangers and Hunter, Hay, McGrain, Connelly and Dalglish from Celtic – it was the Anglos, particularly Bremner, Law and Tommy Hutchison (who was making his international debut), who stole the show.

The Czechs took a shock lead. Big Jim Holton headed an equaliser just before half time. Then the Czechs payed calm, defensive football in the second half and the Scots took their time to raise the tempo. At last Bremner started to show his leadership qualities, and Ormond produced one of the most inspired substitutions I've ever seen, putting on the young and relatively obscure Joe Jordan (then not sure of a first-team place with Leeds) for Kenny Dalglish. With a few minutes to go, Bremner hit the post and the whole of Hampden groaned with a collective fatalism. We knew it was not to be.

We were wrong. In the stramash that followed, the Czechs could not clear their lines. Eventually the ball was played neatly out to Manchester United's Willie Morgan on the right. Willie (who was later to be involved in a dramatic libel action against the Doc) was a winger I'd always regarded as being over-cute. But he was the man for this moment, and how! Amid the mayhem, he was calmness personified. He sent over a controlled, perfectly flighted cross. I can still see Joe Jordan rising to head it sweetly into the net.

The scenes of delirium, of sheer bedlam, of ecstatic emotional release that followed (and lasted non-stop till about fifteen minutes after the end of the game) were more emotive than anything else I've ever experienced at any football stadium, before or since.

The main reason for the incredible display of emotion was the realisation that Scotland were at last going to the most elevated stage in world football, where they truly belonged, and where they without doubt should have been in 1962, 1966 and 1970. The failure to qualify in 1962 was particularly galling; we went out in a European play-off to Czechoslovakia, the eventual finalists. Then in 1966 we'd watched England marching to glory, on their home territory, without Scotland being present to provide even just a little irritation. England's victory in 1966 was, for some of us, hard to take.

At least I was distant and detached from it all. How utterly galling it must have been for the Anglo-Scots players in particular. Denis Law famously went out to play golf on the afternoon of the Wembley final; he could not bear the thought of watching England win, and when he heard the result he apparently threw his golf bag to the ground in abject disgust.

Then, four years later, yet another fine Scotland team narrowly failed to qualify for the Finals in Mexico. That was when the Brazilian team of Pele, Tostao (my particular favourite), Gerson and the rest played the most exhilarating football of all time. And to think that Scots had introduced the game to Brazil in the first place!

But to return to that unforgettable night at Hampden, when suddenly a long litany of failure was expunged in an explosive orgy of relief and joy. At the final whistle the players ran a ragged lap of honour, and eventually disappeared into the venerable old stand. The crowd simply refused to leave. The players reappeared, carrying the small, crumpled, hopelessly happy figure of Willie Ormond, incongruously dressed in a light, shiny suit, on their shoulders. They paraded him round the park; the roar was as loud as it had been when Jordan's goal went in.

In the days and weeks afterwards, it became a commonplace that the fans had willed the team to victory. I'm not so sure. When Billy Bremner's low shot came back off the post, the fans seemed to sense that once again, it was not to be. But there was smeddum in this team.

Looking back on that exceptional night, what amazes me most is the players who *weren't* playing at Hampden. Without trying too hard, I've come up with the following list of Scottish players who were playing at the top level then, and who were all internationalists, but for one reason or another were not in Ormond's team: Eddie Gray, Peter Lorimer, Jimmy Johnstone, Pat Stanton, Derek Parlane, Peter Cormack, Colin Stein, Asa Hartford, Willie Donachie, Joey Harper, John Blackley, Lou Macari, Frank McLintock, John Brownlie, Gordon McQueen, George Graham, Archie Gemmill, Willie Johnston, Martin Buchan, Bobby Clark, David Harvey, Bobby Moncur, John Greig, John O'Hare and Ted McDougall. Such an incredible cornucopia of talent. We produced so many talented players then, but as a nation we would not or could not harness their skills to best effect.

Ormond's team did not let us down in Germany. They beat Zaire 2–0 (a great goal by Peter Lorimer, a simple header by his Leeds team-mate Jordan) and then fought out a heroic goalless draw with Brazil. David Hay, in particular, was colossal that night; Scotland had the moral victory, and deserved to win by at least one goal, if not two. Billy Bremner had one of the worst misses in World Cup history. Then came the crunch game against Yugoslavia. It ended 1–1, and the Scots were unbeaten but out on goal difference. Willie Ormond was in tears. So were half the nation back home, as we watched what seemed like a national tragedy unfold on our tellies.

There was a national solidarity behind that team that I don't think has been equalled since. Partly it was a response to Ormond, whose simple, almost rustic decency was in a paradoxical way inspirational. The fans took to him like no other national team manager since – not even Stein. As for the English, they just patronised him. He was a palpably honest man, and he avoided doublespeak or tactical niceties. He simply said what he felt.

At that time Scottish nationalism was stirring. England's team had not qualified for the finals. A couple of months before the finals Jimmy Johnstone had mysteriously decided to go boating at Largs – and had drifted right out into the Clyde estuary, as dawn was breaking, without a paddle, let alone an oar (maybe he'd had enough of the Queen's Hotel). The English press could hardly contain themselves in their derisive gloating.

Johnstone was a very, very special footballer. I still remember a wonderful phrase of John Rafferty's: 'His was the intricate virtuosity of street football played with a tanner ba and raised to the sublime.'

The fact that Scotland's wing magician, our most iconic player, had been nearly lost at sea was bad enough; the fact that the English press milked the debacle, mocking Ormond's abilities as a man manager, and insinuating that the Scottish squad were a drunken rabble, somehow made it much worse. Of course the story had its comic side. I wrote that Johnstone was bereft of an oar or paddle, but one version had it that when he was rescued he was standing in the rowing boat, waving an oar above his head and yelling Scotland! Scotland! Scotland!

Two days after this happened, I stood happily at Hampden watching the English national team being beaten 2–0 by a Scottish team that included the aberrant boatman.

And yet when that World Cup adventure ended, I did wonder. Had the English commentators, in all their smug condescension, not had a point? Had the Scottish preparations not been haphazard, amateurish, even anarchic? In that era there was not just a tolerated drinking culture in Scottish football; at the highest level, many aspects of clinical, careful professional preparation were deemed to be both boring and unnecessary, but I think that magnificent squad deserved better.

When I had mentioned my doubts about the set-up in Largs to John Rafferty, his reaction was to suggest that the lead-up to games did not matter too much; class would always tell on the pitch. There was some truth in that attitude, but it betrayed a kind of gentle, couthy arrogance.

Now here we were in the summer of 1974, once again pondering on another noble near miss, ruminating on shattered dreams and the glories that might have been. Later on, coaches like Andy Roxburgh and Craig Brown (neither of whom had been distinguished players, though they had been excellent schoolteachers) were sometimes sneered at for being too technical and methodical in their preparations. Yet I wonder what coaches like them would have achieved with the genuinely world-class players that we had in abundance in that earlier era?

And then there was Wembley. Ah, Wembley!

I only joined the great Scottish exodus to London twice, in 1975 and 1977. In 1975 I disgraced myself.

In extenuation, I have to say there were special circumstances that year.

Rarely was the Scottish exodus to London so imbued with a sense of mission. We had played three games without being defeated in the previous year's World Cup Finals, and had outplayed the great Brazilians. So there was a sense of unfinished business. More, a swelling emotional tide swept through Scotland in the weeks before the game, giving it an almost unbearable significance. As I have mentioned, Scottish nationalism was stirring. At this time the Scottish football team, rightly or wrongly, carried the full burden of Scottish national aspiration.

And this was my first visit to Wembley, which was in a way even more exciting than my first visit to Hampden. It was at Wembley 47 years earlier that the most famous Scottish team of all, with a forward line in which no player was taller than five feet seven, ran rings round the bigger and stronger English and walloped them 5–1. These wee men were giants. The team, which included Hughie Gallacher, Alan Morton, Alex James, Alec Jackson, Jimmy Dunn, Jimmy McMullan and Tommy Law, were seen as representing not just a proud wee country but also a special style of football, in which skill and trickery mattered far more than the lesser qualities of strength and brute force.

Alas, for this particular game in 1975 England put out a team that was indeed full of big, strong, forceful players. But the Scots couldn't cope with them. The score was reversed: it was 5–1 to the English.

The day began well enough, with a happy gathering in North Wembley. My old colleague on the *Scotsman* sports desk, David Ross, was now working on the *Sun* in London and he had a house about two miles from the stadium. David, and more to the point, his wife Sheila, generously declared open house, and several of us took up the offer. There was no problem until midway through the Saturday morning, when I started drinking heavily far too soon.

I managed the tartan-draped swagger along to the grand old stadium, but we hadn't been inside for long when I collapsed. I was slumped on the concrete terrace among a sea of feet. David kindly woke me up to see Bruce Rioch's penalty but I happily missed all five of England's goals. Before the last one went in, David was becoming concerned for my safety, and he and two mates nobly shoved their way through the crowd, dragging me with them.

I stumbled away from the stadium and found a tree to sit under. I was woken up by the crowd scailing. I asked the score, and could not take in the bad news. In my befuddled state I managed to convince myself, for an hour or so, that Scotland had won one–nil.

They say the Lord looks after drunks, and somehow I wandered raggedly back to David's house, where I was kindly greeted as a sort of tartan version of the lost sheep or even the prodigal son. Everyone there was gloomy after England's triumph and in addition one or two of them had been gracious enough to be marginally concerned about my safety. So my arrival provided a diversion and in a peculiar way I think I cheered them all up.

I underwent a spectacular recovery and enjoyed our night on the town. But the thing that really pleased me after that debacle was when we were driving back up the M6 on the Sunday afternoon and we overtook a decrepit supporters' bus, belching exhaust as it struggled up the motorway: draped across the back window was an improvised banner reading 'Ye couldnae make it six'. Ah, the splendour of defiance!

Two years later, we were again based at David's house, but this time the circumstances were different. I flew down on the Saturday morning with Dennis Canavan, then the Labour MP for West Stirlingshire, and his agent Harry Dawson. Dennis was, and is, a good guy, a politician who is utterly committed and fights to the hilt for all his constituents.

I'd been covering the annual meeting of the EIS, Scotland's biggest teaching union at Stirling, and Dennis, a former maths teacher, and no mean footballer, had been attending it as an observer. Harry Dawson was a Rangers fan and was delighted, as we were given a lift from Heathrow to north-west London, to see all the red, white and blue bunting in the streets. He took some persuading before he accepted that this was to mark the Queen's 25th jubilee and not the arrival in London of thousands of Rangers-supporting Scotland fans.

This time I was determined to stay (reasonably) sober and I enjoyed the game, which Scotland won 2–1. Bruce Rioch, Asa Hartford, Don Masson and Gordon McQueen were outstanding. But I was becoming uneasy about the growing tribal arrogance of the Tartan Army as we strutted and swaggered round the douce streets of north-west London. In truth, the demeanour of the Scots (including myself) reminded me ominously of the behaviour of Old Firm fans when they had come to Aberdeen in the 1950s and '60s, and taken over the town for a day.

The SNP were doing well then, and had eleven MPs at Westminster. One Scottish Office Minister, Harry Ewing, had gone so far as to link the SNP with what he regarded as the unfortunate tendency of the Scottish fans towards tribal triumphalism. I think the connection was mischievous, yet Ewing was a decent man and not generally one for political point-scoring.

I don't want to be hypocritical; it was smashing to smash the English, albeit by just the one goal. At the end of the game a few, and then a few more, and then literally thousands of Scots fans clambered down and scrambled on to the Wembley pitch. The party that followed on the so-called hallowed turf was essentially innocent and good-natured, although both goal frames were torn down and bits of the pitch were dug up as trophy souvenirs.

The English media had a succession of field days, bemoaning the despoilation of Wembley and much else. The *Daily Telegraph* on the Monday morning pompously reflected on 'a dreadful match spoiled by hordes of puerile drunken Scottish fans'. It was in truth a confused time, as indicated by the reaction of the Scottish Shadow Minister of Sport at the time, a splendid Borderer called Sir Hector Monro, who was essentially more of a rugby than a football man. When a reporter phoned him for his comments on the post-match scenes, he spontaneously said, 'Jolly good show by the fans' or words to that effect. That precipitated him, needless to say, into trouble.

Another MP who nearly got into trouble was Dennis, for he was one of those on the pitch and he too retrieved his wee patch of turf. An hour or so later, when we had reconvened in David and Sheila's house, Dennis was enjoying a snooze when some mischievous English journalists who happened to be there placed his turf on his hands and took a picture. When they were convinced that the snoring figure was indeed an MP, they wanted to sell the picture to the highest bidder. Amid some acrimony, we persuaded them not to do so.

In a weird postscript to this episode, I was asked a few days later by a member of the Scotsman newsdesk to investigate persistent rumours that a well-known Scottish Labour MP, thought to be Dennis Canavan, had been one of those who had invaded the Wembley pitch and had gathered a piece of the turf. Needless to say my 'investigations' were not exactly assiduous.

Later that year, in Liverpool, I saw Scotland qualify for the 1978 World Cup finals in Argentina in a tense game against Wales. (The Welsh FA tried to make more money from the fixture by switching it to Anfield). I was by this time distinctly uneasy about the Tartan Army, and the mood in Liverpool seemed almost rabid.

The game had its highlights – notably a superb save by Alan Rough from John Toshack, and Scotland's second goal, a fine header by Kenny Dalglish after a stirring break up the right wing by Martin Buchan, of all people. But

Scotland's first goal, a penalty, was controversial, though it was not till later that I realised that it was apparently Joe Jordan and not a Welshman who had handled the ball.

Liverpool was not a pleasant place that night. Amid the genuine joy there was over-the-top hubris. Still, as ever, there were ludicrous moments. The principal gathering place after the game at Anfield was the Holiday Inn in the centre of town.

The hotel management eventually shut the doors because of serious overcrowding. The man who took it upon himself to plead with the porters and security men to let a few more of us in was none other than Frank McElhone, MP, then Scotland's Minister for Sport. Frank was a lovely man and then, as always, he had the gift of the gab. He managed to get about sixty more folk in before the doors were again closed.

From then till the following summer there was an atmosphere of rising hysteria, which Ally MacLeod, Scotland's new manager, did his best to encourage rather than suppress. It was inevitable that everything would go wrong in Argentina. We were too damn cocky. After all the years of struggle and failure, there was a vainglorious transformation. We collectively believed that success was facile.

Ally was largely to blame. A more mature manager would have tried to lower expectations as it was clear that an alarmingly powerful fantasy was taking hold of the nation. Instead, in between advertising carpets on television and endorsing various other unlikely products, Ally told a hundred different interviewers – or so it seemed – that, yes, Scotland were going to win the World Cup.

There should have been a belated reality check at the time of the home internationals. When I was driving through to Glasgow for the first one against Northern Ireland, I listened to John Toshack on the radio; he was dismissive about Scotland's prospects, both in the home internationals and the World Cup Finals. My instinct was to put this down to sour grapes as a result of the Welsh team being controversially beaten by Scotland at Liverpool, but part of me realised that he was talking sense. While I looked for a parking place in the King's Park area of Glasgow I reflected on his words as the Tartan Army yelled and blustered all around me. Something was wrong, though I could not quite grasp what it was.

At that game Hugh and I were high up in the old North Stand at Hampden. It was a depressing experience. Ally had given John Robertson of

Nottingham Forest an outing on the left wing. Robertson looked a wee bit portly but perceptive students of the English game knew that something was stirring at Forest under the spectacular if noisy tutelage of Brian Clough, who had been emphasising the key role Robertson played in his set-up. Some Scots fans perversely and stupidly interpreted this as Clough mischievously trying to talk up a dud, so as to scupper Scotland's chances in Argentina. In other words, as well as arrogance, paranoia was abroad too.

Unfortunately, in these circumstances, Robertson did not play well. But what really worried me was the way many of the Scottish fans turned on him, with real venom. The game was an undistinguished 1–1 draw, and I left it feeling sour.

That week Scotland had the unusual privilege of playing all three home internationals at Hampden (the Northern Ireland game had been switched from Belfast because of the troubles). Ominously Scotland drew with Wales as well as Northern Ireland, and then lost to England. But Ally remained as gung-ho as ever and he presided over an absurd farewell for the boys in blue as they paraded at Hampden, with over 35,000 fans present, before their journey to South America. Instead of quietly doing his tactical groundwork for the three first-round games there, against Peru, Iran and Holland, Ally was intent on ratcheting up the nation's expectations yet further.

By this time I was features and literary editor of the *Scotsman* and I was getting to know Alan Bold, the artist, poet, man of letters and Hibs fan. Alan was actually a very distinguished poet, but to match the mood of the times, he produced some doggerel verses which we displayed, tongue in cheek – well, that's the construction that I put on it, now – all over the front page of the paper's weekend section. There were several poems, but the one that is best-remembered anticipated Scotland's first game in Argentina, against Peru. It ran:

> Poor poor Peru
> If you only knew
> What the Boys in Blue
> Are going to do to you
> Too true

When asked to justify this eccentric presentation by surprised, even affronted, *Scotsman* readers, I intoned that the poems represented a clever and vernacular fusion of the two most crucial and quintessential components in Scottish cultural life: poetry and football. The extraordinary thing, in these extraordinary times, was that one or two people seemed to believe me.

And so we come to the black debacle of the Peru game. That terrible night, Julie Davidson, who was by this time living with me, and I threw a party for some friends at our flat. We watched the events in Cordoba unfold with growing disbelief, then despair, then anger. Scotland's tactical ineptitude was blatant; the sheer unpreparedness of the team was horrible to behold. (Needless to say, Ally hadn't even bothered to watch Peru in advance of the game. He seemed to know even less about the fine forward Teofilio Cubillas than we did.) Back home, our 'party' deteriorated. Grisly disillusion led to strife among our small squad of the Tartan Army and there was a minor punch-up.

Things got worse, if that were possible, in the next game against the supposed minnows, Iran. We drew 1–1. We were lucky.

The final game, against Holland, brought a victory. But it was not enough to allow us to qualify for the next stage. Holland, the masters of total football and managed by the finest coach of them all, Rinus Michels, were in 1978 the best team in the world (they were very unfortunate that summer to lose to the home team Argentina, in one of the better World Cup finals). Yet Scotland, for several sustained passages in the game, played the superior football.

The game was remarkable for one of the finest individual goals ever scored in any World Cup. Archie Gemmill's solo effort, early in the second half, when he cut in from the right, jinking past three players with perfect balance, and then chipped the ball past the bamboozled Dutch goalie, was a masterpiece. A goal made in heaven, right enough, but I'm not taking anything away from Archie himself or the marvellous quality of the strike when I suggest that it's somehow pathetic that we have seized on that goal as some kind of consoling icon of Scottish footballing greatness.

In this memoir of what might be called my footballing fanhood I've fallen into the trap, often enough, of celebrating individual skills, of presenting the indulgent old-fashioned inside forwards as the ultimate entertainers – thus conveniently forgetting that football is a team game. I suppose in a way I'm trying to make amends now by regretting the endless fuss that was made of Archie's goal.

I'm neither belittling it, nor suggesting that he was other than a first-rate team player, a dedicated as well as a generously gifted contributor to the cause. He was both of these, and much more. He was not a self-indulgent player. It's not his fault that our national obsession with that constantly celebrated goal, wonderful as it was, has become marginally ridiculous. I do not excuse myself from this tendency. Many years later, I happily sat in the Scottish Football Museum at Hampden, watching an endless replay of the goal, again and again and again.

Off the field, the Argentinian adventure was a sour shambles. The press reports were mixed, for there was something of a war going on between the news reporters and the football writers. Once it became clear that Ally himself, and his squad, had feet of clay, the news-boys were out for blood, looking for all the bad stories they could get. (That is a mixed metaphor but my memory is that spectacular mixed metaphors abounded at that particular time.) And, boy, they did find some bad stories.

As for the football specialists, motivated by perhaps a misguided concern for their own interests, but also by an enlightened, even altruistic, sense of patriotism, they tended to be more protective. So internecine strife among the press corps broke out, exacerbating the tensions. You could gather this from the confused nature of some of the despatches from Argentina – and later, when colleagues returned home, I had this impression confirmed. Argentina was a scarring experience, not just for the players and the fans, but for many of the pressmen too.

What made things even worse was the fact that for the second time running, England had not qualified and were not present. Thus the English media gleefully switched their attention to Scotland, and how they relished the ongoing pantomime, as fiasco after fiasco was presented to them on a great big plate. Worst of all was when Willie Johnston, by now at the veteran stage, had to be sent home in disgrace for taking a banned performance-enhancing stimulant.

And so the decade which I thought had promised such high hopes for Scottish football in general and the Scottish national team in particular looked like ending amid acrimony, backbiting, humiliation and the bitterest of extended post-mortems. Willie Kemp's foreboding had been justified. Maybe athletics were better after all.

Tacked on to it all was the political dimension. Some commentators suggested that Scots did not vote enthusiastically for their own Assembly in the referendum of early 1979 because national self-confidence had been shattered by the events in South America.

Following the national humiliation, Jock Stein, by then in the evening of his career, took over from Ally MacLeod towards the end of 1978. Immediately Stein set about doing the exact opposite of what Ally had done. He systematically played down expectations. The man who in his own words had won the European Cup for Celtic with 'pure, beautiful, inventive, positive football' now exercised a wary caution. He was conservative, not adventurous. Scotland ended that roller-coaster decade with two defeats, home and away, to Belgium. At least realism now ruled. It was almost as if defeat was expected.

Happily, at this time the Tartan Army began to reinvent itself. It would take time, and the process had its ups and downs, but the braggadocio was being replaced by something gentler and softer, something humorous, friendly and self-effacing.

Cautiously and cannily, Stein led Scotland to the World Cup Finals in Spain in 1982. What transpired amounted to yet another near miss in that infuriating catalogue of near misses. Scotland played well against a poor New Zealand team, winning 5–2, but then succumbed to the fabulous Brazil of Zico, Socrates, et al, 4–1. As usual, the crunch came in the third game, against Russia. (The Tartan Army presented this game as Alcoholism versus Communism).

This was a 2–2 draw; impressive, but, as always, not quite good enough. There was an uneasy sense that Stein's tactical acumen was not what it had been. For example, he had introduced a relatively untried – at international level – defender, a big Fifer called Allan Evans, who played for Aston Villa, for the New Zealand game – and then dropped him. At the same time, he had suddenly shed his caution and picked teams that scored eight goals in three games.

Stein could not lead Scotland to the finals of the European Nations Championship in 1984, but he succeeded (as the first Scotland manager to preside over two consecutive World Cup-qualifying campaigns) in leading us to the Mexico finals in 1986. But there was a terrible twist.

Stein, aged 62, saw his side eliminate Wales in a tense final qualifier at Ninian Park, Cardiff. The 1–1 draw (Scotland equalised with a very late Davie Cooper penalty) gave us the point we needed to ensure a play-off against Australia, winners of the Oceania group, which we had every chance of winning. The measured approach was paying off.

Moments after the game ended, Stein collapsed. Alex Ferguson, who as well as managing Aberdeen was Stein's assistant as Scotland coach, was beside the big man as he died. What was developing into a night of relief and joy had suddenly and cruelly metamorphosed into a time of trauma and national sorrow.

Alex took over and guided Scotland through the two play-off games against Australia. But somehow Stein's death in such tragic circumstances compounded my growing feeling that international football was not for me. I was at Hampden to see Scotland beat Australia 2–0 in the first leg of the play-off. It was, as far as I can remember, the last time I ever watched Scotland in the flesh.

I can, however, recall the 1986 World Cup campaign in Mexico very clearly. Alex Ferguson had prepared everything with his usual sedulous thoroughness, even travelling down to England to canvass Sir Alf Ramsey's view on the problems, climatic and other, that would be faced in Mexico. But the fact that he was also managing Aberdeen took its toll, although the SFA rather than Ferguson himself should be blamed for the fact that the team's hotel in Mexico City was ill-chosen. When I heard about this, I thought back to my first impression of the Scotland set-up in Largs fourteen years earlier.

Alex himself felt that he maybe lacked his usual touch when the squad got to Mexico. He admitted later that fears of any hint of favouritism toward his Aberdeen or ex-Aberdeen players possibly influenced at least one of his selections adversely. Further, one of Scotland's key players, Graeme Souness, had just been made manager of Rangers, an appointment that was to have a dramatic effect on the Scottish club game.

Souness was thus now the boss of Walter Smith, the new Rangers assistant manager who was also Ferguson's assistant manager in Mexico. To add to this complicated mix, Ferguson had bravely, after much heartsearching, decided not to include Alan Hansen in his squad, a decision that was brutally criticised in the English press. There was also a devastating blow when Kenny Dalglish, now player-manager with Liverpool, but still Scotland's most talismanic player, called off with a knee injury.

Despite all this, it seemed to me, from a great distance, that Alex got the majority of his decisions spot-on and that unlucky Scotland were actually unluckier than ever in this campaign.

The first game was against a fine Denmark team. I watched it with my family in a remote cottage in the Dumfriesshire hills, where the television reception was dodgy. But not dodgy enough to hide the fact that Scotland in no way deserved to lose 1–0. Paul Sturrock, a surprise choice by Ferguson, played well, as did Charlie Nicholas, and Roy Aitken scored a goal that replays showed was perfectly valid. It was disallowed for offside.

Gordon Strachan put Scotland ahead in the second game, against yet another strong and ultra-professional West German team. What I remember most about that strike is not the goal but Strachan's improvised celebration afterwards, when he mocked his lack of height by pretending that the advertising board at the side of the goal was too high for him to leap over. Germany recovered and muscled their way to a 2–1 win. Even after two defeats, however, a win against Uruguay in the final game would put us through to the next stage.

I believe that Brazil and Argentina produce the world's best footballers and are the teams to watch above all others. This alas does not apply to their neighbours, Uruguay. The Uruguayans played against Scotland with a nastiness that was wicked in its cynicism. Indeed, the referee had no option but to send off one of their players for a horrible assault on Strachan with only a minute played.

Eighty-nine minutes against ten men? Surely we couldn't lose this one. Well, we didn't, but we didn't win it either. I watched the game in the Press Bar in Albion Street, Glasgow. It was a hot, sticky evening, the bar was packed, and as we sank our pints, somehow the play thousands of miles away across the Atlantic got more and more sticky too. The French referee, having started strongly, could not cope with the South Americans' relentless malevolence. Scotland tried to keep their discipline in the face of constant provocation, but they became nervous and edgy as the game wore on and the Uruguayans became ever more sneakily vicious and disruptive.

Scotland carved out a few chances; the best fell to Stevie Nicol of Liverpool, the result of a fine pass from Roy Aitken. Nicol was a terrifically hard-working player but not a natural stiker. So it was a goalless draw and Scotland retreated from Mexico without even the usual compensating sense of glorious failure. Yet I feel we came closer in that campaign than in any other. The record looks bad; three games without a win and only one goal scored. But there were no humiliations and in the first and third games the Scots undoubtedly deserved more than they got.

Those World Cup Finals lacked an exceptional team. Had Scotland managed to beat the contemptible Uruguayans they would have gone on to play Maradona's Argentina, and who knows what might have happened? Had we burst through the huge barrier of qualifying from the first round, we could have surprised everybody. And Gordon Strachan, I feel, was poised to become the player of the tournament. That might seem farcical, in retrospect: it was obviously Maradona's tournament. And yet Strachan had played well in each of Scotland's games; he was 28 then, and at his absolute peak. (Such speculation is the habitual compensation of Scotland fans through the ages.)

In truth, I wasn't really too bothered about Scotland's by now customary exit after the first three games. Like many Aberdeen fans I had selfishly, even disgracefully, resented the fact that our exceptional manager, Alex Ferguson, had been managing Scotland as well as Aberdeen for nearly a year. (There was a precedent: Jock Stein managed Scotland for nine games, including five World Cup qualifiers, in 1965, at the very time when he was building his all-conquering Celtic team. Stein's teams beat Finland and Italy but also lost to Poland and Italy. Thus we did not qualify for the 1966 finals in England).

After Mexico, I was confident that the SFA would appoint a new Scotland manager and that Fergie would be able to concentrate solely on the new season with Aberdeen. I had, however, been aware of intimations that Alex was becoming frustrated at Aberdeen. Pittodrie was too small a stage for his huge talents. I suspect that, if anything, the Scotland experience had compounded his growing restlessness.

I was also coming to realise, with some surprise and perhaps a little shame, that supporting Aberdeen FC meant more to me than supporting Scotland. Obviously I continued to take an interest in the Scottish national team, and I often, but not always, watched their games on television. The national coaches, Andy Roxburgh and then Craig Brown, did well with limited resources and managed to qualify for the World Cup finals in 1990 and again in 1998. But I could not get enthused.

A particular low point came in the finals of 1998. Scotland played creditably in the opening match, against Brazil, and went down 2–1. Then there was a sound, if grim, 1–1 draw with Norway. Everything, as usual, depended on the third game, against Morocco. Scotland were abject; they lost 3–0 and thus finished ignominiously at the bottom of the group, three points behind Morocco, who were second bottom.

I remember the campaigns in the finals of 1974, 1978, 1982 and 1986 as if they took place yesterday; I wasn't there, but I lived through the games with terrible intensity, often in the company of people who cared about it all even more than I did. I can recall exactly where I was and with whom I watched each of these twelve games. But I can remember remarkably little about the six games of 1990 and 1998. Somehow, my passion for Scotland had evaporated.

The nadir was still to come, in the disastrous reign of Berti Vogts. This ridiculous appointment said little for the acumen of the SFA. Berti had many faults, one of the worst being a penchant for redundant, totally meaningless friendlies. In one of these, against Romania at Hampden in March 2004, the excellent young Celtic defender, John Kennedy, suffered a horrendous injury to his left knee after a crass tackle by the Romanian Ioan Ganea.

Kennedy had not been in Berti's original squad, but two consecutive displays of composed defending, in central defence against Barcelona and then at left back against Rangers, persuaded Berti to bring him in, not just into the squad but into the team. It would have been bad enough had Kennedy suffered this terrible injury in a meaningful game; that it happened in a spurious friendly made things even worse. That for me was the final confirmation of Berti's wrong-headedness, and the ridiculous nature of some so-called international football.

Berti at last departed and Walter Smith, the wise choice, was installed as his successor. Walter's first game, a 2–0 defeat against Italy in the San Siro, Milan, gave immediate indications of improvement. The team looked organised, the players appeared to know what they were supposed to be doing and they played with spirit.

I remain a proud Scot. I've spent almost all of my working life in Scotland, which I love dearly. On the other hand I am not an Aberdonian (I was born in Glasgow; my family moved to Aberdeen when I was four) and I am not that often in Aberdeen these days. And if you asked that somewhat absurd but still necessary question, would I rather see Scotland win the World Cup or Aberdeen win the European Champions' League, I'd unhesitatingly plump for the first, for Scotland. And so how on earth, after that, can I say that a club side, Aberdeen FC, mean more to me than the national team? But I can, and it's true.

How? Why? I only wish I knew.

CHAPTER 4

IAN BUCHAN

In 1971 a rather louche, heavily moustached newcomer arrived on the *Scotsman* editorial floor, from the *Guardian* in Manchester. He quickly let it be known that he had little time for the somnolent atmosphere that prevailed. Some resented him; others appreciated the fact that at last here was someone with the personality to liven the place up. His name was Ian Buchan. I immediately responded to his Rabelaisian presence. Even better, Ian came originally from the North-East – and he was an Aberdeen supporter. I had been surrounded by Hibs and Hearts devotees; now the cavalry had arrived.

Over the next few years Ian and I would visit, as well as the three Glasgow temples of Hampden, Ibrox and Parkhead, all sorts of grounds in all sorts of places – Methil, Ayr, Dundee, Paisley, Stirling, Falkirk, Hamilton, Greenock, Arbroath, Dumbarton and so on, as we followed Aberdeen round Scotland. Ian liked a good drink before and after a game and he had an unfailing penchant for sniffing out convivial bars in the most unlikely of contexts. A typical Buchan pub would be a smallish free house, quiet and well run without being in any way grim or austere, and dedicated to the business of drinking without too many other distractions. He didn't particularly like pubs that were full of football fans. But he enjoyed his football and he had a droll perspective on everything, which made him a superb companion.

But first I had to get my stint as a full-time sportswriter on the *Scotsman* out of the way. It did not last too long. A new post had been created for me, mainly to cover the so-called minor sports with big one-off features. This was pleasant work – both the people running these sports and the participants were incredibly grateful for any kind of publicity – and I could not help contrasting their civility and openness with the closed and blinkered boorishness that too often then characterised the world of Scottish professional football.

I also had the privilege of meeting some truly great sportsmen, some of whom appeared to train with a dedication and application that were perhaps not always prevalent among Scottish professional footballers. One of them was an Edinburgh teenager who was getting up at five every morning to train with his coach Frank Thomas at Warrender Park Baths for two and a half hours before school. His name was David Wilkie; he went on to win a silver medal at the Munich Olympics in 1972 and a gold medal four years later.

But I was allowed to cover football too, and, as John Rafferty was the only other staff writer covering the game, I got quite a lot of significant matches to cover. The biggest night came in April 1972 when Rangers and Celtic both had European semi-finals on the same night in Glasgow. John, obviously enough, was reporting on the second leg of the European Cup semi-final at Parkhead. I had the lesser fixture to cover, the second leg of the European Cup Winners' Cup semi-final at Ibrox. The aggregate attendance at the two games was over 155,000, so more than 150,000 fans were watching two club games at the same time in the same Scottish city.

Celtic had drawn 0–0 with Inter in Milan and were slight favourites to go through to their third European Cup final in five years. Sadly, after another 0–0 draw, including extra time, the game ended in a penalty shoot-out. (Aberdeen, funnily enough, had gone out of Europe to Honved of Hungary in the first-ever European penalty shoot-out in season 1970–71.) Dixie Deans ballooned his penalty over the bar, and that was Celtic out.

Four miles across town, I was covering the Rangers game. They were not doing that well in the league that season (they finished fourth) but they were marching through Europe in fine style. They had drawn with Bayern Munich in the first leg of their semi-final, and they too were slight favourites to go through.

That European semi-final was the biggest game I ever reported. Rangers played with power and panache. In the first twenty minutes they almost overwhelmed Bayern with their forceful, precise football. Sandy Jardine scored in the very first minute, with a deceptive cross-shot that almost floated into the net. Then young Derek Parlane blasted in a spectacular second.

The Germans, athletic and physically strong, like all leading German sides, were no match for Rangers that night. Partly because the two goals were scored early and Rangers had such a grip on the game that there was little chance of a Munich revival, it was a relatively easy game to cover.

In a postcript to that game, a few days later Rangers played Dunfermline at Ibrox in a league game. The crowd was 5,000. In other words, 75,000 fans had simply disappeared. Not much loyalty there.

I was delighted when Rangers went on to win the Cup-Winners' Cup at the Nou Camp in Barcelona, beating Moscow Dynamo 3–2 – a game that was of course covered by John Rafferty. The man of the match was the old Pittodrie favourite, Dave Smith, who made the first two Rangers goals and also played a part in the build-up to the third. I've already mentioned that for some reason the Ibrox supporters never seemed to take to him, but that night Dave excelled.

The victory over Dynamo was vitiated by crowd trouble. The Rangers fans and the Spanish police had skirmished in the hours leading up to the match, and when there was a pitch invasion by Rangers fans at the final whistle, the tension which had been simmering erupted into a full-scale riot. Sadly, the ceremony for the public presentation of the trophy and medals at the Nou Camp had to be abandoned. As a result of the misbehaviour of a minority of their fans, Rangers were banned from European football for a season, so they could not defend the trophy.

I think I made quite an impact as a sportswriter, not because of my football writing – John Rafferty was clearly in a different class – but because of the enthusiasm with which I covered so many of the so-called minor sports. Even so, it was a big surprise when Eric Mackay, who had recently become editor of the *Scotsman*, called me to his room and made me a remarkable offer. Eric was a great racing man and I still remember the phrase he used when he told me that John Rafferty was nearing the end of his career. He said that John was 'on his final furlong'. Eric wanted me to commit to being John's eventual successor. I was flattered, but some atavistic caution made me ask for time to think about it.

As I mulled the offer over I realised that I was not as enthusiastic as I might have expected myself to be. The world of Scottish football was small, intense and incestuous. Sometimes it seemed that there was too little fresh air; the atmosphere could be fetid and claustrophobic, as in a bad pub.

Also, I was beginning to realise that the football writers inhabited a peculiar no-man's-land. On the one hand there were the fans, passionate and obsessively involved, yet wholly removed from the running of the game and unaware of much of what was going on behind the scenes. Then there were the insiders, the managers, coaches, players and directors, who tended to exclude everyone else, including the pressmen. It is true that some of these pressmen – Jim Rodger for example – were complete insiders, and others were partial insiders. But for the most part the football writers worked in a kind of awkward halfway house between the territory of the fans on the terraces and the territory where the real insiders operated, the bowels of the stands.

I sensed that John Rafferty was a particularly happy and sanguine football writer (unless Bobby Davidson was refereeing a cup final) because he'd come to the job relatively late in life, after a career as a teacher. He was also covering his beloved Celtic as they dominated Scottish football, season after season.

Many of the other sportswriters I'd met were, after long years of dreich afternoons at Cappielow and Stark's Park, and drearier nights at Love Street or Boghead, essentially defeated men. I'm not just talking about drab games. I'm talking about the frustration of hanging around, sometimes for as long as sixty minutes after a game, for quotes and angles that maybe never materialised. They were decent men – some of them former players – and they disguised any bitterness as best they could with a rather bruised, forced bonhomie. But underneath this outward cheerfulness there often lay a deep cynicism. Many of them drank very heavily; indeed, looking back on these days, it seems that the whole game was awash with booze. There has always been a drinking culture in Scottish professional football; less so nowadays, but the problem is now transferred to aspiring footballers, some of them as young as twelve or thirteen.

Many of these journalists wrote exceptionally well and the more prescient of them anticipated the way that their influence was beginning to decline. Although most of them sincerely loved the game they wrote about day in, day out, they somehow sensed that they were trapped. Once a football writer, always a football writer.

The thought of inhabiting this introverted, insular world, possibly for the rest of my life, at once enthralled and appalled me. Scotland had many outstanding footballers then. I thought, as I have shown, that the national team were on the verge of great things. But I had the foresight to realise that one World Cup might be wonderful – but the fifth or sixth? Football was a demanding, greedy specialism. Some of the football writers I knew actually longed to be golf writers. They reckoned the world of golf was purer, cleaner, more glamorous and more rewarding than the rather grubby world of football. I was not in the slightest interested in golf, but the essential disillusion with football that I had witnessed among the writers made me wonder.

Eventually I decided to say no. Eric Mackay was not best pleased. He called me in again a few weeks later and announced that I was to become the *Scotsman's* first full-time education correspondent. This time the offer was unconditional. I did not have the option of refusal.

I was not particularly pleased as I eased into my new job but I soon realised that the role had three great advantages. First, I had a significant pay rise. Secondly, my Saturdays and most midweek nights were free. I could watch Aberdeen all the time and yes, that actually seemed like a treat. Thirdly, I soon realised that I was getting an insight into how Scotland functioned. I learned about the working of the Scottish Office and local government.

For the first time I got to know politicians, at both national and local level (including an ambitious and bright young Raith Rovers supporter who was the very political student rector of Edinburgh University, one Gordon Brown). As I went about my work I was getting an extended lesson in the anatomy of my country, how it was governed and how the various public parts interacted.

At this time, an unprecedented anger was simmering away in Scottish education. What did this have to do with Scottish football? Well, it was not obvious at the time, but what was stirring in the schools was to have a profound and deleterious effect on our national game. It is no exaggeration to write that the consequences of the teacher militancy that began in the mid-1970s were to be disastrous for Scottish football.

The 1970s were a decade of general industrial trouble. Early in 1974 the miners effectively brought down Ted Heath's Tory Government. Harold Wilson then got them back to work with what many regarded as a policy of appeasement. There followed a steady build-up of industrial strife that culminated in the 'winter of discontent' of 1978–79 which helped to put paid to Jim Callaghan's Labour Government and ushered in Mrs Thatcher – and 18 years of Tory rule.

At the beginning of the 1970s few involved in Scottish education could have predicted that Scottish schools were to be ravaged by industrial action. But a small group of militants, some of them in the so-called Rank and File group, was gaining power in local branches of the Educational Institute of Scotland, which was, by far, Scotland's largest teaching union, with a membership of well over 40,000.

The militants were pushing at an open door, for Scotland's teachers were grotesquely underpaid. They were also being asked, as the decade progressed, to cope with the often problematic consequences of two highly controversial policies – the raising of the school-leaving age, and the phasing out of corporal punishment. The rights and wrongs of these issues are not germane here; what is relevant is that teachers felt they were overburdened, under-valued and, in particular, underpaid.

A big charismatic man (with much of the aura of Jock Stein about him) from Ayrshire, called John Pollock, became leader of the EIS in 1974. He was elected general secretary designate at the start of the year, but he soon assumed control from the retiring general secretary, a rather academic and aloof figure called Gilbert Bryden. John had been headmaster of Mainholm Academy, Ayr (he was the first secondary head in Scotland without an honours degree). He was well versed in Labour politics. Many observers wondered why he switched to a career in the EIS instead of standing for Parliament.

Pollock was more streetwise than Bryden and he sensed that the militants within his union had to be defeated before they took control. He also understood that even his most moderate members – the so-called blue-rinse brigade, the lady primary teachers, many of whom voted Tory – were also agitated about their disgracefully low levels of pay.

So John decided to defeat militancy by embracing it himself. As the winter term of 1974 started, Scotland was surprised by a series of increasingly bellicose threats emanating from the EIS headquarters at Moray Place in the douce purlieus of Edinburgh's New Town. Various directors of education, local councillors, Labour MPs and others chose to characterise this as mere bluster. An exception to this complacency emerged in the form of George Foulkes, the young chairman of Edinburgh Council's education committee. George, who thirty years later was to become chairman of Hearts, did not underestimate the teachers' anger.

John Pollock kept assuring me, and one or two other journalists, that he meant business. I was not surprised when his threats transmuted into action.

Pollock's main adversary in the protracted fight that followed was a formidable politician called Willie Ross. A former teacher in Ayrshire, a former major in the Highland Light Infantry, a hard man with a *basso profundo* voice, a chain-smoker but a non-drinker, Ross was a Scottish Labour MP of the old school. At this time he was a Cabinet Minister, and Secretary of State for Scotland. He had been John Pollock's mentor in Ayrshire. Willie Ross was appalled by John's aggressive stance, and he ratcheted up the stakes with his furious denunciations of EIS militancy.

John's main operational adviser in the EIS was a thoughtful man called Fred Forrester, an intellectual whose official title was Organising Secretary. Fred now describes his boss, John Pollock, as 'a spin doctor before the term was invented', but Fred was no mean spin doctor himself. He had a mastery of tactics and he was given to making the odd blood-curdling speech or holding the occasional apocalyptic press conference. We journalists came to appreciate his consistent ability to raise the stakes.

The other principal player on the scene was Jimmy Docherty, the leader of the SSTA, a secondary-teachers-only union with a much smaller membership than the EIS. Docherty, known as 'Papa Doc', was a shrewd man, more forensic than many lawyers, and a cleverer negotiator than Pollock. He had a grasp of detail and he too knew the value of publicity. He understood that his own membership was seriously disgruntled and that he could not allow the EIS to take on the high ground of the struggle.

It is wrong to look at history solely through personality, but these four principals, with their strong personalities and conflicting agendas, played out a drama of gathering intensity. The winter term of 1974 ended with most of Scotland's schools closed and most teachers on strike. There were to be even more serious strikes later in the decade and again in the 1980s, but this was when even conservative country dominies and matronly lady primary teachers embraced industrial militancy for the first time.

In the early weeks of the dispute the EIS used as its preferred weapon the work-to-rule, which was Fred Forrester's brainchild. When this did not have the desired effect, strikes – intended to be the weapon of last resort – became more and more prevalent. Eventually the Government caved in (I always suspected that the obdurate Willie Ross was under pressure from his more emollient master in London, Harold Wilson). A senior member of the great and the good, Lord Houghton, was told to undertake an urgent review of Scottish teachers' pay and conditions. Houghton worked with speed and produced his report early in 1975. Its main recommendation was a raft of substantial pay increases for teachers at all levels. The minority of extreme militants was still not satisfied, but within a week or so almost all the schools were back to normal. Looking back on these momentous events, Fred Forrester told me:

> Our preferred weapon in 1974 was the work-to-rule. That eventually spilled into strikes when we could not contain our members' justifiable anger any more. The strikes, while unprecedented, were not as prolonged as those that were to follow in the 1980s.
>
> The work-to-rule tactic was significant in that it concentrated on the teachers' precise contractual obligations. At the beginning of the dispute there was a very strong linkage between your powerful grievance and confining your activities to the absolute minimum you were required to do in the working day.

What happened as a result of the work-to-rule was that voluntary activity at the weekend, and that mainly involved schools football on Saturdays, more or less stopped. Then, when the grievance was eventually resolved, it was very difficult indeed to get teachers to resume their voluntary activities. They found that they enjoyed having their weekends to themselves. They asked themselves the simple question: 'Why should I bother?' They thought: 'I'm really enjoying my weekends now.' . . . The effect of this on schools football was seriously harmful, but I would not wish the teachers of the 1970s to be presented as the villains in your book. You must realise that their working day had become so crowded, so overburdened, that even when their pay grievance was removed, they quite understandably saw no need to resume extra-curricular activities.

Football was without doubt the number one extra-curricular activity. So football indubitably suffered most. In the space of a few months, Saturday school sport dwindled away, till it became not a mainstream activity but just the responsibility of a small number of enthusiasts. It did revive again, but the seeds had been sown. Schools football was never to be the same again, particularly in the great breeding grounds of Lanarkshire and Ayrshire, Glasgow and Fife.

At this time, 1974–75, Bob Crampsey, the eminent Scottish football historian, was a tyro secondary head in Coatbridge. He confirmed Fred's view of events. Bob told me: 'Teachers had this understandable sense of liberation, but the decline of schools football was disastrous. It was not just about producing great players. The not-so-good footballer played too, and while he might not go on to make his mark as a professional, he learned to understand and appreciate the game, and he might well go on to become a referee, or an official, or just a good, well-informed supporter. All that was lost.'

The decline of Scottish schools football was not inexorable. There were revivals. But overall the tendency, over the next thirty years, was negative. Some secondary schools, which had been wont to put out as many as ten or twelve teams on a Saturday morning, were eventually hard pressed to produce one or two.

I had no idea that the events I was covering in the autumn and winter of 1974–75 were to have an indirect but nonetheless devastating effect on our national game. At the time, as far as football was concerned, I was more interested in Aberdeen FC's league games on Saturday afternoons than in what was going on, or not going on, in the parks and fields of Lanarkshire and Renfrewshire, Glasgow and Aberdeen, on Saturday mornings. When the

Houghton settlement was accepted, schooling returned to normal – from Monday to Friday. That was good enough for most people. Only a few prescient figures voiced concern about what was happening, or not happening, in schools football.

Meanwhile Aberdeen fans were suffering more betrayals. I've already mentioned that the club's star defender, Martin Buchan, was sold to Manchester United in February 1972. Just nine months later came an event that made me almost physically sick, a sale that most of the club's older supporters to this day regard as the bitterest betrayal of them all.

Joey Harper, who had scored 95 goals for the club in just 3 seasons, was sold to Everton for what seemed the knockdown price of £200,000. The word 'idol' is over-used in football, but Harper was a genuine idol at Pittodrie. There is no other valid word. A fortnight before he was sold, he'd won his first Scotland cap, scoring in a World Cup qualifier in Denmark.

The only, very minor, compensation was the arrival of a Hungarian forward called Zoltan Varga. Zoltan had been implicated in a scandal with his previous club in Berlin, but all the Dons fans cared about were his extraordinary skills. Although I never saw him seize a game by the throat, he was eminently watchable – a bit like Charlie Cooke in that sense. Had Varga not arrived on the scene a few weeks before Harper departed, I believe that there might well have been major riots outside Pittodrie when Joey went.

Aberdeen were deteriorating at an alarming rate. Rangers had taken over as the main challengers to Jock Stein's Celtic in the league. That season Aberdeen did have two intense struggles with Celtic in the two domestic cups. They lost 3–2 to Celtic in the League Cup semi-final at Hampden, a game that was played on a foul November night. They were unlucky, hitting the woodwork three times. (It was one of the very few times that Varga and Harper played in the same team, and there was much promise in their partnership.)

Ian Buchan took me to the Glasgow Press Club after the game – he thought the ambience there would cheer me up. It didn't. In fact much later that night I ended up being detained in Rutherglen police station, but that is another story for another time.

In the Scottish Cup itself a dour defensive display by the Dons – one I was not particularly proud to watch – enabled them to scrape a 0–0 draw at Parkhead, but Celtic won the replay at Pittodrie with a Billy McNeill header.

I was still watching the occasional English game. In 1970 I'd returned to Newcastle to see the wonderful Manchester United team with Denis Law,

Georgie Best and Bobby Charlton (arguably each of them the greatest player their country ever produced) in a forward line of almost fantasy excellence. Once or twice after that I'd driven down to Newcastle with Hugh to see Jimmy Smith, who was still in and out of the United side. I watched the odd game when I was in London. In these days Scottish league football was not markedly inferior to the English product. How things were to change, a generation or so later.

But Aberdeen were going nowhere. The next season, 1973–74, there was more doom and gloom; the only bright development was that a young man from the Bridgeton area of Glasgow, called Willie Miller, established himself in the team as a classy, consistent defender. By now I was probably watching Hibs as often as Aberdeen, not least because Joey Harper was now playing for them, having been surprisingly transferred from Everton.

I was becoming friendly with Arnold Kemp, the *Scotsman*'s deputy editor and the best all-round journalist I've known. Arnold was in his bohemian way a dedicated Hibs fan and he and his wife Sandra used to hold open house in their home just half a mile or so from Easter Road, for an hour or so before Hibs home games. Among those who attended regularly were Ian Wood (later to become the *Scotsman*'s sports editor) and other *Scotsman* stalwarts like Jim Dow and Ronnie Munro. Afterwards Arnold and I would sometimes have a drink in the Windsor Buffet or Sinclair's Bar.

People like Arnold and Ian Wood seemed to take the business of following their team less seriously than I did. They were, to use one of Arnold's preferred words, 'Corinthian'. Hibs, like Aberdeen, were in decline, but Arnold and Ian didn't resent this; they accepted it. During a dull game Arnold had various ways of entertaining himself. He had a theory that in any team there'd always be a player who for one reason or another was hiding. Sometimes he tried to get us to spot who it was. I disliked this game and it led to one my many arguments with Arnold; we had a combustible friendship.

Perhaps I had an exaggerated respect for professional footballers. But I never forgot my inability to play the game with any skill. I also remembered the tales I'd heard about John White, the great Scottish inside forward from Musselburgh who was killed by lightning on a golf course near Enfield in 1964. White would float on the periphery of a game, apparently having zero impact; then he'd suddenly receive the ball, ghost into space, and hit a game-changing pass.

In these years when I was trying to convince Arnold of the importance of football journalism I was on weak ground, having turned down the chance to be John Rafferty's successor, but I felt Arnold had a somewhat dismissive attitude. He called the sports pages on the *Scotsman* the paper's 'raffish endpiece'. This was a common attitude of newspaper executives then; even the most perceptive of them seemed unaware of how avidly the sports pages were picked over by players and fans alike.

To be fair to Arnold, he changed his ways. When he became editor of the *Glasgow Herald*, he was an enormous supporter of the paper's sportsdesk. He also built up a storehouse of stories about football journalism. My favourite concerned the well-known *Herald* feature writer who for years had been moonlighting as an anonymous sports reporter for a Sunday paper. When he eventually decided he'd had enough, he mischievously filled his final report with every single football writing cliché he could think of. His intro actually read 'This was a game of two halves.' That night the Sunday paper's sports editor phoned him to say he'd never read such a well-written piece and he could have a staff job if he wanted it.

Another of Arnold's stories was of how on a visit to the North-East, he was roped in by the *Scotsman's* redoubtable North of Scotland correspondent, Harry Dunn, to be his phonist at a big game at Pittodrie. Harry was busy scribbling his final takes when a dramatic late goal was scored. Arnold had been watching the play carefully and he gave Harry a detailed account of the intricate build-up to the goal. He was miffed to read Harry's next take: 'Jarvie then scored after a goalmouth scramble.'

Anyway, the following season, 1974–75, Aberdeen slipped a little more, to fifth place in the league, just eight points away from tenth spot. I mention tenth place because that was the cut-off point for the new Premier Division. At last, reconstruction had taken place.

Aberdeen's response to the new streamlined 'Premier Division' of ten clubs in season 1975–76 was pitiful. By October they were fighting it out with St Johnstone at the bottom of the league, adrift from the other eight. As two clubs were to be relegated, this was ominous. Already people – not least Ian Buchan and myself – were talking about Aberdeen being relegated for the first time in their history.

Aberdeen's manager, the affable and decent but too tractable Jimmy Bonthrone, did the proper thing and resigned. A month later the new man took over, the manager of Ayr United. His name was Ally MacLeod. Ally had first made his name as a left winger with Third Lanark. He'd been sold to Blackburn Rovers in 1956 for a big fee, which wiped out Thirds' accumulated debts. Ally was known as a cheeky chappy, a supreme enthusiast.

Because of the World Cup debacle he was later to preside over in Argentina, when he was Scotland's manager, Ally MacLeod will always be associated with spectacular football failure. The paradox is that from the Aberdeen perspective he will always be associated with success. He cheered Pittodrie up; he made some shrewd signings and he revived the team. And he made a lot of noise. That was enough, so bad had things been, to grant him saviour status.

Shortly before his appointment I'd written an indulgent and irascible piece for the *Scotsman* attacking Aberdeen's directors for steering the club ever downwards and throwing away Eddie Turnbull's legacy. It was, I think, the only time I abused my position as a journalist. I was astonished to get a call from the club's vice-chairman, Chris Anderson. His tone was emollient. He said that he and the chairman Dick Donald felt that the piece was unfair and its tone worried them because they had ambitious plans for the club. He'd like to meet me.

Chris and I had lunch in an Italian restaurant in Aberdeen a fortnight later and we hit it off straightway. He was a fresh-faced, soft-spoken man, with a deceptively gentle manner (Chris had his hard side. He had been a rugged, uncompromising right half for the Dons in the 1950s). He soon dispensed with his irritation about the piece in the *Scotsman*. Having established that I was a genuine Dons fan, and not some fly-by-night controversialist, he spelt out his ideas for the club, not least the fact that he wanted Pittodrie to be an all-seated stadium – in the mid-seventies a revolutionary concept. He was also, I learned, one of the architects of the new ten-team premier division.

That was the first of many conversations I had with Chris. He drilled into me his belief that Scottish football was in the grip of those he called hardcore conservatives, backward-looking men who were not receptive to new ideas, who were not thinking ahead. He also said that most club boards were too big, filled with reactionary timeservers. Buggins ruled.

I quickly realised that Chris was very different. I was in the presence of that rare breed, a Scottish football visionary. He was keen for me to do an exclusive extended interview with Ally MacLeod, who was beginning to make his mark at Pittodrie, not least with a series of outrageous predictions: Aberdeen could not just win the league, they could win the European Cup. I kid you not.

When we met a few days later, Ally and I did not exactly have a meeting of minds. Ally was aware that I was the *Scotsman*'s education correspondent and was now only writing about football as a sideline. He seemed determined to impress with me with his ideas about secondary education (Ally had ideas about everything under the sun) and to talk about football as little as possible. I kept steering him round to football; he kept steering me back to education. He emphasised the need for freshness and surprise in all walks of life, and education in particular. Routine was the enemy. Timetabling was the curse of school life. Timetables should be ripped up. Schoolkids should turn up in the morning not knowing what lessons or teachers they were going to have. That would solve all educational problems at a stroke.

This was typical Ally; the germ of an idea, but not thought through, and if implemented without planning, a recipe for complete anarchy.

After a bright start, Ally began to hit problems at Pittodrie. His team struggled and they very narrowly avoided relegation in the spring of 1976. Then he made the signing that for me and most Dons fans, really mattered. He persuaded Joey Harper to return to Pittodrie from Easter Road in time for the 1976–77 season.

In that season it was the League Cup, the least important of the three domestic competitions, that gave Ally success and helped to propel him to a job he was not suited for – that of Scotland manager. The first game of the season was a League Cup-tie against Kilmarnock at Pittodrie. With a typical piece of showmanship Ally made the returned Harper captain for the day and Joey duly responded with a goal after just three minutes. He went on to score another twenty-seven that season.

In the quarter-final of the League Cup, in the autumn, Aberdeen were drawn against Stirling Albion. They managed to beat Alex Smith's team with a single Harper goal in the first leg at Pittodrie. I watched the second leg on the terracing at Anfield with Ian Buchan on a wild night of lashing rain and hailstorms. Just 3,000 were present. Stirling deservedly went 1–0 up and the game dragged into extra time as the weather became even more foul. Stirling did everything but score a second. Aberdeen struggled desperately to hold on. They did, just, and this meant a third tie at neutral Dens Park, Dundee.

Ian and I drove up on another wet and dismal night to see Aberdeen ease through 2–0, before another pitifully small crowd. That paved the way for the semi-final against Rangers at Hampden. After standing on dilapidated terraces watching these two earlier games in the grimmest of conditions, I would have been well rewarded had I been at Hampden that night. But I had to be in England, so I missed Aberdeen thumping Rangers 5–1 in what some observers thought was Aberdeen's finest post-war performance. Ally's sides were never consistent; they could struggle desperately against Stirling Albion and then sweep the mighty Rangers aside.

Anyway, it was on to the final against Celtic at Hampden. Aberdeen won the final, and thus the trophy, despite going behind to an early Kenny Dalglish penalty. They triumphed 2–1 with an extra-time winner from Davie Robb, but standing on the north terrace with Ian and my brother Hugh, I was embarrassed. Celtic were in complete control of the game and the result was no reflection of the play. Willie Miller, already emerging as a dignified captain, admitted as much.

Yet the record showed that Ally had won a trophy less than a year after taking over at Pittodrie. He had beaten the Old Firm by an aggregate of 7–2 in two consecutive games at Hampden. This indicated a managerial prowess he didn't really possess. When, at the end of the season, Willie Ormond quit as Scotland manager, Ally was offered the job. It is harsh to write this, but I sincerely feel that Aberdeen had a great escape; Ally left before he was found out. Aberdeen's gain was Scotland's loss.

Aberdeen's next manager was Billy McNeill, captain of the glorious Celtic team that had won the European Cup exactly ten years earlier, and a man who'd always played superbly against the Dons. He is one of the undoubted all-time giants of Scottish football. In his one season in charge at Pittodrie, he took Aberdeen close to Rangers in both the league and the cup. In the league Aberdeen finished second, two points behind the men from Ibrox; in the cup they were beaten 2–1 by Rangers in the final at Hampden, when, despite the narrow scoreline, Aberdeen were outclassed.

McNeill's most important contribution as Aberdeen manager was two inspired signings for a total of less than £100,000: Gordon Strachan from Dundee and Steve Archibald from Clyde. Aberdeen, always a selling club, had suddenly plundered two other Scottish clubs for a couple of special players of infinite potential. Strachan and Archibald are up there with the all-time greats. They were to star in World Cups and European Finals, to excel for clubs like Manchester United, Leeds, Spurs and Barcelona and to amass 87 Scottish caps between them.

I doubt if any other British manager has ever spent as little for so much talent. Archibald only stayed at Pittodrie for three seasons before he was off to Spurs for £800,000, but he gave the club sterling service in this short time, scoring many crucial goals. Strachan, a world class player, stayed for seven seasons and played a key role in the club's finest years.

In the summer of 1978 Jock Stein was ungraciously removed from the managerial chair at Parkhead. That was the cue for McNeill to be summoned to Glasgow as his replacement. Dick Donald and Chris Anderson did not try to make him stay but wasted no time in signing their third manager in less than a year. Their choice was controversial: Alex Ferguson, who had just been fired by St Mirren. The man who acted as the go-between was that superb journalistic fixer Jim Rodger, now with the *Daily Mirror*. When I heard the news in the *Scotsman* offices I remember turning to my colleague Jim Seaton and saying I thought it was a bad appointment. That was the stupidest thing I ever said.

CHAPTER 5

THE NEW FIRM

Although I was, and remain, awestruck by Alex Ferguson's achievements during his 8 years at Pittodrie, it is important to emphasise his relatively strong inheritance. On the playing side he had Joey Harper, then the most natural goalscorer in Scotland (in Ferguson's first season Harper scored 33 goals) and in Willie Miller the Scottish game's most tenacious tackler, a supremely consistent defender and a captain with a maturity way beyond his years.

Among the others he inherited were the McNeill signings Archibald and Strachan and that most underrated right back Stuart Kennedy. Plus a very cultured midfielder called John McMaster. (Kennedy played just 8 times for Scotland, McMaster not once. Fast-forward 27 or 28 years, and I wonder how many caps they'd be getting today?)

And then there was Alex McLeish, a big wholehearted centre half whom Billy McNeill had 'blooded' when he was just 17. McNeill probably saw something of himself in the young McLeish; it took Alex Ferguson a good 18 months before he was playing McLeish regularly, and that was often in midfield. But this midfield experience gave Alex an all-round edge to his game that was to be invaluable when he at last formed his legendary partnership with Miller.

There was also a young goalkeeper called Jim Leighton, who had been farmed out to the Highland side Devronvale. Circumstances immediately catapulted this raw, inexperienced goalie into the first team in place of Bobby Clark and he starred in Ferguson's first game, a 4–1 victory over Hearts at Tynecastle.

I was at that game, and you did not need to be particularly perceptive to see that Leighton was special. He let in a goal, by Eamonn Bannon, after just three minutes, but he did not allow the early setback to unsettle him, despite the appalling conditions (the entire game was played in torrential rain). Indeed, without Leighton's exceptional performance, the score would probably have been 4–4.

Players of the calibre of Miller and Strachan and so on were quite an inheritance, but even more importantly, Alex Ferguson had the support of a sensible and progressive board. Then, and possibly even now, the phrase 'a sensible and progressive board' is, in the context of Scottish football, an oxymoron. But Aberdeen's three-man board was motivated not by personal ambition or diseased egotism but, purely and simply, by the best interests of the club. Board meetings would be held informally at lunchtimes. The shrewd geniality and businesslike caution of Chairman Donald perfectly balanced the more expansive, forward-looking approach of Chris Anderson.

Ferguson was also lucky in that he had to advise him the best of the many unsung backroom boys in Scottish football. Teddy Scott was in his time both reserve team coach and kit manager, but his main role was that of all-round back-of-the-house factotum.

It was Teddy who spotted Willie Miller's potential as a defender. When Willie arrived at Aberdeen from Eastercraigs he was a forward, and indeed the club farmed the 17-year-old striker out to Peterhead where he hit 23 goals in one Highland League season. But the perceptive Teddy Scott noted something in his play that convinced him that Willie could become a first-class defender. Teddy Scott had been at Pittodrie since 1954 and there were not enough hours in the day for him to do all his work for the club. Sometimes he slept overnight at the ground. If I were asked to name Aberdeen FC's greatest servants, I'd unhesitatingly cite two names: Teddy Scott and his greatest protégé, Willie Miller.

Significantly, Scott noted that one of Ferguson's very first requests was for all the morning papers to be delivered to Pittodrie. The manager would peruse the sports pages carefully before most of the staff had arrived at the ground.

Ferguson's first season was not especially propitious. In September, Aberdeen drew with Rangers at Ibrox, scoring a late equaliser. I did not know this at the time, but evidently Alex had one of his famous rages after the game. He was furious that the players were celebrating a draw; he told them that celebrations would be reserved for victories. This was an early indication of his determination not to be overawed by the Old Firm. He would take on Rangers and Celtic, and beat them on their own territory, and treat them as equals or even inferiors.

A week or so later Aberdeen beat Celtic 4–1 at Pittodrie, with Archibald and Harper playing superbly. The following Monday that astute sportswriter Alan Davidson wrote in the Glasgow *Evening Times* that this kind of performance was all very well, but Aberdeen needed consistency. They could produce the odd fine result, but they seemed destined to be perpetual nearly men of Scottish football. I worried about this analysis and in truth that season bore it out. Aberdeen finished fourth in the league; they were beaten by Rangers in an ill-tempered League Cup final and in the Scottish Cup they were knocked out by Hibs in a hard-fought semi-final.

The next season was to be Aberdeen's and Ferguson's breakthrough, but most of it looked like being yet another chapter in the sad saga of the nearly men. At the end of December Aberdeen were languishing in fourth place in the league, quite a few points behind the leaders, Celtic. In the League Cup they beat Rangers home and away, and repeated the feat against Celtic. Having done the hard work, surely the cup would be theirs?

Well, in the semi-final against an Andy Ritchie-inspired Morton (then, remarkably, the league leaders) at Hampden they were incredibly lucky. In one of the most nerve-wracking finales I ever watched, they clung on to their 2–1 lead.

It was a different story in the final at Hampden, just a week later. The opposition were Dundee United. Aberdeen dominated, but they missed the injured Harper, and United held out for a dour 0–0 draw. There were only 27,000 in the ground (most of them Dons fans, but even so it was a pitiful attendance for a national final). This raised one of the perennial issues in Scottish football, much raised in Glasgow; if teams other than the Old Firm cannot produce decent crowds for even cup finals, what right have they to moan about the ascendancy of the two great Glasgow teams? The answer, at least in part, might be that the big games – finals and semi-finals – should be spread around geographically.

And certainly, when the replay was played in midweek at Dens Park, Dundee, after pressure from both clubs to have the game moved from Hampden, the attendance was up slightly, at 29,000, but the atmosphere was better because of the smaller ground.

I was at that game on my own, Ian Buchan having called off at the last minute, and it was one of the most depressing nights of my football-watching career. For a start, the rain was teeming down. (For some reason, many of both the worst and best football matches I have seen have been played in torrential rain.) I was stuck in a crowded open terrace at the side of the south enclosure, and I was thoroughly soaked before the game even started.

Like most supporters I like to watch the game with a friend or friends, but you watch the game with greater intensity if you are on your own. That night

I confidently expected the Dons to sweep United aside. After all, they had beaten Rangers and Celtic, home and away, in four games on the way to the final, scoring nine goals and conceding only three. United had on the other hand reached the final without having had to play a single Premier League opponent.

The pitch was so wet it looked unplayable, but that is not an excuse. Aberdeen were outclassed. United's Paul Hegarty, David Narey and in particular Paul Sturrock played like the thoroughbreds they were. United scored early, and although Aberdeen rarely looked like equalising, it was not until midway through the second half that United scored their second. Then, fifteen minutes from the end, the outstanding Sturrock scored an absolute beauty to clinch the trophy.

I had a perfect view of that goal, and as the ball hit the net my immediate instinct was to quit the ground there and then. But I remained stubbornly on the rapidly thinning terrace, hoping irrationally, as fans do, for a late goal. Even a fluke would have done – anything to spark the most unlikely of comebacks. I was really just hoping for that most forlorn of scores, the so-called 'consolation' goal. It was not to be. Aberdeen's destiny seemed confirmed: Ferguson wasn't going to change anything. Aberdeen were just a nearly team, doomed to be always second or third. Thereabouts. Never quite there.

Actually, that night was important and historic. It was the pivotal point in the creation of the new dispensation which was about to dominate Scottish football. On the night, Ferguson lost graciously; the next morning he reacted to the debacle with renewed vigour. To use the jargon, he regrouped. He shook hands with each of his players as they arrived at Pittodrie and assured them that they would not lose another final. He was as good as his word. I sense that was the moment when he finally knew that he could not tolerate being second best.

As for United, they had won their first-ever trophy. Their canny manager, Jim McLean, had won the tactical battle with his old friend and rival Ferguson. The triumph gave United confidence. So that game at Dens was United's launchpad, the platform they needed to give them the drive to combine with Aberdeen in creating the so-called New Firm who were to change Scottish football in such spectacular fashion.

United were to go on and win the league and sweep through Europe, enjoying many illustrious feats. They were to reach the final of the UEFA

Cup, a run that included a titanic away victory against Barcelona. Even more impressively, they were to reach the semi-finals of the European Cup, going out unluckily on a 2–3 aggregate to Roma.

Thus, on that dreich, dismal night at Dens, the New Firm were born. For United, the triumph gave them belief. For the losers, Aberdeen, adversity gave them determination and a renewed will.

If someone had told me as I left Dens, bedraggled, wet to the bone, and worse, bludgeoned by my team's comprehensive defeat, that all that United success lay ahead, then I might – just – have believed him. If the same someone had told me that Aberdeen were about to go on a run which included two European trophies, three league titles and three successive Scottish Cup wins, I'd have told him in the Scottish vernacular to 'Awa an boil yer heid.'

At this time, a most remarkable development occurred in Scottish football. It showed, among other things, that the press still had considerable influence.

Stewart Brown, the senior football writer for the Edinburgh *Evening News*, proposed that Hibs, struggling against relegation and playing before depressingly meagre crowds, should sign Georgie Best. A few years earlier Best had been an exceptional celebrity forward but now, at 33, his love of the high life had taken its toll. He had left Manchester United in 1975, having scored 137 goals for them over 10 seasons. Some of these goals were among the most impish and cheeky ever scored.

He had drifted round the world, a nomad of fitful brilliance, playing for teams as varied as Los Angles Aztecs, Cork Celtic and Fulham. He had recently returned to the UK from Florida, where he had been starring for Fort Lauderdale Strikers. Best went everywhere with a lot of baggage but Brown shrewdly argued that his very presence would boost the club and be worth all the attendant risks.

Luckily, in Tom Hart, a controversial and dictatorial director of the old school, Hibs had a chairman who was prepared to gamble. Hart ran his own building business and was used to getting his own way, and was not given to paying much attention to anyone else. But he was a friend of Stewart Brown, and he took everything that Stewart wrote seriously. Within two or three weeks of Brown's first article, Best had signed a game by game contract. He was to be paid £2,000 per appearance (a small fortune in those days).

To some extent, the gamble paid off. Best only played about twenty games, and he could not save Hibs from relegation; but for the most part he gave value for the big money. On one notorious occasion he went missing on the match-day, and Hart fired him. But he was back in action a week or so later.

I remember seeing him score a spectacular goal against Celtic. Even better, one night, after an interminable meeting at North Bridge I slipped down to Easter Road, almost as an afterthought, to see Hibs in a midweek league game against Dundee. Best was playing in midfield and it was his passing, not his dribbling, that caught the eye. His touch and his vision were little short of miraculous. It was one of the finest individual displays I've seen. I stood on the old high terrace opposite the main stand utterly spellbound. I still cherish the memory of that night. Hibs won 2–0, but that is not the point. It is not fanciful or ridiculous, just the plain truth, to state that I'd seen a genius at work.

These days my preferred bar was the Halfway House, halfway down Fleshmarket Close behind the *Scotsman* building in North Bridge. It was a gem of a pub, superbly run by an old-fashioned landlord called Alex Lannie, who once famously told two of the *Scotsman*'s more dilettante graduate trainees to drink faster or get out. The Halfway House was patronised by journalists, detectives, railway workers from Waverley and production staff from the *Scotsman*'s case room and machine room. A few yards further up the close was the more upmarket Jinglin Geordie, whose clientele consisted of more pretentious journalists, city councillors, advocates, lawyers and footballers. Georgie chose this pub as one of his watering holes and I confess that once or twice some of us forsook the Halfway House in order to be in the same pub as the great man. But I am happy to say that I never bought him a drink.

It was sad to see people crowding around Georgie, desperate to inflict hospitality on him. He accepted the attention – and adulation – with gracious charm, and that was part of the trouble. It was no wonder that his problems with alcohol steadily worsened. The Easter Road experiment lasted just a few months. By the middle of April 1980, Georgie was off on his travels once more, to San Jose Earthquakes in California. Well, it was warmer there.

Meanwhile, as the bitterly cold winter of 1980 gave way reluctantly to spring, there was no indication of the pyrotechnics to come in the climax to that season's league. In late February Aberdeen were third in the league, behind Celtic and Morton. Celtic had eight points more than the Dons (at that time a win was worth only two points) although they had played two games more. They looked certainties to be champions.

It was during a pretty dismal mid-week game against Dundee at Pittodrie a month later that I had an inkling that something special might be about to happen. Again, this was a game I watched on my own and I can recall its course clearly. Andy Watson, an unsung player if ever there was one, scored early on, but although the Dons were the better team they could not press home their advantage. The attendance was poor – less than 7,000 – and, as all too often happened at Pittodrie when the Dons could not raise their game, the fans vented their irritation on the team.

I remember thinking that this was remarkably similar to the games I'd watched about twenty years earlier: the atmosphere was flat and most of the play was drab to a degree. I thought that the Dons would do well to hold on for a dour 1–0 win. Worse, I became fatefully certain, as did the fans around me, that Dundee would somehow equalise, though their stodgy play did not suggest any attacking prowess. It was almost as if, with that perversity that can overtake frustrated football fans, the crowd actually *wanted* Dundee to score, to justify the feeling that such a development had a grisly inevitability.

But this Aberdeen team were different. From somewhere (the dugout?) they found the will to express their class. Two players turned the game: John McMaster, who started to spray lovely passes around, and Andy Watson, whose dogged determination in midfield was quietly inspirational. The Dons scored two very late goals, by Drew Jarvie and Willie Miller, and ended the game looking like champions.

That game was the catalyst for an incredible run. Because of bad weather earlier in the season, the Dons had to play Celtic twice at Parkhead in the space of three weeks. They won both games, with Strachan outstanding. This signalled that something extraordinary was happening. You were not supposed to beat the Old Firm on their home territory. To do so twice in a month, in crucial games, was unheard of. At the beginning of May Aberdeen went to Easter Road for the second-last game of the season. If they beat Hibs (now, sadly, without Best) and Celtic dropped a point at St Mirren, the title was theirs – for the first time in 25 years.

Hibs were the bottom club and already relegated; they offered scant resistance. Aberdeen smashed in five goals without reply, one of them coming from man-of-the-moment, Andy Watson. We stood on the terrace behind the south goal at Easter Road waiting for the news from Love St. It was OK, Celtic were drawing. There was a false alarm when someone said they'd been given a last-minute penalty. Then the official news came through; they'd definitely dropped a point. The Dons were champions.

I'd like again to mention Andy Watson (now Alex McLeish's assistant at Ibrox) because he played a significant, if largely forgotten, holding role in midfield during Aberdeen's dramatic charge for the title. The other special hero was Bobby Clark, who had reclaimed his place in goal from Jim Leighton, and made several crucial saves in the key games in April, including stopping a Bobby Lennox penalty at Parkhead.

When Celtic's draw at Paisley was confirmed, Alex Ferguson sprinted on to the pitch, exactly as Willie Waddell had done fifteen years before at Tynecastle when his Kilmarnock team won the league against all the odds. Alex headed straight for Bobby Clark, who was the first player he embraced.

Many of the Aberdeen fans followed his lead and invaded the pitch, and there was no attempt to stop them. I remember looking up at the old Easter Road main stand where many of the Hibs supporters stood, applauding and cheering enthusiastically. I could not imagine a similar scene in similar circumstances in Glasgow. The mood was one of celebration and bonhomie, and for that the Hibs supporters must take enormous credit.

That night Arnold and Sandra Kemp (who was an Aberdonian) held a party for visiting Aberdeen supporters at their home up the hill from the top of Easter Road. There were actually considerably more Hibs than Aberdeen fans present but they were all remarkably generous to us, considering that their team were relegated and had just been thumped by five goals. I suspect that they were almost as happy as the Dons supporters, for they too relished the fact that for the first time since Kilmarnock had prevailed in 1965, neither Rangers nor Celtic were league champions.

In a slightly downbeat postscript to that point, however, it is worth noting that when Aberdeen officially clinched the league title in a game against Partick Thistle at Firhill the following Wednesday, there were fewer than 7,000 fans present. My memory is that by far the bulk – at least 5,000 – of these fans were Aberdeen supporters. The implication is that very few Thistle supporters, or indeed neutral Glaswegians, bothered to come out and celebrate the 'democratisation' of the league championship.

After the tragic demise of Third Lanark in 1967, Partick had supposedly become established as the preferred club for Glasgow football folk who did not want to support the Old Firm. I'd be a very wealthy man if I had a fiver for every Glaswegian I've met who has told me he is a Partick Thistle supporter. The fact is that Partick Thistle have been lamentably supported (in terms of numbers, if not spirit) for many years. The alternative option to the Old Firm in the Glasgow area hardly exists in any meaningful sense at all.

That night in May 1980, Thistle had to beat the Dons by ten goals if Celtic were to win the title. This was obviously never going to happen, but early in the game, Jim Melrose scored for Thistle and a slightly indulgent frisson of anxiety spread through the Aberdeen ranks on the terraces. But the Dons soon equalised and the game petered out, a tame 1–1 draw. There was a half-hearted pitch invasion at the end, by celebrating Dons supporters, but the whole occasion was rather flat.

There was a more spectacular and ominous pitch invasion at Hampden Park a few days later, at the end of the Scottish Cup final. It was the first Old Firm final for three years, and I remember that in advance of it there were some arrogant suggestions in the Glasgow media that this gave Celtic and Rangers the opportunity to present a showcase spectacle. They would remind the punters of what Scottish football was all about – and at the same time put these usurpers from the North-East who had just appropriated the league championship in their place.

The two famous teams played out a tedious 0–0 draw, so the final dragged into extra time. Then Danny McGrain hit a shot which George McCluskey deflected into the net, and Rangers were too spent to equalise. Celtic thus reclaimed the cup that they hadn't won since 1977. At the end of one of the most boring games in the history of Hampden, everything suddenly livened up – in the wrong manner. A group of Celtic fans ran on to the pitch to acclaim their victory. This was the signal for the venerable old park to become, literally, a battleground. In the words of the official description of the incident in the Scottish Football Museum, 'Rangers fans responded by swarming onto the field to vent their anger.'

The consequent brawling on the pitch was so serious that mounted police were deployed to charge up and down the park in an attempt to clear the marauding fans. The scenes were undoubtedly ugly, and images of the unacceptable face of Scottish football were beamed round the world.

It was a sad day for anyone involved in any way with Scottish football and I could not help comparing the unfortunate events at Hampden with the more modest but essentially benign scenes on the Easter Road pitch exactly a week earlier.

Rangers and Celtic were deemed equally responsible for the trouble and were fined £20,000 each. The official inquiry blamed sectarianism as the root cause of the hatred and bitterness. One beneficial residue of the debacle was the passing of the Criminal Justice (Scotland) Act. This made it an offence to be drunk within a Scottish ground, or trying to enter one; to transport alcohol to grounds on buses or special trains; or to carry any drink container into a ground. Fair enough, though before long Scottish teams were advertising alcoholic products on their strips, many of which were bought by or for youngsters.

Anyway, for a few days I had nursed the illusion that Aberdeen's breakthrough might herald a brave new era in Scottish football. In some respects it did, but on the other hand the poison of hooliganism was never far away. And as the events of the coming decade were to make clear, the North-East was by no means bereft of this particular scourge either.

CHAPTER 6

GOTHENBURG

One consequence of Aberdeen's historic victory in the league was that the Dons were to represent Scotland in the European Cup. Since the club's debut in European competition in 1967 they had qualified for Europe a few times and generally stuttered through a couple of rounds before bowing out the first time they met a class team, usually, for some reason, from Germany.

I recall the odd exciting European night at Pittodrie; I watched a stirring 2–0 defeat of Slavia Sofia in a crowd of 29,000 in 1969, for example. But overall the performances had been pretty dire and there was a certain apprehension among Dons supporters that we would let Scotland down in the prestige competition. A nondescript Austrian team were dispatched, not without difficulty, in the first round, and in the second round Aberdeen drew Liverpool, who had recently twice won the European Cup and were by a country mile England's top team at the time.

I was not at the first leg at Pittodrie which the Dons lost 1–0 in a game which is mainly remembered for a nasty foul by Ray Kennedy on John McMaster, which put the Aberdeen player out of the game for a year. But a group of us drove down to Liverpool for the second leg and we witnessed nothing short of a masterclass. Aberdeen put up a fight for the first half hour or so, but Mark McGhee – now established as Joey Harper's replacement – missed an excellent chance and then a Willie Miller own goal was followed quickly by a second goal by that superlative full back, Phil Neal.

Liverpool were thus 3–0 up on aggregate at half time and I thought that the second half would be painful to watch. Although Alan Hansen and Kenny Dalglish scored two more goals and the Dons were on the brink of humiliation, the spectacle was actually pleasing to watch; I've rarely seen players pass with such precision, and combine strength and subtlety so effectively as these Liverpool superstars did. There was no point in fretting; Aberdeen were clearly out of the competition, so why not sit back and enjoy a display of power football at its smoothest? And that's just what we did. It was suprisingly enjoyable. The three Scots musketeers, Dalglish, Hansen and Souness, were in their pomp. I remember wondering what it must be like to watch football of this class on a regular basis.

That night we revisited the Holiday Inn in the city centre, the scene of that night of mayhem after Scotland's World Cup victory over Wales exactly three years earlier. This time the atmosphere was restrained, almost sophisticated. Some of the Liverpool players turned up and we admired their sleek demeanour. They seemed as classy off the pitch as they had been on it. I confess that that night we felt well and truly provincial.

But we were lucky in that Aberdeen had a resilient manager who was very special. I heard later that the main lesson Alex Ferguson drummed into his team in the aftermath of that game, in which the Dons had enough spirit to avoid complete surrender, was the importance of retaining possession. And indeed that had been the most impressive aspect of Liverpool's mastery: the way they kept the ball. It was not effortless; it was the result of sheer hard work. Every time a Liverpool player had the ball, he had several options, several colleagues in space, several mates he could pass to. It sounds simple, but how often do you actually see it? Liverpool duly went on to win the European Cup, beating Real Madrid in the final. It was the third time they won the trophy in five years.

That night at Anfield, Liverpool had seemed to us to be some kind of footballing Valhalla. But nemesis was to come for this fine club, in the form of Heysel and Hillsborough. In football, as in life itself, you must take nothing for granted.

Around this time my own life was changing significantly, and in the early 1980s I was finding it more difficult to find the time to watch football, just when Aberdeen were embarking on the most glorious passage in their history.

I'd married Julie in 1980, and the demands of marriage and then fatherhood, combined with the exigencies of executive journalism, meant that I had to manage my time much more carefully.

In 1977 I'd been appointed to my first executive job: features editor of the *Scotsman*. Then in the beginning of 1981 I got a call from a man called Charlie Wilson, who had been editor of the *Evening Times* in Glasgow and had just become editor of the *Glasgow Herald*.

Charlie hailed from the Shettleston area of Glasgow and had a reputation as one of journalism's hard men. He went on to edit the London *Times*, and was involved in the controversial move to Wapping. I always found him decent and fair and I reckon he was a bit like Alex Ferguson in his management techniques; he shouted at those who required such treatment; whereas he put an arm round, and even mollycoddled, those who responded more to gentle persuasion.

Leading a team, or a club, involves not just looking after the collective; it involves dealing with people as individuals. The likes of Jock Stein and Alex Ferguson seemed to understand this intuitively.

Charlie Wilson was reputed to have a phenomenal temper, and although I did witness a few theatrical explosions, I suspected that most of them were planned rather than spontaneous. Another trait Charlie shared with Fergie was his extraordinary energy.

Charlie told me in confidence that he was about to launch a new Sunday paper, as a sister to the *Herald* and the *Times*. He wanted me to be the features editor. We had a pleasant exploratory discussion in the NB Hotel in Glasgow's George Square (it has since changed its name about six times) and agreed to meet again. The second time, he told me he'd prefer me to be sports editor. (I later heard that he'd another preferred candidate as features editor.) I was astounded, but pleased. He was offering me far more money than I was earning on the *Scotsman* and although I knew it would be a huge wrench to leave North Bridge after eleven happy years there, I was pretty certain that I wanted the job.

But I told Charlie, candidly, that I'd little production experience. Charlie, like most Glaswegians, had a way with words and he told me not to worry: all the production would be taken care of. He wanted me to motivate the writers, to come up with ideas for innovatory sports journalism and plan imaginative sports features. As simple as that. I wouldn't even need to work Saturdays!

Two months later I found myself reporting for duty at Albion Street at 8 a.m. on a Saturday, and I was lucky if I was away by midnight. That was to be my Saturday routine for the next eighteen months. Newspapers are like that. Over the years I've worked on quite a few Christmas Days, on many hundreds of Sundays, on many public holidays, and I've done shifts that didn't finish till 3.30 in the morning. No complaints.

The *Sunday Standard*, as it turned out to be called, was a wonderful paper to work on during its brief life, and an undoubted success editorially. Charlie assembled a terrific team of journalists. Unfortunately the commercial side was not so well organised, and worse, the paper was launched in the midst of a serious recession. The *Standard* folded after just two years. It was being heavily subsidised by the *Herald*, which, although hugely profitable, needed some investment itself. Thus it was coming to the stage where one or other of the papers had to go. The *Herald*, with its 200-year history, was obviously not going to die. So the *Standard* succumbed.

But in the heady days of spring 1981, there was a buzz about the infant paper that I've never known before or since in journalism. The three principal sportswriters were Ian Archer (universally called Dan), my old colleague on the *Scotsman*, Norman Mair and Doug Gillon.

Doug was, and is, the greatest all-round sports enthusiast I've ever known. His first love was athletics – he was no mean athlete in his time – but he had an encyclopaedic and insightful knowledge of everything from boxing to volleyball.

Norman was a wordsmith of the old school, and a genuine sporting insider. He had played for Scotland at both rugby and cricket. He had an impressive range of trusted friends – from Carwyn James to Jack Nicklaus – in his specialist sports of rugby and golf, a bulging contact book and a rich treasury of offbeat sporting anecdotes and insights. He had just been voted Scotland's first-ever sportswriter of the year.

And Dan, the football expert – well, he was a naturally gracious and charismatic man who had worked on the *Scottish Daily Mail*, the *Glasgow Herald* and the *Scottish Daily Express*. He was the inheritor of the tradition of McIlvanney and Rafferty. He wrote about football with wit and panache. He was greatly respected by many key people in the game, such as Billy McNeill. But, as I got to know him over the next year or so, I realised that he was, to put it bluntly, fed up with football. Golf was the sport he had come to love. He saw golf as bereft of the pettiness and parochialism he detested in Scottish football. There was in Dan the same disillusion that I'd noticed in other football writers, though in him it was both deeper and better disguised.

I still retained something of the innocent enthusiasm of the football fan, but privately – Dan was always respectful to me in public – he told me I was ingenuous. Dan himself did not anticipate how football was to change, to come in thrall to television and to explode – at the top end – with mega-money and spurious glitz, but I'm sure he'd have regarded the new glamour as tacky. He was conscious of the other side, a rottenness gnawing away at the game.

Dan was gently cynical, and like many cynics he was a frustrated romantic. He had in his time loved football, but he was beginning to believe that the game was beset by some incurable malaise. His growing disillusion was fuelled by many factors. He did not like the Old Firm and he worried about the scourge of sectarianism, but that was by no means all of it. Like many others, Dan was having doubts about the tribal arrogance with which the supporters of the Scottish national team had disported themselves in the 1970s. We had in our different ways been part of it all, but now we were having second thoughts.

And Dan was a writer who needed a broad canvas, a bigger stage. Scottish football could be frighteningly, intensively introverted. In some ways his frustrations were similar to those that Alex Ferguson was to experience at Aberdeen in 1985 and 1986.

Further, the nature of sports journalism was changing. Success had come to Dan when he was young and he confessed to me that he had become somewhat written out as far as football was concerned. At that time the newspaper world was becoming less stable and more competitive. Journalists were under more pressure. There was a new watchfulness, the old camaraderie was no longer guaranteed and football writers were wary of each other. They did not always help each other out. There was a growing demand for exclusives, no matter how spurious. Dan had a natural disdain for this kind of news- and story-driven journalism, yet the old John Rafferty credo, 'It's not true until I write it', now seemed seriously out of time.

We tried to find offbeat features to help him through his angst. His first piece was a cracker, a beautifully written and revelatory interview with Alan Hansen. But I soon realised that he was at his happiest doing pieces that were unconnected with football, though that was his staple. So I did my best to steer our star football writer away from football, wherever possible. For example, 1981 was Ian Botham's *annus mirabilis* and the best interview I read with the great cricketer was Dan's in the *Sunday Standard*.

A bonus for me on the *Standard* was that one of the newly recruited staff in the newsroom was Jack Webster, who had for long been the star feature writer on the *Scottish Daily Express*, during that paper's great years in the 1960s and '70s, before going freelance. Jack was a Dons superfan; he had followed Aberdeen since the 1940s and had written many perceptive pieces about the ups and downs of the club he loved. He had an encyclopaedic knowledge of both the club and the city of Aberdeen. I had met him briefly on one or two occasions as the crowds milled around before games, but now we got to know each other. Jack was very well-in with both Chris Anderson and Dick Donald and he often watched games from the directors' box. He was to write the definitive history of the club.

Another colleague was Roddy Forsyth, who later in his career was to specialise in football but was then an investigative reporter working on deep background. Roddy was a bright spark. He was always hanging around the sports desk and his infectious good humour brightened many a day on the *Standard*.

On Saturdays the sports pages were put together by a squad of production journalists from the *Evening Times*. They were a cheerful, wisecracking crew, led by Rod Ramsay, Crawford Brankin and Russell Kyle, with an immense knowledge of football (and an immense disdain for the Dons). They worked hard and well for a paper that was not their main professional concern. I shall always be incredibly grateful for their support. At that time we started using various other journalists to do match reports; among them was young James Traynor from the *Herald*. He too made a notable contribution to some excellent pages.

I did a little writing myself on the *Standard*. I went down to London to interview Steve Archibald, now starring for Spurs, and his psychologist, John Syer. I'd known John when he was working as a sports psychologist in Scotland a decade earlier, and he was eager to set up the feature, but Steve was very wary. Eventually he was persuaded and the three of us had a long conversation over and after dinner at a hotel at Enfield Chase, near the Spurs training ground.

Steve adored the bigger stage of English football and made it clear that he felt liberated from the constricted context of the Scottish game. He spent four seasons at Spurs and managed almost a goal every other game, a fine record in an era when defences generally predominated. He helped Spurs win the UEFA Cup and then went on to Barcelona for five successful years. Despite his sense of having made the great escape, he returned to Scotland many years later, briefly as a player with Hibs, then as manager of East Fife; and then he tried, unsuccessfully, to revive Airdrieonians.

Meanwhile, Dan Archer was keen that I should meet Jock Stein and he arranged a lunch for the three of us at the Ambassador, then Glasgow's plushest restaurant, early in 1982. I was nervous about meeting the most inspirational figure in the Scottish game, but I needn't have worried. In the flesh, Jock reminded me of my old colleague John Rafferty. He could not have been more affable.

Dan and Jock engaged in some inside-track banter and then Dan started to tease the big man about his alleged teetotalism. Jock actually did take a very little wine, less than half a glass. Stein talked about the state of Scottish club football. He was convinced that, with a fair wind, the country could sustain at least five clubs capable of mounting regular good runs in Europe, though obviously not all at the same time.

What interested me most in our chat was Stein's almost boyish enthusiasm once he started discussing tactics for the forthcoming World Cup Finals in Spain. He started pushing the condiments round the pristine linen, trying to explain various abstruse tactical possibilities to me. It was as if he was arguing with himself. I became aware of a slight foreboding, for I formed the impression that he was over-preparing in his mind.He seemed in considerable doubt as to which was his ideal line-up and what tactics he should deploy. He seemed to be over-complicating things. (This contradicted everything I'd heard about him as a manager: that he liked to keep things simple. Possibly he kept it simple with the players, while his mind was in a torment.) Overall, his intense and passionate enthusiasm for the game was awe-inspiring.

I also went up to Aberdeen to do an interview with Alex Ferguson. He generously gave me two hours of his time. It was the first time I'd met him, though I reminded him I'd done a phone interview with him when he was chairman of the players' union, away back in 1972.

I was struck by the wide range of his football chat, and in particular by his incredible recall. He could remember games he'd played in, including the one in the evening of his playing career when he put two goals past the Dons' defence at Brockville, with amazing clarity. He spoke modestly but intensely about his ambitions for Aberdeen. I understood that I was listening to someone who thought deeply about the game, and who analysed everything in his football life carefully. He was determined to draw lessons from every footballing experience, good and bad, trivial and momentous.

Another person I was getting to know at this time was a very different personality, Terry Cassidy. He had been appointed managing director of the *Herald* group in 1981. He hailed from Tees-side and he was a former professional footballer (with Nottingham Forest). He had also been a television salesman and had been involved in clubs (night not football). Then he had moved into the advertising side of newspapers, and had rapidly made his name as a commercial manager. He came to Glasgow from Dublin, where he'd turned round the *Irish Times* group.

Terry was rude, shrewd, abrasive, sharp and at times distinctly boorish. Despite that I liked him. Early on in his time at Albion Street he had to close down the *Sunday Standard*, a difficult task which he accomplished with finesse and sensitivity. He then proceeded to apply his somewhat unorthodox management skills to the *Herald* and the *Evening Times*. At that time Arnold Kemp was reviving the *Herald* editorially, and Cassidy backed him commercially. He and Arnold did not always get on; indeed they had some blazing rows. (It was impossible to avoid rows with Terry, unless you were a total wimp.) But there was a strange kind of mutual respect there, and these were fat years for the *Herald*.

I had a crisis with Terry in the summer of 1985. I was then deputy editor of the *Herald* and there was a serious journalists' dispute that stopped production of the paper. Arnold was away, and late that night, at about 11.30, Terry summoned me to his office and said he'd reached a deal with the print unions. If the most senior executive journalist around – me – appeared in the caseroom, the paper – a sort of paper – would be produced. There would be no editorial in it, just adverts. I thought this was an absurd proposition, and declined.

With quiet menace Terry told me that this was not a request – it was an instruction. To buy time I asked for ten minutes to think about it, but I knew I had no option. What would be produced would be a dog's breakfast and anyway I'd lose all credibility with my striking journalistic colleagues. So I told Terry no, though I seriously feared for my job. No 'paper' was produced and a lot of revenue was lost. Terry was very angry.

Twenty-four hours later the dispute was settled and Terry called me back to his room. He said that as far as he was concerned the events of the previous forty-eight hours had never happened and the slate was clean. I thought that was a big, magnanimous gesture.

I relate this, because several years later, at the end of 1990, Terry was appointed chief executive of Celtic. It was a surprise appointment, and I have no idea how Terry – who, as I say, could be rude, even offensive, in his management style – handled things inside the club. What I do know is that he wanted, rightly or wrongly, to run Celtic as a business, not as an old-fashioned family-run football club.

He was associated with grandiose plans to develop a new stadium complex at Cambuslang, complete with a 250-bedroom hotel, a multiplex cinema and other leisure facilities. This option was rejected and later it was decided to undertake a comprehensive redevelopment of the existing Parkhead site, though without the hotel, cinema and so on. The majority of Celtic fans did not want to see the ground relocated, so the Cambuslang plan was one component of what rapidly became Terry's acute unpopularity. (As a complete outsider, my own hunch is that in the long-term the Cambuslang development would probably have been the better option.)

The point is that Terry was hardly given a chance, externally anyway. Almost as soon as he started at Parkhead he was subjected to some of the most sustained vilification that any management figure in Scotland has ever suffered. I invited him as one of the guests at my table at the Willie Miller West of Scotland testimonial dinner in February 1991 and was surprised, and disgusted, by the abuse he got from various people who should have known better. I also heard him consistently and nastily abused on an extended Radio Clyde phone-in.

Eventually, towards the end of 1992, Terry left Parkhead. One of his last gestures was to leave a couple of complimentary tickets for a Celtic–Aberdeen league game for Jack Webster and myself. (It was a cracking game, a 2–2 draw that could easily have been 6–6.)

All this was salutary. People in football can be a bit naïve about the outside world. They appear to want to operate in a bubble that is insulated from all outside practice and to exclude the demanding commercial and business pressures that so many other people have to live with day in, day out. I accept that Terry had a difficult persona. I accept that his style was not 'normal' in that it was very much *ad hominem* and I also emphasise that I have no awareness of what was going on internally at Parkhead during his time there. But he was subjected to a public campaign of vilification that seemed to me both hysterical and vicious. This anticipated some of the personality-driven malice and unpleasantness that was to infest and besmirch football twenty years later.

To rewind to season 1981–82. This was a peculiar time in Scottish football. Aberdeen and Celtic, who won the league, were way ahead of Rangers. Arguably the most exciting player at the time was Davie Cooper, the Rangers winger. For some reason the Ibrox club rarely played him, though it was clear that they desperately required his skills. The most consistent player in the league that season was a right back – Celtic's Danny McGrain. As for Aberdeen, their best midfield player was a centre half playing out of position – Alex McLeish – and their leading scorer was not one of their out-and-out strikers – Mark McGhee and Eric Black – but the playmaker Gordon Strachan.

Looking back on that era, I realise that that I should not be too surprised that McLeish and Strachan ended up as mangers of Rangers and Celtic respectively. You could tell that they were more than very talented players; they thought their way through games and always seemed aware of everything that was going on around them.

This was the season when Aberdeen's European progress began in earnest. In season 1981–2, they were no longer champions, so they were now in the UEFA Cup. In the first round they were paired against Bobby Robson's Ipswich, the holders of the trophy. The English pundits went into overdrive. Aberdeen would be humiliated. It would be Liverpool all over again, or worse. The first game was at Ipswich, and the Dons gained a creditable 1–1 draw. My brother Hugh, who was there, recalls that the Suffolk police were particularly high-handed and repressive in their handling of the Dons fans. In the second leg, before a full house at Pittodrie, Aberdeen won 3–1. The English experts could not work out what had happened.

In the next round the Dons met an obscure Romanian outfit, whom they disposed of, although not without a little difficulty in the away leg. In the third round Aberdeen were drawn against Hamburg, a team crammed with internationals, not least the greatest of all German footballers, Franz Beckenbauer. Aberdeen won the first leg at Pittodrie 3–2, and they would have had a two-goal margin of victory had Strachan not had a penalty saved. In the second leg Hamburg won 3–1, and thus eased through 5–4 on goal aggregate. I saw none of these games because of various commitments, but I was all the more determined to enjoy some European football the next season.

I saw Aberdeen beat Rangers 4–1 in the 1982 Scottish Cup final at Hampden. They thus qualified for the 1982–83 European Cup-Winners' Cup. In the event I saw just four games in the campaign, but what a magnificent quartet they were. These four games in themselves were a sufficient justification for a lifetime's support of the club.

At the beginning of 1983 Alex Ferguson was newly forty-one. He had been in charge of Aberdeen for four and a half years, and they had won two trophies: the league championship in 1980 and the Scottish Cup in 1982. A few journalists were suggesting that he was too raw and impetuous to be a truly great manager; it was being put about that he'd be lucky to win anything else with Aberdeen. Early in January, Aberdeen had played a game more than Celtic in the league, but were three points behind.

So there was current a certain reservation about Fergie; not a whispering campaign, more an insidious scepticism. Some of this was blown away when at the beginning of February he took the Dons to Glasgow and they beat Celtic 3–1, thanks to a powerful hat-trick by the precocious centre forward Eric Black. Few could recall when a visiting player had last scored a hat-trick at Parkhead. Yet even after that victory, doubts were still expressed. Two trophies in four and a half years was regarded as a meagre haul for a team that was now packed with international players. (Alex went on to win eight more trophies in his remaining three and half years at Pittodrie: another indication of the truism that all managers, even the best ones, require time.)

I had a long chat with Arnold Kemp, the editor of the *Glasgow Herald*, which I had just joined, and Eddie Rodger, the sports editor. We wanted to establish whether Ferguson was one of those managers, like Eddie Turnbull, who'd threatened to smash the dominance of the Old Firm but would ultimately fail to deliver.

We agreed that I'd go up to Aberdeen to do an in-depth profile of Fergie. The intention was, without getting into the realms of amateur psychology, to probe his persona. I was to try to determine if he had the capacity to become both the consistent winner and the outstanding manager he clearly wanted to be.

I had a long chat with Alex himself. I also talked to many other people, including Bob Shaw, who had been director/secretary at East Stirling during Alex's time there, Ricky McFarlane, his assistant when he was manager at St Mirren, Pat Stanton, who had been his first assistant at Pittodrie, and Chris Anderson.

I listened to fascinating stories about his obsessive need to learn everything possible about all aspects of the game, and how to improve himself constantly as a manager. For example, I was told that when he was at St Mirren he used to attend afternoon schoolboy matches. This was not so much to spot potential talent as to eavesdrop on the English scouts who were present, to try to find out how they went about their work and to gauge precisely what they were looking for.

It became clear that Alex Ferguson Senior, his father, had been the most potent influence in his life. His dad had died in 1978, before he had won anything, and he was convinced that he'd never be as good a man as the father he venerated. Ferguson Senior was a Govan shipyard worker who had been hard on Alex when he was a player. Now, at Aberdeen, Alex had in a way installed Dick Donald, his chairman, as a kind of substitute father figure. Donald was presiding over his 'mellowing'.

I put a lot of work into the piece and it was published in the *Herald* in March 1983. My conclusion was cautious, but I think it stands the test of time:

> It would be pleasant if he were to stay at Aberdeen indefinitely; there would be nothing that he and the club might not achieve were he to do so. But for all his new contentment, he remains a restless, febrile man, driven on by a relentless ambition.

In the quarter-finals of the European Cup-Winners' Cup Aberdeen were paired with Bayern Munich, a club that had won the European Cup three times in a row in the mid-1970s, had slumped a little and were now recovering strongly. They were the clear favourites for the trophy.

The first leg was at Munich. This was one of the few games I went to with my wife Julie; we made a holiday of it, travelling to Munich by train after a few days in Paris. In Munich we met up with various well-kent faces, including Jack Webster and my brother Hugh. The match was played on a bitterly cold night; there were almost 40,000 in the vast Olympic stadium but there was little atmosphere. I have never liked stadia like this one, with a running track between the spectators and the pitch, so that you are far from the action.

The Dons produced the most controlled performance I ever saw by an Aberdeen team. Their discipline was awesome. They evinced a composure that spoke volumes for Ferguson's preparation. It was only two and half years on from that 4–0 defeat at Anfield, but now they were more than matching a team that was on the same level as that excellent Liverpool outfit.

One of the joys of watching top class European football was the chance to see world class players (though I think it is fair to say that at that time Aberdeen had their own world class players: Miller, McLeish and Strachan). Bayern were dripping with experienced internationalists such as Dremmler, Hoeness, Breitner and the great goalscorer Karl-Heinz Rummenigge – players who had all starred in the World Cup Finals the previous year. But that night in Munich, the only players who really caught the eye for Bayern were Rummenigge, Breitner and Klaus Augenthaler. It was a particular privilege to watch the two superstars, Rummenigge and Breitner, trying all they knew against the Dons.

Rummenigge won ninety-five caps for his country. He was a thoroughbred, and in both the games against the Dons he was the danger man. As for Paul Breitner, he had played in two World Cup Finals.

Amazingly, for a midfielder, he scored in both (against Holland in 1974 and against Italy in 1982). He was one of the tiny number of élite players who had simultaneously held winners' medals in the World Cup, European Nations' Championship and European Cup. In short, he was a true football aristocrat.

As it was, that night in Munich Mark McGhee came very close to snatching victory for the Dons. But the 0–0 draw set up what proved to be a monumental night at Pittodrie. After the game the Bayern manager opined that Aberdeen were better than Barcelona or Inter Milan. They were certainly much better than Spurs, who had gone down 4–1 to Bayern in the previous round.

The night of 16 March 1983 marked the finest Aberdeen performance I ever saw. Dons crowds over the years have been criticised, with some validity, for lack of vocal support, but not that night. Even twenty minutes before kick-off the atmosphere was tumultuous.

Bayern scored early on, and for much of the first half were in control of the game. Then towards half time the Dons at last built up momentum. Eric Black hit the bar with a header and then he got another header past Muller, the goalie, but it did not look like crossing the line. Neil Simpson appeared from nowhere to scramble it in: 1–1 at the break.

About twenty minutes into the second half Bayern's Pfugler hit an incredible volley from way out on the left. I was right behind him as he hit it and it was a goal from the moment the ball left his boot, 30 yards out. A wonder goal, without doubt. I turned to my brother in the shocked silence and said: 'We can still hit them with two late goals.' Yes, I did say that.

With less than fifteen minutes to go, Strachan and McMaster worked their botched freekick routine. The Dons fans knew it well, but the Germans didn't. They'd lost concentration when Strachan suddenly swung the ball over and McLeish headed it into the net: 2–2. This was one of the most crucial goals in Aberdeen's history, made and scored by the men who are now leading the Old Firm.

We were still off our seats roaring with joy when two minutes later supersub John Hewitt scrambled in goal number three. Somehow the celebrations became even louder, the pandemonium even wilder . . . but there was still work to be done. Willie Miller had to perform like the world class defender he was in the final desperate minutes. Twice the wily, elusive Rummenigge – a quicksilver player if ever there was one – almost broke clear; twice Willie saved the day with the sweetest of tackles.

The orgy of relief and joy at the end reminded me of that night at Hampden ten years earlier, when Scotland qualified for the 1974 World Cup Finals. These were the two most thrilling games I ever saw.

Aberdeen were now the only British team left in European competition and thus the focus of rare all-UK attention. Alex Ferguson handled the next few weeks with panache, talking to the media judiciously and shrewdly. The first leg of the semi-final against little-known Belgians from Genk – the club was called Waterschei – was an anti-climax. They were a physical, well-organised team, utterly lacking the glamour of the likes of Bayern or Real Madrid. Just the kind of outfit Aberdeen might slip up against, in other words: but not that season.

Indeed I almost felt sorry for Waterschei, as they were two goals down after only three minutes at Pittodrie. I've never seen a team blitz the opposition straight from kick-off as Aberdeen did that night. The football was almost brutal in its power, but there was subtlety there too. We realised that Ferguson was orchestrating something very special. The man of the match was the buccaneering Dougie Bell, a fringe player who always looked classy when he was called on. Even then, Ferguson was deploying the squad tactics he was later to use with such devastating effect at Manchester United.

Aberdeen won 5–1. A fortnight later they lost 1–0 in Belgium, the only time they lost a game in the entire campaign. And so it was on to Gothenburg, and the final against Real Madrid, the club team with the greatest pedigree of them all. This was to be their eleventh European final. They were managed by the legendary Alfredo di Stefano, who 23 years earlier had hit a hat-trick for Real in the European Cup final at Hampden and who vied with Pele as the most celebrated player in the history of the game. Luckily, he was better at playing than managing.

Forty-four planes flew over to Sweden from Aberdeen in the 48 hours before the game. I went over on the team plane. At the front were the players, directors and back-up staff. In the middle were the press. At the back were the superfans and assorted insiders, or to put it less delicately, the élite of the hangers-on. I could have been in the middle or the back, but chose the middle. As we flew out from Dyce, I looked down on Aberdeen and thought how neat and trig the city looked between its two fine rivers, with its vast agricultural hinterland behind it and the sea on the other side. It was and is an organic city, having developed as a port and fishing town to serve the seaboard side, and as a market centre, serving the landward side.

It looked too small and somehow too innocent to produce a football team that could win a European trophy. That sort of stuff was for big, teeming cities, cosmopolitan capitals like Madrid or Rome, or sprawling post-industrial centres like Glasgow or Liverpool or Turin – certainly not neat little burghs like Aberdeen. I was sitting beside Mike Aitken of the *Scotsman*, and I remember Mike shaking me out of these musings with some entertaining tales of life at my old paper.

Gothenburg was awash with Aberdeen supporters. People had literally come from all over the world, like my brother Hugh's old friend Sandy Tait, now a doctor in Australia. I'd stood on the Pittodrie terraces with Sandy in the early sixties. Hugh himself had now arrived in town, having sailed over in the special chartered ferryboat the *St Clair*, with, among others, Dan Archer. Some of us sat in one of the bars of the Europa Hotel reminiscing into the night about the likes of Jimmy Smith and Charlie Cooke. Among the company was George Duthie, a scion of the Glasgow Press Club and one of the kenspeckle characters of the city's journalistic fraternity. Sadly George drank too much over lunch on the day of the game; he went to his room for a nap and nobody thought to wake him up, so he missed the game.

Gothenburg is a handsome city, with wide streets and plenty of café life, and for two days we wandered through it. It seemed that around every corner you encountered a half-remembered face from way back. There was hardly a Spaniard in sight.

On the afternoon of the big day there was torrential rain and we feared the game would be off. The rain eventually eased but the pitch was terribly sodden and perhaps militated against the quality of the play. Aberdeen were clearly the better team. Young Eric Black, who was in my opinion Aberdeen's most consistent forward that season, crashed a volley against the bar early on. Then he scored, after Augustin, the Real goalkeeper, fumbled a McLeish header.

Midway through the first half Real equalised with a penalty. After that the Spaniards were bereft of ambition, playing cynically for a penalty shoot-out. The game went into extra time. Then Peter Weir went on a wonderful run on the left; he beat a couple of men and sent an exquisite chip forward to Mark McGhee, who had intelligently run into space further up the left flank. McGhee sent over a perfectly judged cross and there was supersub Hewitt heading the ball into the net. Hallelujah! Aberdeen had won a European trophy, and they had won it with an intelligently constructed goal of supreme quality.

Later that night Jack Webster and myself and one or two other supporters were allowed into the team's celebration dinner in the Fars Hatt hotel at Kungalv, about twelve miles outside Gothenburg. It was a low-key, almost homely occasion. I recall Dick Donald standing beside Willie Miller at the buffet and saying simply, 'Quite a night, eh Willie?' It was the night of nights, although somehow it did not produce the emotional turmoil associated with the victory against Bayern a couple of months earlier. But the trophy had been won in style. Eleven games played, and only one defeat; twenty-five goals scored, and only six conceded; and significantly, only one booking. Aberdeen were a strong but clean team. They had done Scotland, and the game of football, proud. Alfredo di Stefano, dignified in defeat, said: 'Aberdeen have what money can't buy – a soul.'

On the plane back the next day the Cup itself, filled with champagne, was passed around. The mood was one of modest, even subdued, satisfaction rather than triumphalism. I don't think anyone on that plane was prepared for the reception that the people of Aberdeen, normally reserved and restrained, gave their team that afternoon. All the schools had been granted a special holiday and many employers had allowed their staff the afternoon off. The airport was jam-packed with well-wishers. I got a taxi into town with Mike Aitken and the streets on the route the team bus was to take an hour or so later were lined with crowds.

They say that there were nearly half a million people on the streets of Aberdeen that afternoon, though given that the population of Aberdeen and its environs was barely 250,000, that meant that an awful lot of people must have come in from much further afield. Whatever; the city was *en fête*. It was as if there was a collective realisation that the word Aberdeen no longer signified a place, but a football team.

On the train south I was drained. Mike was talking intelligently about the pressures that would now be on Aberdeen, but I was not concentrating properly. I did realise though that I was incredibly lucky. Scottish supporters outside the Old Firm were not supposed to have experiences such as this. It was not in any script. Enjoy it while you can, I ordered myself.

Later that year, Aberdeen played their old opponents Hamburg home and away in the Super Cup. The European Super Cup had been launched eleven years earlier as a showpiece showdown between the European Cup winners and the holders of the European Cup-Winners' Cup, to establish the best club team in Europe. Ajax were the first team to win the trophy, beating

Rangers 6–3 over the two legs in 1972 (although Rangers were banned from Europe after the trouble in Barcelona, they were given a dispensation to take part in the Super Cup).

Hamburg had qualified for the Super Cup by beating Juventus of Turin in the 1983 European Cup final. So the Dons now had their chance to avenge the 5–4 defeat in the UEFA Cup two years previously, and they did so in style, winning 2–0 on aggregate. They were kings of Europe.

By this time, as I've mentioned, I was deputy editor of the *Glasgow Herald*, and I was unable to attend either of the Super Cup games because of work commitments. This annoyed me because I wanted to be present if and when Aberdeen were officially confirmed as the top team in Europe.

At this time Rangers tried very hard to persuade Alex Ferguson to take over at Ibrox. Many Scottish pundits decided it was a done deal, but Fergie took his time and eventually decided to stay with the Dons, signing a new five-year contract. I decided, foolishly, that he'd stay at Aberdeen for very many years to come. I briefly (and no doubt equally foolishly) thought of ending my formal career and trying to make a living as a freelance, so that I would have more flexibility in my life and more time to follow the Dons. I was missing too many of the big games. Luckily, this idea – of giving up the security of salaried employment to become a more committed football supporter – was a fantasy that I did not entertain for long.

Meanwhile, this glorious period in the Dons' history was sullied by the canker of hooliganism, something Aberdeen had hardly ever been associated with in the past.

In August 1982 I had popped over to Fife to take in a rather meaningless League Cup tie at Stark's Park, Kirkcaldy. Aberdeen had won the first leg 9–0. There was a pitiful attendance and the game was dreary. Midway through the second half I noticed a group of smartly dressed youths standing around under the railway embankment, at the corner of the ground near the north enclosure.

There were about twenty of them and they clearly were not watching the game. There was something vaguely unsettling about their demeanour, but I thought nothing more of it till a few weeks later I heard there had been serious trouble at a Motherwell–Dons game instigated by the so-called Aberdeen Casuals. From the descriptions of the hooligans I realised they were the squad I'd seen at Kirkcaldy. This was the first I had heard of them, although they had been around for a year or so.

For the next couple of years the casuals visited enormous embarrassment and shame on Aberdeen FC during the finest period in the club's history. They were not from deprived backgrounds; they had no grievance, either imagined or genuine, against society. Their sick desire for violence was channelled into cold and calculated organisation. Their main tactic was to set up pre-arranged fights with other 'crews' on match-days, often quite far from the actual grounds. Thus what happened at Motherwell was not typical.

The Aberdeen casuals were probably the most violent, but other clubs were also contaminated by their unwanted 'crews'. Among the more notorious were the Capital City Service (Hibs), Her Majesty's Service (Rangers), and the Love St Division (St Mirren). The police got on top of the problem; there were convictions and custodial sentences, and the worst seems to be over. But there are still casuals around, even today.

CHAPTER 7

CUP WOES

The season 1983–84 was the one in which Aberdeen, as well as winning the European Super Cup, turned their grip on the Scottish game into the tightest of strangleholds. They won the league at the proverbial canter, finishing seven points ahead of Celtic, twelve ahead of Dundee United, their sparring partners in the New Firm, and an amazing twenty-one points ahead of Rangers. And they won their third successive Scottish Cup final. Having beaten Rangers in the two previous finals, they now took on Celtic, and beat them 2–1 in a hard contest, after extra time. It was the first time a team outside the Old Firm had completed the league and cup double.

Meanwhile Dundee United, who had won the league the previous season, were performing heroics in the European Cup, progressing to the semi-finals. Aberdeen were defending the Cup-Winners' Cup. They too reached the semi-finals, but they met their match in Porto, who won both legs 1–0. The second leg, at Pittodrie, was a curiously subdued, low-key affair. The stadium was shrouded in a thick haar, which didn't help.

During this season I watched several games from the comfort of the directors' box, in the company of Jack Webster and Chris Anderson. I do not wish to decry in any way the hospitality of Chris and Dick Donald, but I was ill at ease in the box. It is not really a place for fans. Some of the best directors are fans, but they have to subsume their partisanship, which means that they are no longer proper fans. You cannot misbehave in the box. I do not write that frivolously. I simply mean that you cannot rant and shout and vent your anger, as football fans do.

In a way I believe fans should be slightly detached from their clubs. If they get too close to the people who run it, they lose the detachment which is a crucial component of proper fanhood. And as for the box, there is something too cosy and muffled about that little island of constraint in the middle of the main stand. There is now a trend for supporters' representatives to serve on the boards, and this is obviously a progressive tendency. Yet I feel it must be very difficult to be both a fan and a director.

At this period I was gaining fascinating insights into the psychology of Old

Firm supporters. Many of my colleagues, and indeed many of the people I met both socially and professionally in Glasgow, were supporters of either Rangers or Celtic. I am certain that in those years, roughly from 1980 to 1986, these supporters came closer together than they have been before or since. This uneasy solidarity was based on a resentment of Aberdeen, who were regarded as insolent upstarts, or worse.

There was a general belief that the Dons had no right to come to Glasgow – whether it was to Parkhead, Ibrox or Hampden – with every expectation of winning. The odd aberrant victory could be tolerated, but it was not ordained that a team from the sticks could come to Glasgow and play the big boys off the park, time and time and time again.

I'm afraid that this attitude spread through the Glasgow-based media, though I'm pleased to say that the *Herald* was pretty well immune from it: Eddie Rodger, the sports editor, was a dyed-in-the-wool Rangers man, yet he treated Aberdeen's achievements generously and graciously. And the editor, that fine Corinthian Arnold Kemp, would not have tolerated any pettiness.

Meanwhile, up in Aberdeen Alex Ferguson, developing his considerable skills at mind games and the psychology of football management, exploited the West of Scotland media's disdain for the Dons' progress to spur his team on to yet greater efforts.

By this time I had a good understanding of the intensity of the average Rangers or Celtic fan's commitment to their club and I did not especially object to their irritation at Aberdeen's achievements in Scotland, though I found their annoyance at the club's European success peculiar and wrong-headed. On the other hand, all football fans can be small and parochial; it is part of being a fan. I've already confessed to my grudging attitude when Alex Ferguson was asked to divide his time between Aberdeen and Scotland. A properly patriotic Scot would surely have placed Scotland's interests before Aberdeen's, but in my own mindset I could not bring myself to do that.

I noticed, with wry amusement, that Dundee United, while also resented in Glasgow, were not regarded with as much animus. This was because they did not beat the Old Firm anything like as frequently as Aberdeen did. Aberdeen found it much easier to beat Rangers and Celtic than to beat Dundee United. On the other hand, United had a very disappointing record against the Old Firm.

What made me angry (and made it easy for some of my Glasgow friends to wind me up) was the suggestion that I was some kind of Johnny-come-lately glory hunter. I had, after all, been an Aberdeen supporter for well over twenty years. I'd done my time. I think I suffered enough, watching terrible games in terrible conditions at Pittodrie in the early 1960s, to have earned some right to enjoy the good years while they lasted.

Anyway, the perverse thought occurred at this time that one way to end the sectarian scourge that bedevils the Old Firm rivalry is for some other team in Scotland – Aberdeen, Hearts, Hibs, Dundee United, whoever – to start winning all the trophies consistently, over an extended period of time. I cannot think of anything else that would so readily bring the fans of Glasgow's bitter rivals together as their mutual loathing of an upstart 'provincial' team.

This attitude of resentment and disdain for Aberdeen was unique to Glasgow. In Edinburgh I found Hearts and Hibs fans were warm in their appreciation of Aberdeen's success, especially their triumphs in the Cup-Winners' Cup and the Super Cup. They had an intuitive understanding of what Willie Hunter, that crabbit but much-loved *Herald* journalist who was a St Mirren man through and through, meant when he wrote that a good Saturday was one when at least one half, and preferably both, of the Old Firm did not win.

A disappointing aspect of Aberdeen's success that was mocked in Glasgow was their lack of crowd support. I had to grant some merit to the view that the team were less well supported than they should have been. A case in point was the Scottish Cup semi-final replay against Dundee United in April 1985. The first game (a frenetic encounter that somehow finished without a goal) was played at Tynecastle in Edinburgh; it should of course have been played at Dens Park, Dundee.

The replay, the following Wednesday evening, was also at Tynecastle. The attendance of 10,770 was abject. There was a rail dispute at the time but most fans would have come by bus or car, so that was no excuse. And the build-up to the game was feverish: Aberdeen were aiming for an unprecedented fourth successive appearance in the Scottish Cup final. The fact that it would be the hundredth Cup final added to the media interest.

The game itself was an absolute belter. (My father's Uncle Willie, an affable Glasgow businessman who served for a time as a director of Clyde, told me when I first started following Aberdeen in the early 1960s that the only time you ever saw two Scottish teams going at each other was in an Old Firm derby. He may have had a point then, but the New Firm games had an intensity and passion all of their own. The other point was why people like him were presiding at clubs that did not 'go at' Rangers and Celtic.)

It was in this semi-final replay that the Dons' four-year run of twenty-three circumstances. United started brilliantly, with the wispy and elusive Paul Sturrock, so often the bane of the Dons, in rampant form. He scored early on, and for the rest of the first half United were by far the better team. Just after half time Neale Cooper was sent off and so the Dons were down to ten men. Soon United scored their second goal, a thundering volley by Beedie, and the game should have been over.

As so often, Ferguson's men defied logic and the odds. United's Dodds was sent off, and we were back to numerical parity. At last, Aberdeen were pushing United back. Jim McLean's men lost their composure. They began to panic.

With five minutes left, the Dons scored the goal they deserved through Angus, who had come on for Bell. Then in the last minute Malpas clearly handled in the box. How and why Aberdeen were denied such an obvious penalty I'll never know. Alex Ferguson went berserk on the touchline, and the next day received much pompous press admonition for his antics.

It was not an enjoyable game for an Aberdeen fan, yet it was one of the most exhilarating I've ever attended, and the quality and the commitment were awesome. As a spectacle of top-class sport it deserved an attendance of far, far more than 11,000. The previous season both Aberdeen and United had been European semi-finalists. Here then were undisputed class acts, playing to a two-thirds empty house. The blame for that must mainly lie with the Aberdeen and Dundee United fans. Aberdeen supporters had some excuse: to travel on a round trip of over 250 miles for an evening game is never easy.

But another question arose; where were the capital's fans? I've praised Hearts and Hibs supporters for their open-minded response to Aberdeen's success. Here they had a chance to see two of the leading teams in Europe, evenly matched and crammed with outstanding players of the calibre of Malpas, Gough, Narey, Sturrock, Black, McLeish, Miller and Leighton.

It was pitiful that more neutral Edinburgh fans did not show up for that game. It was a lovely April evening, balmy and unseasonably warm. Old Firm fans have a valid point when they say, as they often do, that Scotland's other fans are very slow to get off their backsides and attend games.

One neutral who did attend the game was my former colleague Norman

Mair. Rugby and golf were Norman's main interests, but he had been no mean footballer in his day and he was a sharp and wise observer of the game. He'd played for his country in two different sports and he brought a special perception to any sporting action he watched.

Norman told me a couple of days later that he was most impressed by the standard of the play and the almost superhuman commitment of both teams. What struck him most was the pace at which the game was played for the entire ninety minutes. He annoyed me by joking that he presumed the ref. had refused to give Aberdeen their deserved penalty because extra time would have been too much to ask of players who had already given so much.

And so Aberdeen were out of the Cup, after that explosive and exhilarating New Firm encounter, but they won the league easily, again by seven points over Celtic. That put them back into the European Cup and they eased through to the quarter-finals, early in 1986. They were drawn against Gothenburg, which meant a sentimental return to the scene of their finest triumph.

The first leg was at Pittodrie and again the issue of support arose. The ground was nothing like full, which for a European Cup quarter-final was disgraceful. Alex Ferguson, with every justification, was displeased. He later wrote of his suspicion that the Dons supporters were becoming spoiled and were taking success for granted.

It was an exciting game, with Aberdeen missing several good chances, though they did score twice, the first of their goals being a cracker by Willie Miller. The Swedes equalised in the last minute. A fortnight later I flew out to Gothenburg on the team plane with Jack Webster. Jack, normally the most cheery of companions, was in quiet, reflective mode.

It was only the second time I'd seen both legs of a European tie. Sadly, far too few Dons fans made the effort to get to Gothenburg. The occasion was flat. I remember a Swedish TV crew making desperate efforts to get the Dons fans to make at least some noise in the Ullevi Stadium just before kick-off. The contrast with three years earlier was painful. The game was a dour 0–0 draw, though Jim Bett nearly got the goal the Dons needed. Aberdeen were out of Europe, and Fergie was out of sorts.

At the airport and then on the plane back the manager's unease was not too apparent, yet you could tell that Alex was frustrated. He was friendly and gregarious and he moved around in an almost feverish way, chatting with just about everyone in the party. I sensed that he was trying to disguise his growing disillusion. I had already divined that he was becoming restless, and who could blame him? There were some chirpy characters in the party, including Roddy Forsyth and the great Denis Law, but even they could not dispel the feeling that somehow we were drifting to the end of an extra-ordinary era.

I'd sensed that Alex was beginning to realise that he needed a bigger stage towards the end of 1985. I'd been invited up to Pittodrie for the launch of his first book, *A Light in the North*. After the party at Pittodrie I went across town to see Chris Anderson, who was very unwell. He had that cruellest of illnesses, motor neurone disease. The next morning, a Saturday, I attended Fergie's first major book signing. It was at a bookstore in Aberdeen city centre. The crowd waiting for him to sign copies was phenomenal; it snaked out the shop and round the streets for several hundred yards.

Aberdeen were playing Motherwell that afternoon and Alex had agreed to give Bill Campbell and Pete Mackenzie, his publishers, and myself, a lift down to Fir Park. As he belted down the A92 in his Merc, driving in his customary white-knuckle manner, he played us his favourite Bill Shankly tapes. He mentioned that Shankly had found at Anfield the big stage he'd needed to express his managerial talents to the full. It was a casual remark, but later I played it over in my mind. That was the first intimation I had that he might be on his way before too long.

At that time Alex was also acting as Scotland manager, and after the Motherwell game he supervised the loading of the Aberdeen internationalists' kit into the boot of his car. He was going on to Glasgow to prepare the Scotland squad for the forthcoming World Cup play-off with Australia. This was understandably giving him a buzz that Aberdeen could no longer provide. He was, and is, a world-class manager. He needed a fresh environ-ment, a larger challenge.

I reckon that the final factor in Alex's growing unease was Aberdeen's remaining inability, despite their success, to retain some of their best players. At the end of the 1983–84 season, when the Cup and League double had been won and the team had reached a European semi-final, three players had decamped: Strachan to Manchester United, McGhee to Hamburg and the big full back and folk-hero Doug Rougvie to Chelsea.

In May 1986 Aberdeen won the Scottish Cup for the fourth time in Alex Ferguson's reign. It was to be the last trophy he led them to; and that particular Cup final, in which the Dons beat Hearts 3–0, was not an altogether joyous occasion. I watched the game in the main stand at Hampden with my brother Hugh and both of us had more than the usual modicum of sympathy for losing opponents.

Aberdeen won with comparative ease because, without being too corny, Hearts had been broken a week earlier. The Edinburgh team had put together a superb 27-match unbeaten run in the league, only to lose 2–0 to Dundee at Dens Park in the final match. At the same time Celtic were beating St Mirren 5–0, which allowed them to become champions by the narrowest of margins, on goal difference.

In the cruellest of twists, Hearts would actually have won the league had it been decided on goal average rather than goal difference. Twenty-one years earlier, Hearts had lost the league at Tynecastle when, in the last day of the season, they were beaten 2–0 by Kilmarnock, and thus lost the title on goal average, which was the rule then. Had it been decided on goal difference in 1965, Hearts would have been champions.

I've indicated that, of the two capital-city clubs, my sympathies have generally been with Hibs. Yet I have no doubt that Hearts are the unluckiest of Scottish clubs.

After presiding over that defeat of Hearts in that Cup final, Alex Ferguson had to switch his attention to international matters, for he was about to take charge of Scotland's campaign in the World Cup Finals in Mexico. It was not surprising that his mind was wandering from Pittodrie for other reasons. Many commentators were now openly suggesting that it was just a matter of time before he left Aberdeen. As well as Rangers, he had rebuffed distinguished English clubs when they had come looking for his services – clubs of the standing of Arsenal and Spurs. He had served Aberdeen magnificently for over seven years. Nobody could grudge him going.

As it happened, the terrible moment did not come till November 1986. I was having a lunchtime pint in Babbity Bowster's in Glasgow's Merchant City when Bob Shields, then with the *Evening Times*, came up to me and said laconically: 'Ferguson's on his way to Manchester United.' At first the enormity of what I'd been told didn't sink in. When it did, a few seconds later, I knew this was a disaster. Fergie was irreplaceable.

I wrote a piece for the *Herald*, attempting to assess his gargantuan achievement at Pittodrie. I also wrote him a short personal letter, thanking him for all the wonderful times he had given me and other Aberdeen supporters over the past eight years. I still have the letter he sent from Old Trafford a fortnight later. In it he wrote, among other things:

> I must say, Harry, I am enjoying it and fully realise now how much I've needed this, this type of challenge with the risk and uncertainty and even the agony. It is a magnificent club and doesn't need an awful lot to get it going and I'm looking forward to it.

These almost poetic words serve as a suitable preface to a great chapter in the career of the finest British manager of modern times. Fergie's finest adventure was now about to begin. As for Aberdeen, after he left the decline was inexorable.

CHAPTER 8

GRAEME SOUNESS

One of the great imponderables of modern Scottish football is how Alex Ferguson, had he stayed at Aberdeen, would have responded to the Souness revolution at Rangers.

When Graeme Souness was appointed the new player-manager at Ibrox in the spring of 1986, few, perhaps not even the man himself, could have anticipated the effects of the revolution he was to instigate, although some of the more perceptive media commentators sensed that this was more than just a high-profile appointment, that something significant and unusual was stirring. One of the more far-sighted pieces written about the possible consequences of his arrival at Ibrox was in the *Herald*, by Jack Webster, who would be the first to admit that he was never likely to win a contest as Rangers No. 1 fan, but was always an authoritative and prescient journalist.

Souness was a bold and inspirational appointment. (Incidentally, many people seem to believe, almost 20 years on, that it was David Murray who brought Souness to Ibrox, but Murray was not yet the owner of Rangers. It was the Lawrence family, through their executive, David Holmes, who appointed Souness.)

Never a man likely to be modest in his demeanour, on or off the park, Souness had always walked with controversy. As a schoolboy, he trained with Celtic. Then as a teenager with Spurs, in 1970, he made headlines when he walked out on the club before he had played a first-team game, supposedly because he was homesick. Souness had the knack of attracting publicity. That incident became a national news story, with questions being asked in the House of Commons by the young Tam Dalyell, MP.

Two years later Souness was sold to Middlesborough and he played many 'muck and nettles' games in central midfield in the hard school of the English second division. Middlesborough, managed by Jack Charlton, were promoted in 1974. Four years later, Souness joined Kenny Dalglish at Liverpool, who paid Middlesborough £350,000 for his services. Souness soon became skipper of that marvellous Liverpool team and he won four European Cups with them.

He also won over fifty caps for Scotland, and in the Stein era – the late 1970s to the mid 1980s – he was one of Scotland's outstanding players, along with Willie Miller, Kenny Dalglish, Alan Hansen, Gordon Strachan, Davie Cooper, David Narey, Alex McLeish and Danny McGrain. The Tartan Army had an ambivalent relationship with him; they liked his class, and in particular his lovely passing, but the more fastidious Scotland supporters worried about his penchant for ferocious tackling, and this aspect of his game was not always controlled. But his combination of creativity and hardness made him a commanding, world class midfielder.

(In an extended aside here I must note that, to my enormous regret, I never saw Dave Mackay play, though I heard about him – interminably – from the Hearts supporters I worked beside on the *Scotsman*. Mackay had left Hearts for Spurs in 1959, when he was twenty-four. He had already won Scottish Cup and League medals. When I joined the *Scotsman* ten years later, people were still talking about his phenomenally committed all-round play for Hearts. It was as if he were still at Tynecastle.

Some players, generally forwards, seem to inspire especially strong affection among supporters. Into this category I'd place, for example, Joey Harper, Jimmy Johnstone, Denis Law, Ally McCoist, Henrik Larsson and Joe Baker. It is more rare for a midfielder or a defender to inspire this kind of devoted retrospective loyalty, and indeed such persistent reminiscence – but I have to say that in the many conversations I've had about Scottish football over the last forty years and more I'm certain that I've heard Dave Mackay praised more than any other single player. That may be surprising, but it's true.

From all that I heard about of Mackay, I reckon that he and Souness were remarkably similar, though Mackay was more controlled; he certainly had a much superior disciplinary record as a player. Despite Mackay's reputation as a physical force as well as a player of finesse, he was never sent off once in a professional career that lasted more than twenty years.

Both players were born in the same area of Edinburgh, a mile or so west of Tynecastle. Neither was particularly tall, but both had robust physiques and could boss games with their combination of tough tackling and precise passing. Both made the transition from being dominant, assertive players into top-level management. It is sometimes forgotten that Dave Mackay had the almost impossible job of succeeding Brian Clough as manager of Derby County, yet he led Derby to the English League Championship in 1975.)

When he arrived at Ibrox in 1986 Souness was given money to spend, more than any other Scottish manager up till then; but it was the way he spent the money, not the amount, that was significant. He used his high standing in international football (he had also played for Sampdoria in Genoa), his many connections in England and his clear ambitions for Rangers to entice English internationals of the calibre of Mark Hateley, Ray Wilkins and Trevor Steven north. Best of all his signings was the redoubtable Terry Butcher, the central defender who had performed heroics over many seasons for Bobby Robson's Ipswich. Butcher was about to sign for Spurs when Souness persuaded him to come north. Butcher, a 'steal' at £750,000, was in all respects a giant of a man. He was to lead England to the semi-finals of the World Cup in Italy in 1990, where they unluckily lost to Germany in a penalty shoot-out.

For decades (and how well I knew this as an Aberdeen supporter) English clubs had been plundering our best players. Now, overnight, this traffic was being reversed. Souness was signalling that Rangers were interested in more than just domestic domination, though that was of course important. They wanted to strut their stuff on a bigger stage. And they had a potent brand, which was to all intents and purposes under-exploited. At a stroke, Souness signified that they *were* a big club, and intended to be even bigger.

This was a revolution. Like many revolutions it did not start auspiciously. In Souness's first game as Rangers player-manager, against Hibs at Easter Road in August 1986, it was his combustible rather than his classy side that was on display. He was sent off after he kicked George McCluskey in the knee and his team lost 2–1. It was a vicious, violent game and at one point it degenerated into a mass brawl, involving twenty players. McCluskey needed nine stitches and Souness was banned for five games.

In an 'offbeat' postscript to this shambles, I recall that Michael Tumelty, the *Herald*'s brilliant music critic, wrote a memorable review of the Edinburgh Festival's opening concert at the Usher Hall that very night. Everything went wrong in the concert, and so Tumelty based his piece on the notion that it was the musical equivalent of the debacle at Easter Road a few hours earlier. Scottish intellectuals constantly try to place football within a wider cultural context and their attempts often don't work, but this was one of the neater efforts.

Anyway, Souness and Alex Ferguson only pitted their tactical wits against each other once in the Scottish Premier Division, in September 1986, at Ibrox. Rangers won 2–0, and if the truth be told, they could have won by more.

Ferguson left Aberdeen at the beginning of November, and he started a revolution at Manchester United not dissimilar to what Souness started at Ibrox, though he made less of an immediate impact. Eventually however, the Ferguson revolution was to be even more far-reaching than even the Souness one.

Both men used success on the pitch to help to create a socio-economic phenomenon of enormous reach, a marketing brand of colossal potential. The main consequence of this was the consolidation of football power and wealth. The same thing is happening all over Europe now; in most domestic leagues only three or four clubs have a meaningful chance of success.

Of course Souness and Ferguson were and are football managers, not marketing men; but it is indisputable that their successful stewardship of Rangers and Manchester United respectively created platforms for the marketeers and commercial executives to exploit in a way that they could not have exploited before.

My hunch is that, had Alex Ferguson stayed on at Aberdeen, he would have demanded more control over all aspects of the club and he would have done his best to match the Souness revolution, in every branch of the club's affairs, though obviously on a smaller scale than what was happening at Ibrox. I suspect that Fergie might have put together a consortium to buy the club. On the playing side, I'm more than confident that he could have given Rangers a run for their money.

Meanwhile, the club that simply had to respond to what Souness was doing was not Aberdeen but Celtic, and this hidebound outfit took their time. Billy McNeill did guide them to a memorable League and Cup double in their centenary year, 1987–88, but then Rangers went on to win the league title nine years in a row.

I've already referred to Terry Cassidy's unhappy stint as Celtic's chief executive at Parkhead in 1990–92, and I reckon that Terry was trying desperately to instigate some kind of management revolution behind the scenes at Parkhead. But he was not allowed to join the board, still dominated by two family dynasties. And Terry had a fraught relationship with two managers: first Billy McNeill, then Liam Brady. His relations with the board were not much better, though the directors appeared happy enough to push him forward as the club's front man when the going got rough, as it often did at that turbulent time. After Terry left, the club's finances deteriorated alarmingly. So did attendances; in 1993 Celtic played one or two home league games before crowds that barely reached five figures.

Celtic were on the brink of bankruptcy in March 1994, when the Canadian entrepreneur Fergus McCann took over. McCann was a ruthless, single-minded businessman. He was devoid of charisma or any kind of flamboyance and was never liked by the bulk of Celtic fans. Some of them seemed to dislike him as much as they had disliked Cassidy.

Many of these fans actually booed McCann, the saviour of their club, when the league flag was unfurled before the Parkhead crowd at the beginning of the 1998–99 season, to mark the winning of the championship the previous season. This was the treatment he received for ensuring that Celtic survived. His canny rebuilding had allowed Celtic, like Rangers, to exploit their global brand.

It had taken several years for Celtic to manage to turn themselves from an introverted, backward-looking club, symbolised by the notorious 'biscuit tin' mentality, and run by two long-standing family dynasties, the Whites and the Kellys, into a modern, forward-looking business that could begin to match Rangers on and off the park.

A key part of what Murray and McCann did at Rangers and Celtic respectively was to persuade supporters to become season ticket holders: in other words, if they wanted to see the big games, they'd have to pay for the lesser ones also.

The most spectacular attempt to respond to the Souness revolution was instigated not in Glasgow but in Edinburgh. Wallace Mercer, a high-profile property developer who then owned Hearts, tried to take over Hibs. The idea was that the combined capital team would be big and powerful enough to take on the new might of Rangers. The problem was of course the Edinburgh fans; their loyalties were based at least partly on their atavistic rivalry; they defined themselves by their dislike of the team on the other side of town. Yet here was a completely new 'brand' being proposed.

I attended a hastily arranged press conference in an Edinburgh hotel (organised, ironically, by my old Hibs-watching colleague Jim Dow) when Mercer admitted that the move was inspired in part by a desire to deal imaginatively with the emerging dominance of Rangers. Needless to say, this did not mollify the fans – particularly those of Hibs – who were under-standably outraged.

A 'Hands Off Hibs' campaign was quickly organised. It had a high media profile and there were very well-attended rallies at which passions ran high; Wallace Mercer seemed able to generate more excitement among Hibs fans than the club's players had managed to do for quite some time. A petition with over 50,000 signatures was raised. Mercer's initiative fizzled out amid rancour and recrimination.

What Graeme Souness started in his five years at Ibrox raised questions that are still germane. The three key ones (which are interrelated) are: Should football clubs be run as brands, with all the attendant commercial exploitation of fans, particularly young fans? And if Rangers and Celtic are to be run as huge international brands, do they lose what is left of their Scottish identity? And now that Rangers and Celtic, thanks to the revolution instigated by Souness, have reached something like their true commercial – if not playing – potential, are they too big for Scottish football, which must be essentially small-time? These are questions I attempt to answer in Part Three.

Alex Ferguson had been eight years at Pittodrie; Graeme Souness lasted almost five years at Ibrox before he was tempted back to Liverpool. Taken together, these thirteen years were remarkable. In the first eight Ferguson effectively 'democratised' the Scottish game, showing that Rangers and Celtic were not invincible, that the prizes need not stay in Glasgow and that a so-called provincial team could consistently outplay the home teams at both Parkhead and Ibrox. Then in turn Souness changed all this by elevating Rangers (and indirectly and later, Celtic) on to a different level so that in a sense all Ferguson's fine work was undone.

Graeme Souness did many good things and one or two bad things during his tempestuous stewardship at Ibrox. He engineered two spectacular coups. First, he persuaded his friend David Murray, the megarich Edinburgh entrepreneur, to buy Rangers from the Lawrence-Marlborough dynasty. Shortly after Murray took charge, Souness joined the Ibrox board. Soon after that, the club announced that at least two-thirds of their income was to come from sources other than gate money.

Secondly, Souness signed Rangers' first high-profile Catholic player (Mo Johnston, from Nantes).

If we look at the downside of his five years, the main failure on the playing side was his inability to make an impact in Europe. This was extraordinary, given his own glittering success on the European stage as a player, and the fact that both Alex Ferguson at Aberdeen and Jim McLean at Dundee United managed to reach European finals with far fewer resources.

The other, and more serious, downside was that the new tendency to sign big players from England – and indeed abroad – meant that Rangers and eventually Celtic had far less incentive to develop their own young players. And when they did sign promising young players from other Scottish teams, they tended to languish in the reserves, bereft of first-team football.

Anyway, Ferguson left the Scottish game in 1986, and Souness followed him early in 1991 when – to the surprise of many – he left Ibrox to take over from Kenny Dalglish at Liverpool. Neither Ferguson nor Souness has ever given any indication of wanting to return, and why should they? It is salutary to note that it is now almost fifteen years since either of these hugely influential personalities has had any involvement in the Scottish game.

A few weeks after Alex Ferguson left Pittodrie, I went down to Old Trafford to do a big 'day-in-the-life' piece for the *Herald* on how he was tackling the task of reviving Manchester United. Alex had taken over a club that were languishing second-bottom of the first division, already in serious danger of relegation, though it was only November. The clubs above them included Luton, Watford, Wimbledon and Oxford. Most of United's players were not exactly household names, even in Lancashire: the likes of Duxbury, Sivebaek, Blackmore, Hogg (son of Aberdeen's fine left back Jimmy Hogg), Higgins, Davenport, Turner and Moses prove the point. When you consider that squad, you realise the enormous scale of Ferguson's achievement.

I write 'to Old Trafford' but we actually spent the bulk of the day at United's two training facilities. Alex, always an early starter, insisted that I had to be at the Cliff training ground at 7.45. I made sure I was there by 7.40, but even so he was there before me.

It was a bitter-sweet day for me, at once elegiac from my point of view, and full of energy and zest and commitment, from Alex's. First, over toast and tea, he talked candidly about the vastness of the challenge facing him. He had many worries, but these were dwarfed by his sheer relish for the immensity of what lay ahead.

Then I stood beside him as he took a training session at the Carrington training ground, a couple of miles from the Cliff. There was not much security – how things have changed since, reflecting the colossal growth in the club, which is almost entirely down to Alex's hard work over nearly twenty years. A few fans wandered in and were allowed to stand beside us. One of them told me about the drinking culture of the club, and I found it hard to believe some of his tales. All Alex said on this subject was that he was aware of the problem and was determined to stamp it out.

Later, towards the end of the afternoon, we did spend some time at Old Trafford, where he introduced me to his chairman, Martin Edwards, a somewhat saturnine man. I sensed that Alex was less at ease in the great stadium, though we did have a marvellous hour or so of banter in the company of his kit man, Norman Davies.

I don't always get my football predictions right (who does?) but when I wrote the piece I pronounced that Alex would build a team and a set-up that would dominate English football for years to come. I thought it would take him two years to win his first trophy. In fact it was to take him almost four years; the rest, to use a cliché that for once is apposite, is footballing history.

Meanwhile, back in Scotland, Aberdeen could not cope with the Ibrox revolution, nor could they cope with the loss of Alex Ferguson. A succession of managers – Ian Porterfield, Alex Smith, Willie Miller, Roy Aitken, Alex Miller, Paul Hegarty, Ebbe Skovdahl, Steve Paterson and Jimmy Calderwood were appointed (and fired) over the next eighteen years. That works out as a new one every other year. As I write, Jimmy Calderwood and his assistant, Jimmy Nicholl, have made a promising start; they have certainly, like Ally MacLeod all these years ago, cheered Pittodrie up.

Two of these managers, Alex Smith and Willie Miller, should have been granted much more time. But the great visionary, Chris Anderson, had died, tragically young, in 1986, and that wise and kind chairman Dick Donald was no longer in the best of health (he died in 1994). Dick's son Ian had been on the board for some time, and was to serve his stint as chairman. An engaging and friendly man, he did not seem to exercise the control that his father had. From a distance, Aberdeen's board seemed to be becoming less cohesive, less confident, more prone to indecision and even panic.

Alex Smith, who had already won the Scottish Cup as manager of St Mirren, won two trophies in his shamefully short stint at Pittodrie: the League and Scottish cups, both in season 1989–90. Alex had a laid-back style and he often diverted credit to his co-manger Jocky Scott and their assistant Drew Jarvie, but shrewd observers well understood his achievements.

The League Cup victory was especially thrilling for it was the third time in a row that Aberdeen had played Rangers in the final, and they were certainly due a win. They had lost on penalties after a 3–3 draw in 1987 and they went down 3–2 to a last-minute Ally McCoist goal the following year.

The final in 1989 was the last time I actually stood on the Hampden terraces. (Despite my earlier praise for Chris Anderson and his belief in the

Above. Tommy Burns (left) playing for Celtic against Aberdeen
Below. Ally MacLeod in Argentina, 1978

Above. Denis Law scoring against England, Hampden 1966
Below. Charlie Cooke

Above. Alex McLeish playing for Aberdeen
Below. Andy Lynch, captain of Celtic

Above. Riot at Hampden after the Old Firm Cup Final, 1980
Opposite. Willie Miller (centre) defending for Aberdeen against Celtic
Below. Steven Pressley, captain of Hearts (right) playing against Hibs

Previous page. Victory celebrations at Wembley, 1977
Above. Graeme Souness, player and manager of Rangers
Below. Gordon Strachan scores against Rangers, Scottish Cup Final, 1982

need for all-seater stadia, I always preferred the freedom to move around that the old terraces gave you, unless of course the crowd was jam-packed. I also enjoyed the old away ritual of 'changing ends' at half time. But as I eased into middle age, I was watching more and more of my football from the 'comfort' of the stands, even when there were still terraces available.)

That 1989 final was notable for some spectacular goalkeeping by the Dons' Dutch goalie Theo Snelders, for a composed and intelligent midfield display by Paul Mason (one of Alex Smith's best signings; an Englishman also plucked from obscurity in Holland) and for a brave performance from the precocious forward, Eoin Jess, only 18 years old.

Alex Smith's other win, the 1990 Scottish Cup final, was a dour goalless game of attrition with Celtic that went to penalties after extra time. Aberdeen held their nerve and won 9–8 in the protracted shoot-out. That fine club servant Brian Irvine fittingly scored the winning penalty.

I was particularly pleased to see the enormously gifted Charlie Nicholas, who had given Aberdeen two and a half good seasons after being signed from Arsenal by Ian Porterfield, blast his penalty high into the net. I write that because we all knew that Charlie was on his way back to Celtic, his first senior club and his first footballing love, the next season, and it was thus a somewhat difficult situation for him. But he took the kick like the fine professional he was.

(I am more mellow than I used to be but I can still be roused to indignation if not to actual anger, and I was none too happy when early in 2005 the Rangers player Nacho Novo responded to some criticism from Charlie Nicholas by asking 'Charlie Nicholas? I don't even know if he played football or not.' You would have thought that someone earning a good living from one of Scotland's most eminent clubs would have bothered to pick up enough about the recent history of the game here to know that in the 1980s Charlie was capped 35 times for Scotland and had a very distinguished playing career with Celtic (twice), Arsenal and Aberdeen. But maybe I'm just ingenuous).

As for Willie Miller's stint as manager of Aberdeen, he started with a serious handicap. His iconic status placed an unreal burden of expectation on him. His playing career, marked by a loyalty undreamt of in today's game, had ended in 1990 after eighteen glorious seasons, fifteen of them as club captain. I'm certain that if the board of Dick Donald and Chris Anderson had still been running the club, he would have been granted the time he needed.

If Willie was a magnificent player for the Dons, by far the best in their history, he was also at times lucky. He had no luck whatsoever as a manager. One example came in the Scottish Cup-tie with Clydebank at Pittodrie in March 1993. I was present with my daughter Catherine (it was her first-ever game) and it got off to a catastrophic start; within ninety seconds Eoin Jess was seriously injured. Jess was Aberdeen's most talismanic player in the early 1990s, a winger cum midfielder who oozed class and also had an eye for goal. The injury was serious; he had a broken leg, and although he made a remarkably quick recovery, there is no doubt that he was never quite the same player thereafter.

Willie brought some decent players to the club, notably the forwards Mixu Paatelainen and Duncan Shearer. Duncan, in particular, became a firm favourite of the fans, the nearest they've had to a truly consistent goalscorer since the days of Joey Harper, Mark McGhee, Eric Black and Frank MacDougall. I recall one dazzling patch towards the end of 1992 when I was lucky enough to see three scintillating consecutive displays (Partick away, Hearts at home, Celtic away) in which Aberdeen hit a total of fifteen goals, with Jess, Shearer and Paul Mason all on fire.

In fact Willie had few problems with Celtic. It was Rangers who were his main adversaries, and they were now benefiting from the enhanced status that had come with the revolution Souness had started. Walter Smith, who succeeded Souness, was a canny and astute manager. He also had resources that Willie couldn't dream of. Even so, Willie ran the Ibrox team very close indeed.

He took Aberdeen to both domestic cup finals in 1992–93, his first full season as manager. They lost the League Cup final, to Rangers, 2–1, in a game they dominated for long periods. In the Scottish Cup final, Rangers beat them, again 2–1, in a game the Ibrox team deserved to win, but at the time the Aberdeen squad had been hit by a series of injuries and were missing key players, notably Jess. In both Willie's two full seasons in charge, Aberdeen finished runners-up to Rangers in the league. I took in a good number of Dons games at that time and I saw enough to conclude that he was making sound progress. While he wasn't getting the breaks, things would surely even out in time.

Willie was, however, fired in February 1995, after two successive away defeats (to Hibs and Kilmarnock) had begun to make relegation look a distinct possibility. Was this just a blip, albeit a serious one? I thought so; the board thought otherwise. Willie had served slightly less than three years as manager.

His departure upset me and indeed prompted an unease which has been nagging at me ever since. I realised that once a manager is under sustained pressure, and some of the fans turn against him, there is hardly anybody around to defend him; maybe the odd iconoclastic pressman, and that's it. Alex Ferguson described Willie as 'simply the best penalty-box defender in the world' but, irony of ironies, who was there to defend Willie?

The case against him was that he had been tinkering with his tactical formations, and I couldn't understand why he seemed to be freezing out Brian Irvine, the central defender, who was Aberdeen's most wholehearted player at the time. On the other hand, his record that season, while unsatisfactory, did not suggest a steady descent to oblivion. When he was dismissed his league record was won six, drawn nine, lost ten. And he'd taken the team to the semi-final of the League Cup, in which they'd lost, again unluckily, 1–0 to Celtic. And they were still in the Scottish Cup.

I believe that a more mature and far-sighted board would have given Willie at the very least another year. I have to be honest: there is an element of sentiment in this belief. I admit it: I venerate Willie Miller. I am happy that he is now back where he belongs, at the heart of the club, as director of football.

Altogether, 1995 was a black year for Scottish football. Willie Miller was fired by Aberdeen; the Rangers player Duncan Ferguson was jailed for three months after assaulting a Raith player on the pitch at Ibrox; and the European Court of Justice came to a momentous decision which was to have a desperately unfortunate effect on Scottish football.

This decision, the Bosman Ruling, was the result of the legalistic stubbornness of an obscure Belgian footballer. Jean-Marc Bosman may not have been anything special as a midfielder with Liège in the late 1980s – most observers reckoned he was at best nondescript – but he was a man who knew his rights. His contract with Liège expired in 1990. The club offered him a new contract, but his wages were to be cut by more than fifty per cent. Understandably, Bosman asked for a transfer. A French club was prepared to sign him, but only on a free transfer. Liège insisted on a fee.

Bosman took the impasse to court, citing his labour rights under European Law. After many hearings and various appeals, in 1995 the European Court of Justice finally endorsed Bosman's freedom of labour. There were two immediate and far-reaching consequences of this ruling. First, all out-of-contract players could now change clubs without transfer fees. Secondly, there could be no restrictions on the number of players from EU countries in any of the member states.

It took a year or so for these implications to sink in as far Scotland was concerned. Then suddenly, and in a way farcically, the floodgates opened. An absurd influx of foreign players swept into Scotland. A few had genuine talent, style and glamour but most were, in retrospect, no better – and in some cases worse – than the Scots they displaced and whose careers they damaged. And these imports did not come cheap. Scottish clubs which had been characterised by canniness – or downright meanness – suddenly swung to the other extreme. Financial responsibility vanished. Several clubs began to spend well over a hundred per cent of their turnover on players' wages.

As for the man himself, Jean-Marc rarely watches games now because he is worried about being spotted and harassed. He accepts that the ramifications of his case went too far. He acknowledges that the issue of poorer clubs across Europe losing their promising young players, often for nothing, is one that must be resolved by UEFA. He condemns some young players, saying they want everything too fast, and he thinks young professionals should be required to stay at their first club for a stipulated amount of time.

Meanwhile, during the 1990s the *Herald* had three different owners. I was closely involved in the ramifications of both changes of ownership, and they were very time-consuming. I became editor of the paper early in 1997, and my time commitments ratcheted up even further. Then in the summer of 2000 we moved premises, from Albion Street to Renfield Street; not a huge distance across central Glasgow as the crow flies, but the planning for the move was again very demanding on time, sometimes eating into Saturdays, normally my one guaranteed day off. These are not excuses, but I found I had less time – and inclination – to watch football. I would have been more inclined to make the time had the fare on offer been more palatable, but most of the games I did see were both poor and predictable.

At Aberdeen the dismissal of Willie Miller did not have the desired effect, though the next manager, Roy Aitken – whom Willie had brought to the club – did win a trophy, the League Cup, the following season. But that apart, matters just continued to deteriorate and I do not want to rehearse the weary litany of decline. Suffice to say that in the games I did go to, I saw the Dons lose far, far more often than I saw them win. And now there was not even a Charlie Cooke around to astonish and infuriate us in equal measure.

One of the few times in the late 1990s when I saw the Dons beat a team emphatically was at Boghead, Dumbarton, in a League Cup-tie at the start of season 1997–98. They won 5–1. I took Catherine there, primarily so that she could stand on the dilapidated Boghead terraces.

There were only about 1,500 fans present, and we could move around easily. Catherine was amazed by the ground, particularly when I told her that not so long ago Dumbarton had been playing in the top division, and that most grounds used to be just like this. When I also told her that thirty years earlier the Dons had played a cup-tie at this small ground in front of more than 10,000 fans, she could hardly believe me. I tried to explain that although the facilities for the fans were often much better now, the standard of play on the park was generally much worse.

In that game in August 1997, incidentally, Mike Newell scored a hat-trick for the Dons. Mike had won an English Premiership medal with Kenny Dalglish's Blackburn two years earlier and he was one of many players who passed through Pittodrie in the late 1990s. At least he played his part for the Dons, and I am pleased to see him now doing well as manager of Luton.

This was of course the period of the post-Bosman frenzy, when many Scottish club directors took leave of their senses and behaved with a crass irresponsibility for which it is difficult to forgive them. They encouraged their managers to spend good money after bad on a succession of execrable foreign imports. In season 1995–96 the Dons had only one foreign player in the first team squad, but over the next five or six seasons a sad succession of mercenaries flitted through Pittodrie, some staying for a couple of seasons, others for just a few months. Most of these players were so forgettable that they have already been completely forgotten, thank goodness.

Other Scottish clubs went down the same route, perhaps most spectacularly Motherwell, during the reign of Harri Kampman. Here are one or two names from that era that may jog some unhappy memories: Holm Kraska (Motherwell), Frank van Eijs (Dundee), Thomas Solberg (Aberdeen), Fabrice Henry (Hibs). Remember them? Congratulations.

Not to be outdone, the Old Firm played their part in this extended fiasco. They were of course able to be more extravagant than anyone else. Two examples will suffice. Rafael Scheidt (yes, that was his name) signed for Celtic in 1999 for almost £5 million on a four-year deal. This John Barnes signing was paid an alleged £20k a week. He made two starts for the Parkhead club. But at least he did appear. The previous year the Rangers manager Dick Advocaat had signed the Romanian Daniel Prodan from Atletico Madrid for £2.5 million. He was at Ibrox for three years, but he never once played for the first team.

I should emphasise here that I don't object to foreign players as such. Quite the contrary. Aberdeen fans of my age still cherish the contributions of the stylish Zoltan Varga. Younger ones have wonderful memories of the late Hicham Zerouali. And of how Scottish football as a whole has been graced by the likes of Brian Laudrup, Henrik Larsson and Franck Sauzee.

Aberdeen fans endured an utterly bizarre season in 1999–2000, a season when I watched far more games than was now usual. The Dons had yet another new manager: Ebbe Skovdahl, a chain-smoking Dane who had an avuncular, laid-back style and who was reputed, like one or two other Dons managers over the years, to have a fondness for the whisky.

Ebbe's first game, at Pittodrie, was a 5–0 defeat by Celtic. It was the first game Celtic played under the ill-fated John Barnes–Kenny Dalglish regime. I remember turning to Catherine as we sat in glorious sunshine at Pittodrie watching this debacle with growing foreboding and saying 'Either Celtic are very very good or we are very very bad.' As it turned out, Celtic were bad, and Aberdeen were simply atrocious. But John Barnes lasted only seven months as Celtic's manager; Ebbe lasted three and a half years at Pittodrie. To be fair to the Aberdeen board, they gave the Dane every chance.

In the early weeks of that 1999–2000 season Aberdeen became, for the only time I can remember, an utter embarrassment, a source of rich pickings to comedians the length of the UK. Amazingly, it took another six games before they managed to score their first league goal. Catherine and I went to see the fourth game of the season, at Tynecastle, when Hearts easily beat them 3–0. It could and should have been 6–0. The following Saturday we drove up to Aberdeen to see the fifth game, against St Johnstone. We journeyed on a sort of desperate mission; neither of us really wanted to see the game, but we went with a kind of bravado, a determination to support the team in their hour of need.

I actually picked up a ticket on the way north, the only time I've ever been caught for speeding. This caused much amusement among my friends, who needless to say thought it would have been more rational to have been caught speeding *away* from Pittodrie. The game itself was dire; Aberdeen again lost

3–0. This made the scoring record, after just five games: Goals for – 0; Goals against – 17.

There was a large and angry demonstration outside the main stand in Pittodrie Street afterwards, and the club chairman, Stewart Milne, was subjected to some appalling abuse. Catherine and I did not take part, but we did observe it. I had mixed feelings; I had every sympathy with the raw, frustrated fury of the fans, who had seen Alex Fergusons' legacy frittered away over thirteen inglorious years; at the same time I felt, maybe sentimentally, that there was a need for solidarity, that everyone in the club was in this together and that bitter division could make things even worse.

It took until late October before the Dons recorded their first league win, a 6–5 victory at Motherwell. Three days earlier they had been beaten 7–0 by Celtic at Parkhead, a game that Catherine went to but I didn't. She was becoming a more committed fan than I was.

I'm not making this up. Celtic beat the Dons 7–0, and seventy-two hours later the Dons went to Motherwell and won 6–5. The next two games were Aberdeen 2, Kilmarnock 2, and Aberdeen 1, Rangers 5. So in the space of three weeks, Aberdeen's four-game record was: Goals for – 9; Goals against – 19. To make it even more surreal, a fortnight later they beat Rangers 1–0 in the quarter-final of the League Cup.

In that crazy season, lit up only by the unlikely talents of the mercurial Moroccan, Hicham Zerouali, Aberdeen actually reached the two domestic cup finals. The semi-finals that took them there rank among the most emotive Dons games I have ever witnessed, partly because of the overall lousiness of the season. The first, in the League Cup, was a 1–0 victory over Dundee United at Dens Park. (In the subsequent final at Hampden, the Dons lost 2–0 to a Celtic team that seemed almost as nervous and ill-prepared as the Dons.)

The other semi-final, in the Scottish Cup, was played at Hampden on a Sunday evening in April 2000 – yes, a Sunday evening; the SFA have never been too thoughtful when it comes to the Dons' travelling support. The attendance was 22,600, which was poor, yet not too bad in the circum-stances. The Dons were up against a hard-working Hibs side. They came back from being a goal down early in the second half, and won 2–1. That was a special night, the one real highlight of Ebbe's surprisingly long stint as manager.

In the Cup Final Rangers won easily, 4–0. The Dons were not helped by the fact that the goalie, Jim Leighton, in his last game in his second stint for the club (he'd made his debut 22 years earlier in 1978, in Alex Ferguson's first game as Aberdeen manager), was seriously injured in the first minute. Ebbe, in his wisdom, had not included a goalkeeper among his substitutes. Aberdeen's main striker, Robbie Winters, went into goal. How Rangers did not score more than just four, I'll never know. Maybe they were being kind.

That grotesque season the Dons were surprisingly well supported and their away support, in particular, developed a perverse and jolly defiance, a cheery and cheeky bravado not unlike that of the reinvented Tartan Army. At first there was anger; then as the season progressed, if that is the correct word, the anger turned to amused defiance. The worse the adversity, the more these loyal away supporters seemed to enjoy it. I deprecated this tendency in so far as it seemed to endorse the inevitability of decline; I felt that the Dons supporters were becoming – how can I put it? – just a tad too philosophical. But on the other hand I realise that cheerfulness in defeat must be better than bitterness.

One bonus in that absurd season was that I was rarely bored. Later on, when Ebbe's teams became more organised, I was all too often bored. During games my mind would drift away from the action (such as it was) taking place before me, and spirit me back to the early days of my fanhood. I'd think of wonderful entertainers like Charlie Cooke and Jinky Smith. They seemed like distant, glorious ghosts.

I'd blot out the rubbish before me and I'd see Charlie, dancing past one, two, three defenders, and then spoiling it by pushing a pointless pass into no-man's-land. That seemed a bit like my football-watching career. Class, artistry, wizardry and genius: I've been privileged to witness and appreciate all of these. Now everything seemed to be petering out in a kind of dreich inconsequence. But the memories are still there, and thank God for them.

CHAPTER 9

FIRST CONCLUSION

Television was to change everything in Scottish football in the 1980s and particularly in the 1990s, and not just because it brought a lot of new money into the game. It completely altered the nature of Scottish football journalism. Television made some (by no means all) of the 'product' it helped to reinvent and reshape more fashionable, more personality-driven, more celebrity-obsessed, more prone to hype rather than considered reflection.

In other words, football – and particularly the Old Firm – became more suitable for marketing. Television is now central to the professional game, and wrangles over television revenues constitute a major part of the task of football administrators. (They often seem to come badly out of the negotiations, but that is another matter.)

When I started in journalism, much of the football writing was high-flown and even literary. I'm thinking of people like Hugh McIlvanney, John Rafferty and Ian Archer. It would not be fanciful to call them artists. Writers like that are still around, but it is more difficult for them now. Many, maybe even most, supporters now primarily experience the game through television. In addition the rise of the 'fanzines' and radio phone-ins in the 1980s and the Internet in the 1990s democratised commentary on the game. This was another revolution, parallel to the television one. Ordinary fans could now air their views and communicate with each other more easily. That was fine, but the downside was that rumours and innuendo, and at times blatant malice, became the common currency of comment.

In response, some football writing became more self-consciously abrasive, critical, combative, crude, unreliable and sensational. There is also a 'look-at-me' stridency in some contemporary football journalism. When I was talking with the Scottish international and captain of Hearts, Steven Pressley, he reflected wryly that some journalists seemed to want to become much bigger celebrities than the star players.

My former colleague on the *Sunday Standard*, Roddy Forsyth, who covers Scottish football for both BBC Radio Five Live and the *Daily Telegraph*, told me: 'What has diminished the standing of parts of the Scottish football press is that some younger journalists are over-influenced by the Internet. You used to have to cultivate your contacts for information, but now some of the younger writers just trawl though the Internet. What you get there is often a frenzy of misinformation, so I don't think that's the best basis from which to start. Some of the stuff on the Internet can be quite vindictive.'

Roddy also suggested that no-one should discount the way in which certain journalists were used by managers, directors and agents. 'This has always happened, of course it has, but some journalists are allowing themselves to be used more and more,' he said.

The 1960s and '70s were a golden era for football journalism. But I would indict some of those involved in that period for not using their potential power and influence to greater and more beneficial effect. Too many of them allowed their growing disillusion to blind them to the good that they might have done.

It ill behoves me, of all people, to be critical of Scottish football writers, because, as I have related, I turned down the chance to become one, and later, when I became an executive journalist, I did not always take sport in general and football in particular seriously enough. I recalled how in my early days on the *Scotsman* I used to berate my good friend Arnold Kemp about what I regarded as his slightly patronising attitude to the sports pages.

I confess that when I became editor of the *Herald* at the beginning of 1997, I did not regard the paper's sports pages as a top priority. My attitude was more or less that these pages looked after themselves. This was because Iain Scott and his writers, who included my former *Standard* colleague ,Doug Gillon, as well as the likes of Ian Paul, Jim Reynolds, Ken Gallacher and the young Darryl Broadfoot, were doing an excellent job. My main concern was to introduce a new sports supplement on Saturdays, and this was soon accomplished, thanks to the splendid efforts of Iain and his production team.

In extenuation, I could argue that this was a time of political ferment, in which politics brushed everything else aside. We were approaching the general election of 1997, which was to end eighteen years of Tory rule, and to bring in a government that had devolution as one of its key priorities. Within a few months, the new government had indeed delivered the referendum on the proposed Scottish Parliament (which has not had the impact on Scottish football it perhaps should have had: this is a point I shall return to in Part Three).

In retrospect, I regret that I took this attitude, that the sports pages would look after themselves. Far too many people in Scottish life talk, and emote, about football; far too few of them actually regard it as a major priority when they have the chance to do something about it, however indirectly. It is almost as if we are a nation obsessed by football, yet at the same time we don't take the game seriously. The veteran politician Donald Gorrie summed up this syndrome for me when he said that most politicians at Holyrood would far rather talk about football than politics; but when it came to taking meaningful political initiatives on football, their interest suddenly evaporated.

The issue of attendances looms large in this book. I still get indignant when I recall that only 10,700 turned up to watch the Scottish Cup semi-final replay between Aberdeen and Dundee United in April 1985. (The game was not live on television, incidentally.) There is no doubt that the Dons and United were then among the élite of the leading club teams in Europe. That attendance was a national disgrace. So much for the glory days of the New Firm. So much for the theory that if the Old Firm played in a different league, Scottish football, having become more 'democratic' and more competitive, would draw bigger crowds.

And what are we to make of the fact that a few days after storming to a European final in 1972, Rangers could only draw 5,000 to a league game at Ibrox? In the 1960s, 1970s and (to a lesser extent) in the 1980s there were some huge crowds; there were also many pitiful crowds. There was no consistency. The fans were more fickle and fastidious than is often allowed. They weren't just fodder, coming along to see whatever was on offer, willy-nilly. They were more picky than the fans of today.

After the revolutions at Rangers and then at Celtic, regular attendances at both Ibrox and Parkhead are now consistently higher than they were twenty and thirty years ago. The stadia are superior and the two clubs have huge cohorts of season-ticket holders. There are however danger signs: some of these season-ticket holders are becoming more choosy, and are no longer prepared to come to watch games they expect to be one-sided and boring.

Yet you could argue that most of the fans that make up the 115,000 or so who generally turn out to watch Scottish professional league football every weekend are more loyal these days. A lot of the people I knew in the 1970s – journalistic colleagues and others – could talk about the game till the cows came home; they had vehement opinions about football, but they rarely bothered to watch a game. Whatever the current ills of Scottish football, they cannot be mainly attributed to the loss of spectators.

I'm conscious that the preceding chapters might read like the chronicle of a fair-weather fan. In the 1960s and '70s I'd routinely watch more than thirty games in a season. In the 1980s this dwindled to about twenty a season. In the 1990s there was a further decline, to about twelve or fifteen per season. And in the new millennium my attendance levels have been frankly pathetic; I'm down to five or six a season.

This reflects the decline in Aberdeen's performances, but it is also symptomatic of a growing and worrying feeling among many fans that Scottish football is becoming dull, predictable, and all too often, putrid. There are fewer individual entertainers around. Teams may be working harder, collectively, but they are providing inferior entertainment. I simply don't think it is true now that even the most diehard fan will happily accept their team grinding out 1-0 results, as long as they are winning.

And many fans nowadays are not so much fans of a team as consumers of a product. When the game is so much about branding, about sponsorship and marketing and merchandising, is it any surprise that the fan is turned into a consumer? I do not often quote anything said by Tony Blair with approval, but in 1995, before he became Prime Minister, he suggested that the dividing line between marketing and exploitation might have been crossed as far as the British football fan was concerned. I agree with that; indeed I might even regard these words as prophetic.

A further negative factor in Scotland (and increasingly elsewhere) is the lopsided nature of the league. There are two (in other countries three or four or five) clubs that are regarded as potential champions – and the rest make up the numbers. The élite clubs are gobbling up most of the fans, most of the money and most of the publicity.

Then there is television. The advent of satellite television cannot be discounted. I watch far more football on television, almost all of it on satellite television, than I did eight or nine years ago. I know that many other people do the same. This again reflects the fact that I have become the consumer of a product, rather than the fan of a team.

Finally, there is the simple process of growing old. I think the best time to be a fan is in your late teens, through your twenties and into your early thirties. (Obviously the best time to play, too, if you are any good at playing.) In these years the complications and annoyances of travelling to and from games loom less large, and the pleasures of drinking before and after the match are greater (and both of these remain, for many, key aspects of the overall football-watching experience).

Also, serious domestic and work pressures start kicking in, generally from the late twenties onwards. These pressures usually become ever more pressing in middle age. Then, when at last you find you are shaking them off, you discover that you are on the threshold of old age. And fewer old men seem to attend football matches nowadays.

In April 2002, Dunfermline and Aberdeen played out a grim and tedious goalless draw. My daughter Catherine and I were sitting high in the East Stand at East End Park, and as the game decayed into meaningless oblivion I looked at the supporters around and below. What struck me about the crowd was that I – then aged fifty-four – must have been, by a considerable distance, the oldest spectator among the fifty or sixty fans in my immediate vicinity. A couple of generations ago the terraces were populated by plenty of old men, usually casting an acerbic and mordant eye on proceedings. I sometimes used to position myself in front of a pair of these oldies; their vitriolic nostalgia and constant disparaging of the present could be more entertaining than the actual game.

My friend Sarah Nelson, a loyal Dons fan over the years, thinks I am too gentle on these old folk. She disapproves of the 'rugs and pan drops' brigade, as she calls them. (Yes, when Pittodrie became all seated in the late 1970s, they actually used to bring rugs to the ground.) They were constantly moaning and could find fault with everybody and everything. For example, a creative player like Gordon Strachan was never in the same league as George Hamilton. A prolific goalscorer like Joey Harper was not in the same class as Harry Yorston.

Whatever; I just note that sociologically, watching football seems to be more and more a pastime for the young, and the early middle-aged. The elderly stay at home, or maybe go to the pub and watch on the telly.

I lost interest in the national team in the late 1980s. I am not decrying the sterling work done by Andy Roxburgh and Craig Brown, national coaches with an ever-decreasing pool of fine players to work with. In the 1990s Scotland's teams became more efficient, but they also became less entertaining to watch. There was for me no incentive to watch players who were regimented and cajoled into systems which, no doubt for perfectly valid tactical reasons, seemed to militate against individual expression and flair.

Also, the nature of the Tartan Army changed. There was too much arrogance and tribalism in the 1970s. But as the Army reinvented itself, we perhaps moved too far in the opposite direction. The connection between the national team and the supporters became more tenuous. Everything was becoming bland. The hunger had gone. The Scottish nationalist politician Kenny MacAskill, a loyal Tartan Army footsoldier, told me: 'Defeat should and must hurt. For too many members of the modern Tartan Army, defeat does not seem to matter. For some of them the game has become almost incidental. It's just one part of a fun away trip.'

Yet I would not wish to disparage the well-behaved nature of the new Tartan Army unduly. That would be crass and irresponsible. They still can and do provide magnificent support. In Walter Smith's first game in charge of Scotland, in Milan in March 2005, 13,000 Scots fans out-shouted and out-sung the Italians. Further, everyone, including the Italian police and neutral observers, agreed that that their behaviour was impeccable. Not one Scot was arrested in the San Siro stadium or its environs. This contrasted with the conduct of the Italian supporters who brawled among themselves in the tier beneath the Scots. (The local police had let in a squad of Verona hooligans at half time. They promptly picked a fight with the local Milan supporters.)

At exactly the same time, thousands of German fans went on a vicious rampage during and after a friendly international in Slovenia. The violence was serious and had a sickening racist dimension.

If the national team plays constant meaningless friendly fixtures, the currency is debased. A Scotland game should be an event; it has, too often in recent years, become a joke. At least the annual fixture against the English used to keep alive a mood of national pride that could be expressed through football. We may not have always beaten the English – though we did so more often than we had any right to – and sometimes we were drubbed. Heaven knows, a 9–3 or a 7–1 defeat rankled, but the nation always regrouped, and recovered.

I saw seven of these games against England (five at Hampden and two, or, more accurately, one and a wee bit) at Wembley and I well understand their importance. The Scottish team usually evinced all sorts of qualities – cheek, pluck, mischief, defiance, disrespect, virtuosity and sheer cocky style – that the English team, even if clearly superior, could never begin to manifest. Somehow it is not possible for a Scotland team to display all these exciting qualities in a meaningless friendly against, say, Egypt.

There is possibly in some of what I have written the odd hint of anti-English prejudice. I disclaim any bigotry or bile. Indeed I revere England and the English, and I think that in many ways they are people more blessed with many of the finer qualities than we Scots are. I think that history shows that they are much better at working collectively than the Scots, who tend to operate best as individuals. I think that characteristic is often reflected in our football.

But when it comes to the English national football team, the English, normally so reasonable and decent, seem to forget themselves. The worst characteristics of diseased nationalism can prevail. I happily confess that I have always been pleased to see the English football team doing badly, whereas, for example, I would be delighted to watch the English cricket team beat Australia in an Ashes series. I discern nothing irrational or inconsistent in this attitude.

Further, I cannot see anything wrong or misguided in resenting the fact that England, not West Germany, won the 1966 World Cup final. For me, that is just part of being Scottish. As I write this, I have just heard of a grandfather in his early seventies who has reluctantly concluded that he will never see a great Scotland team again. So he has decided to do the next best thing. He has decided to have one final fling. He is going to the World Cup finals in Germany in 2006 to support the teams England are playing. Good on you, sir!

It was a particular pleasure for me to live through the glory years at Aberdeen when, for all too short a time, the Scottish game was 'democratised'. But then came the Souness revolution at Ibrox, and Celtic had to respond, and all Alex Ferguson's fine work was undone. Scottish football is now in effect ruled by a duopoly consisting of two international brands which have less and less to do with Scotland, and the life-enhancing community-rooted loyalties of club football at its best.

But I am determined that this book should not develop into an anti-Old Firm rant, tempting as that sometimes is, and anyway I am convinced that there is at least one key figure in the Old Firm set-up – Rangers' director-secretary Campbell Ogilvie – who is working on various projects which may well help the teams who are most likely to present meaningful challenges to Rangers and Celtic: Hearts, Hibs and Aberdeen.

I mention Ferguson and Souness. They, along with Jock Stein, were the three dominating figures of Scottish football in the period 1965–90. There was then a hiatus when the Scottish game was on the cusp, and this was followed by a time of decline, roughly from 1995 to the present. Individuals of their standing were unable, for whatever reason, to make their mark on our game during this period.

Thus the three key figures in Part One of this book are managers. Football is all about complex cross-currents of sociological and financial and cultural as well as sporting change. But it is important not to discount the potentially colossal influence of the outstanding individual; and up till now it is the great manager far more than the great player or the great director or the great fan, who has changed things.

I suspect that we are going to look in a new direction for the architects of much-needed beneficial change. We shall have to look to our legislators and administrators to show the vision – through the development of a proper national youth-development scheme, and though an improved, imaginative and innovative league structure – that can help our game revive.

We also must look to the Scottish Parliament and the local authorities to do much more to help with the provision of all-weather pitches and indoor halls. They also need to get schoolteachers re-involved with the game as part of their professional duties, and to allow more use of school facilities out of school hours. We must also examine radical ways of nurturing our best young talent, and this may involve removing the best young players from school well before the school-leaving age. I hasten to add that their education would not be neglected: far from it. I'd like to see a culture where football development and educational development go hand-in-hand. We need more graduate footballers.

It is significant that two of the great trio of managers – Souness and Ferguson – were able to do momentous things because they had the support of that rare breed, progressive directors. Alas, Jock Stein had no such support during the glory years at Parkhead. That makes his achievement all the greater.

I have been chronicling lost opportunities. Inevitably, in the preceding pages there has been much about short-sightedness, incompetence and parochialism. For some of this, the media may be blamed. But mostly I'd blame the directors and the so-called legislators who could not capitalise, who would not invest and think ahead, at the very time when we were producing world class footballers for fun. So there is irony in the fact that I'm now looking to the legislators and directors to save our game.

There were shining exceptions, but most of the bad guys in Scottish football were to be found in the boardrooms. Hardly any of them were downright villains, like the rogue who presided over the death of Third Lanark. But too many of them were mean, petty and myopic. They left behind a mess, which was then compounded by other factors such as the teachers' strikes and the reckless, profligate buying of second-rate foreign players in the aftermath of Bosman.

Can our Scottish game be great again, or even better than it ever was before? I am certain that it can. Even as this is written, towards the end of season 2004–05, there are definite signs of revival. But it will be a long haul. It will require three qualities in particular: hard work, imagination and patience. Perhaps surprisingly, the third may be the most difficult to summon. For too long our Scottish game has been bedevilled by an obsession with the quick fix, which generally fixes nothing.

PART TWO
THE FORUM

INTRODUCTION

This is the age of the soundbite, the text message, the instant quote. I thought it would be rewarding to ask a disparate collection of football folk to ventilate their views at greater length on any aspects of our Scottish professional game and its travails that they wished to address.

Some of these people are young; some are old. Some are household names, others are obscure and unsung. Some of them have given a lifetime of distinguished service to football; for some of the others football does not mean that much any more. But all of them – even Jack McLean, despite what he claims – have this in common: the Scottish game is, or has been, a meaningful part of their lives, and they care about its future.

First, here is an evocative mini-celebration of the place football has in our national folk memory from Richard Holloway, the former Bishop of Edinburgh who is now chairman of the Scottish Arts Council. Brought up in the west of Scotland, Richard has long been fascinated by the way in which football infatuates the Scottish psyche. He has insisted publicly on more than one occasion that football is a quintessential part not just of Scottish culture, but of Scottish life. Here is Richard Holloway on the essence of Scottish football:

> Keepy uppy in the back court. Dribbling with a tin can down the street.
>
> Five-a-side during the tea break, jackets for goal posts. The exultant exhilaration of clearing a dangerous ball from your own penalty area all the way down to theirs.
>
> The rooks settling in the trees nearby on dreich November afternoons.
>
> Your father doing the pools as the scores come in over the wireless: och, maybe next week.
>
> Wee men with bowly legs weaving magic circles round blond gods from places faraway. And the roar, the roar. The beautiful game is part of the collective memory of Scotland. It's the worst of us; but it's also the best of us.

CHAPTER 1

The Renegade
JACK McLEAN

Jack McLean, the 'Urban Voltaire', is a great Glasgow *flaneur*, man about town and sometime commentator on the city's many idiosyncrasies. He was a supporter of Third Lanark. He used to love football; now he hates it.

> Football? Damn the game. I say: God damn it. It's so fucking relentless. I go to my local – but this is true of most other pubs too – and it's on every night, on two tellies, both showing football, and the punters say 'sh sh sh' or words to that effect, if you get my drift, if my mates and me dare to talk about anything other than football. It's being forced on us, rammed down our throats.
>
> God, how I hate football. I'm now strongly, fervently anti-football. I detest it. When I hear George W Bush speaking on the radio I switch it off; but I can't switch off the tellies in the pub, can I?
>
> Tonight, there's an Old Firm game, and there will be violence in the streets. Not just in Glasgow, but in Lanarkshire, Ayrshire, all over. I won't go to my pub tonight: I'd be put out, for I insist on talking through the game. By the way, Harry: your book won't sell unless it's all about Celtic and Rangers. No-one cares about any other teams now. Don't you kid yourself.
>
> I'm a republican but for heaven's sake, even the Royal Family is not forced down my throat like football and the Old Firm in particular.
>
> OK, for all that, I admit: A wee part of me does still care about the game. And so how would I revive it? Simple: I'd levy a compulsory percentage – say 30 per cent or even 40 per cent – of the wages of the big earning players and I'd put all that cash straight back into the game at grass-roots level.

Jack, despite his tirade (delivered in a surprisingly dulcet tone over our lunch in Newton Mearns, not a place he normally frequents) made a sentimental suggestion when we drove back into town. He said we should visit Cathkin Park, the former home of Third Lanark. When we got there, his mood changed dramatically, he became mellow and wistful. There were tears in his eyes as he looked round. He said that for him, and many Glaswegians, football died when Third Lanark died.

CHAPTER 2

The Administrator
CAMPBELL OGILVIE

Campbell Ogilvie, the son of a former Rangers club doctor, has been secretary of the Ibrox club since 1979. In 1989, when the David Murray/ Graeme Souness revolution was beginning to take shape, he became a director of the club.

He is also a vice-president of UEFA, and serves on various panels of that body, including the national teams committee and the administrative panel. He is vice-president of the SFA and crucially, chairman of the National Youth Initiative. It is not generally known that he was an architect of the European Champions' League. He is now developing radical proposals for improving the league structure in Scotland. His commitment to Rangers is exemplary, but he is also deeply concerned about the general health of the overall Scottish game and he is constantly thinking about new initiatives that might advance our national standing. He is a modest, low-profile visionary, but a visionary nonetheless.

Working for a football club, it is too easy to become insular. There are so many pressures on you not to look ahead; it's all about the next game, about the coming transfer window, and so on. It is difficult to look three or four seasons ahead. Whereas that is exactly what you have to do, or should be doing, with the SFA, or with UEFA.

In Scotland six or seven years ago, everybody was trying to keep up with each other when it came to buying foreign players, and it just became crazy. We all neglected youth development and didn't give our own players a chance. Talent without opportunity is meaningless. The wage bills were ridiculous. Rangers had a squad of 33 or 34 players, which was far too many, and it's now significantly lower. UEFA, as you know, are working on proposals to make clubs develop home-grown players.

In the past SFA committees were made up of club directors, who might be garage owners or whatever. Now we have brought in working groups with the football people, the managers and coaches and former players, involved. This is all to the good. Under the SFA umbrella we have a unified approach for the first time in our Youth Initiative. We have specific criteria in place for the clubs. We insist that they work to meet strict criteria for facilities, coaching, sports science and so on. We are trying to provide clarity, particularly in the area of coaching. With all this progressing, I am utterly confident that before too long you will see more and more good young players breaking through.

We are doing this within the game but I think the Scottish Executive must help too. I understand that football must be down the list after health and education, but youth development can pay dividends in these very areas. The Executive and the local authorities can help with facilities, with opening up the schools and the parks. And grant aid should be given to the clubs to improve their facilities. The criteria would be whether players were coming though at under-21 and full national level. Everybody benefits at this point. The whole country benefits if the national game is booming.

In the short term, we simply have to improve our domestic game. We keep decrying our product – it's not a word I like, but I have to admit, it is a product now. I'd love to see Rangers with a hard core of home-based players, and all our supporters would love that. The players who come through the ranks are those who are appreciated most by the fans. I'd like at least 50 per cent of our squad to be Scottish.

Before we developed Murray Park (Rangers' £14 million training facility at Milngavie) European players would come here and ask to see our training facilities. It was embarrassing. In Europe most clubs don't own their grounds but they have invested in really impressive training facilities. Other clubs in Scotland cannot be expected to create facilities on the scale of Murray Park, but access to proper facilities is a key aspect of our SFA Youth Initiative. The club do not need to own the facility, but they must have an arrangement for proper access to some kind of community facility. And if facilities are important, coaching is equally important. We need more qualified coaches. This is an area where the Executive could assist with grant aid; for the whole community, not just the clubs, would benefit from better coaching.

And then there are the structures. The financing and the football must be developed hand in hand. If you get the footballing structure right, the finance will follow. The Champions' League is not responsible for the situation you have in most countries, not just Scotland, where just two or three clubs have a meaningful chance of winning the league. But I agree that it is essential that we increase the quality of our domestic competition. More and more of our season-ticket holders here at Ibrox are not turning up for league games that they regard as meaningless. Along with others, I am working on proposals for new league structures, and I believe that we must be open-minded and radical as we develop these.

CHAPTER 3

The Manager
SIR ALEX FERGUSON

There is much about Sir Alex Ferguson in Part One of this book. As far as I am concerned he is by far the greatest British manager of modern times. He is the only manager in football history to have achieved extended success at the highest level in both Scotland and England. Between 1958 and 1974 he played for Queen's Park, St Johnstone, Dunfermline, Rangers, Falkirk and Ayr United. He then managed East Stirlingshire (July–October 1974), St Mirren (1974 –78), Aberdeen (1978–86), and Manchester United from November 1986 till the present. He also managed Scotland in 1985–86. In 1999 he was knighted for his services to football.

> There has been this constant problem ever since the war in Scotland in that we just haven't had the training facilities needed for development. There was no investment in training grounds when land was readily available, for buttons. I remember Dick Donald at Aberdeen telling me that in the early 1960s the club had a chance to buy some land for a training ground just north of the Bridge of Don, but for one reason or another they didn't. Rangers sold their training ground and it became a car park. That hardly helped.
>
> The biggest single difference between Scotland and England was that in England even quite small clubs had their training facilities. In Scotland managers had to beg, steal or borrow their training grounds. You had to scrape around, ferrying players round town from place to place in cars and minibuses. So the current difficulties were always going to happen.
>
> Then there was the growth of boys' club football at the same time as the schools football was dying. You have to understand that most players are manufactured. Only the very best ones, the really special ones, aren't. That means you need really good coaching, to develop any players other than the outstanding ones – but with the growth of the boys' clubs there was this emphasis on playing, not coaching and practice. Some boys were playing 140, 150 games a season when they were 15. That was ridiculous. How can you develop physically if you're playing that many games? It was miraculous that anyone came through at all. There were so many games, there just weren't enough opportunities for practice. The practice ethic was taken away, and it's all-important.

When a boy is fifteen, round about then, there are a lot of distractions. Boys are being introduced to a different life. To make it in football requires sacrifice, and only the determined ones get through this stage, but they need help, support and above all, good coaching.

The best time in Scottish football for boys of this age was probably in the 1950s. Schools football in the 1950s was terrific. I was lucky enough to play for the Scottish schoolboys with players like Willie Henderson. Youngsters were not playing too many games then and they were being sensibly coached. The Scottish schools set-up was excellent then. The emphasis was on practice, practice, and more practice.

But the most important learning curve comes even before that. In fact I'd say as early as six or seven. That's when the kids learn the natural skills. I remember when we went on our family holidays to Saltcoats, my Dad would always take a ball. And he'd keep emphasising the usual stuff, use both feet, practise your passing, and so on.

Much later in Scotland there was this tendency after Bosman to buy cheap foreign players. Scottish home-grown talent wasn't looked at properly. A lot of talent was just dumped, it was just dismissed. That was a terrible, terrible time. The way young Scottish players were treated created apathy, a lack of ambition, and a loss of hope. At last, one or two decent players are starting to come through again.

It's the league clubs who engage the youngsters' attention, it's the league clubs that are always going to have most influence on them. As I said, there are many distractions when they are fifteen, but they'll pay attention to the clubs all right. Every club needs to have good training facilities, floodlit pitches, indoor pitches. And proper coaching. This can make a contribution to the community, too.

Since devolution, we've got the Parliament but we need to get it more involved. So I look to the Parliament. I notice every time I'm back in Scotland how able people are, the Scots people still have this quality about them. It's up to the Parliament to harness this quality for the good of the game because it is a matter of national importance. You motivate people in all sorts of ways and if the country is good at sport, it booms through the whole country, it gives a general uplift. In Scottish football we've got pride, we've got reputation, we've got tradition. We must build on these. The future of our football is a national issue.

CHAPTER 4

The Former Chairman
JAMIE MOFFAT

Jamie Moffat stood down as chairman of Kilmarnock FC in the summer of 2005. Jamie is an affable figure, an engaging businessman who always seemed slightly bemused by his involvement in football. In truth, he is not a football man at heart; golf is his first sporting love (he is a past Ayrshire County champion). He became involved in Kilmarnock FC after his late father, the entrepreneur who founded the AT Mays travel empire, rescued the club in the late 1980s. Between them, Jamie and his mother Margie own 90 per cent of the club.

When I interviewed him in the headquarters of his travel company in Saltcoats, Jamie was remarkably honest about his uncertainties. Most football people have dogmatic opinions; Jamie was a refreshing change. He was cautious, reflective, pensive. I formed the impression that he had maintained his commitment to Kilmarnock out of respect, more than anything else, for his late father's memory.

He presided over the completion of a superb venue: Rugby Park, with its 18,000 capacity, is now one of the most pleasant grounds in Scotland, not least because of the excellent large hotel that has been constructed alongside the stadium. I sensed that, although he had introduced much more realistic budgeting, he remained worried that because people knew he was a wealthy man, they would always assume that he was there to 'save' the club, even if there was continued overspending.

I did find the financial responsibility very taxing. My late father and I between us have put over £4 million into the club. I don't for one moment regret this, but the responsibilities are enormous. The club is such an important part of the community. We have 3,500 season-ticket holders. There should be far more; I wish there were more, and I have been contsantly saying to the community, quite frankly, please come and help, please come and support us. The club means so much to the loyal supporters we do have.

When we won the Scottish Cup in 1997, I was amazed at the emotion of it all. I've never seen so many grown men crying. We took over 25,000 to Ibrox that day. The win gave a terrific fillip to the community. But as I say, I really do wish that more of these supporters would attend more regularly. It would make a huge difference.*

As chairman, the buck stopped with me. The biggest demands were on my time, not my pocket. I just thank God I didn't have to pick the team!

When I watched a game, as chairman, I did not really enjoy it. I felt this constant tension.

As the game swings one way and the next, you see big amounts of money coming and then going. I remember watching a cup game when we were holding Rangers to a draw. I was thinking of the replay at Ibrox, and then a possible game at Parkhead. I was thinking: this will balance the books! But then we went down late in the game.†

I'm chairman of ATM Travel, but I spent more than fifty per cent of my working week on the football club. Football is so demanding. It is relentless. It swallows up your time. It's a unique kind of business. There is so much media interest. And the supporters, your customers, are so vocal, so involved. Joe Punter keeps firing off. And bizarre things keep happening. Football is not like a normal business at all, although most clubs do now try to operate as normal businesses. Nothing, nothing about football would ever surprise me. The players' wage demands, the constant media interest, the chance nature of the actual game – the difference between success and failure is tiny – and the passion of the supporters: it all adds up to a very volatile mix.

The Bank of Scotland have been incredibly supportive to most of the clubs in the SPL. Without this one bank, our football would be in much deeper trouble. We've had these huge losses. The business is in better health now but we cannot be complacent and we must never let our costs rise again. We must not anticipate income. That is the most important thing. Budgets must be realistic and must be kept to.

After the SPL was set up, the first TV deal was very lucrative. Clubs started spending far too much on players. Budgets were set far, far too optimistically. People – directors – were spending money that just wasn't there. Players' contracts were not realistic. Over the last three years or so, we reduced the players' contracts by at least 50 per cent.

What football directors must do now is work collectively to get more fans back watching live games. Success at Rugby Park makes a difference to the

* Towards the end of season 2003–04, league attendances at Rugby Park slipped under the 5,000 mark.

† The draw for the next round had already been made.

community that is almost immeasurable. But of course not every club can be successful. That's football.

There is too much football on television, yet the television money is essential. But there won't be so much TV money in the future. We must be ready for that. Players themselves are, as I say, becoming more realistic, but are their agents?

And you ask about the Old Firm. Should they stay, should they go? I'm sitting on the fence on that one. Attendances at Rugby Park would increase in a more competitive league. But, without the Old Firm, average attendances would still fall. That is the conundrum. A new TV deal would be even more difficult to negotiate. More people from the Kilmarnock catchment area go to Glasgow to support the Old Firm than support their local club. This is despite our new hotel at the ground, with its excellent restaurant and bar facilities, and the all-round improvements to the stadium.

CHAPTER 5

The Politician(1)
DONALD GORRIE

Donald Gorrie is Lib. Dem. MSP for Central Scotland, and his party's official spokesman on sport and culture. He has reached the veteran stage (he is 72) but after many years of service at local council level, Westminster, and now Holyrood he manages to remain enthusiastic, energetic and independent-minded. He has a long record of community engagement, particularly in the areas of youth sport and drama. His fastidious and non-demotic style makes some people who should know better query whether he has a genuine concern about football, but anyone who knows him well realises that he longs fervently for a revival of our national game. Unusually for a Scot who cares about football, he has no personal baggage in terms of supporting a particular team.

There is a limit to what politicians can do. It is a good rule that sports bodies should be independent of the Executive. And it is right that there should be no direct political interference in Scottish football. So to that extent I sympathise with the First Minister: he can't say, 'We'll do this, we'll do that.' On the other hand much more public money needs to be put into the game, and that is something that the Executive can and should do.

For example, large tracts of Glasgow have no proper facilities. Yet the schools are often lying empty in the evenings, at the weekends, in the holidays. We must start paying the teachers to go back in the evenings and at weekends. The Scottish Executive should attend to this immediately. Get the teachers back, plus qualified coaches from the professional teams to help too, working in partnership with the teachers. At present far too much is left to the parents, and while I do not wish to disparage their enthusiasm, parents often want to relive what they imagine their youth was all about and they do abuse referees, and send out the wrong signals. Parental enthusiasm is not necessarily conducive to the teaching of good footballing habits. Parents are often not objective and professional in their approach to coaching in the way that teachers are.

While the Scottish Executive cannot tell the SFA or the other football bodies what they must or must not do, the Executive simply must find money to promote and organise sport, and football in particular, at the bottom level. If we were to put an extra £10 million into the health service it would disappear without trace. But if it were put into sport, it would have an effect – it might even do much good. The Executive could find £10 million easily enough, and I'd say eighty per cent of this should go to youth football. But I've never managed to persuade my colleagues to go down this route. MSPs are far more interested in sport than politics, but they just will not take political initiatives on sport.

The first thing to do is to get young people using school facilities for structured football – both coaching and games – on a regular, organised basis. Then you need to develop a career path. Old Firm teams often take the field with one, two, three Scottish players at the most. This applies to some of the other league teams too. There are not nearly enough opportunities in Scottish professional football for seriously talented young Scottish players. This lack of a career path is at the heart of the problem. Somehow, the clubs must be persuaded to employ more young Scots, and to give them a fair chance.

CHAPTER 6

The Youth Coach
GRAHAM BIRSE

Graham is forty-seven, married, with three children: two boys and a girl. His second boy, Gordon, has just signed for Dunfermline

Many of the people I talked to while researching this book were genuinely concerned about the revival of Scottish youth football. They spoke with vehemence and passion. But not one person spoke to me with more commitment and more ardour on this subject than Graham Birse. He is an optimist and he says that in his area of Fife there is a plentiful supply of boys – and girls – who want to play football in an organised way.

Graham lives in South Fife and commutes every day to Edinburgh, where he holds down a responsible and time-consuming job. Even so he manages to find at least twelve hours a week to devote to youth football. He coaches the under-14s in the Norrie McCathie Development Squad. They are based at Pitreavie, and at the Dalgety Bay sports centre. He takes two coaching sessions a week, supervises his team at a game and has a considerable amount of admin. and paperwork on top of that.

Incidentally, Graham spoke highly of Jim Sinclair, the SFA's director of football development. Although it is fashionable to knock the SFA, Graham insisted that the support he and his colleagues received from the SFA was on the right lines.

> Our youngsters must have qualified coaches from the earliest stage. You wouldn't take golf lessons from an amateur. We simply must introduce new coaching qualifications. At the moment, if you just turn up and complete the course you pass. So we need coaching qualifications that are more difficult to attain. Having said that, I don't want over-qualified coaches. I'd say the most important qualification for a coach is never having grown up. Being a coach takes me back to when I was 12 or 13, and playing endlessly with my mates – the nicknames and everything.

> And whatever people may say about over-committed parents and over-enthusiastic dads, they should not be eliminated from the game. You just want to make sure that they are properly trained, that they have gained proper

coaching qualifications. In a good set-up parental behaviour will be monitored, anyway. I do accept that the decline in schools football has been little short of tragic, and I'd certainly want to see the teachers involved as they used to be.

There should be élite coaches for élite players. The élite kids should be identified as early as 8 or 9 and pulled out and placed in an élite regional set-up. We must not be scared of this concept of élitism. On the other hand, we must not make things too competitive too soon. My view is that it's natural to want to win. Why add to the pressures? A game is public enough. If a kid makes a mistake, he doesn't need the coach getting on his back.

Young players don't have the tanner ba skills any more so they need to be coached. There should be an emphasis on personal skill from a very early age. Kids should be encouraged and empowered to do the likes of Cruyff turns during games. There has been too much emphasis on physical strength. Skills must be developed in all positions, including centre back.

The tradition of Scottish football from away back, the idea that you had to play hard to win, well, I don't think that wears any more. With all due respect to the mining villages and the industrial cities and junior football; the players who emerged came through despite rather than because of their environment. Also you must remember that what happened in Scotland in the 1940s and 1950s and 1960s, when we did produce so many great players, is happening in Africa now. It's happening in Turkey now. It's happening in many parts of the world, but not here. It's happening, as it always has, in South America.

Kids can dream. In Scotland football was once the alternative to the pit or the army. In every street, every pend, every close, the kids were playing till it got dark. Football was the only thing. Now kids are often not allowed out, for reasons we all know. So that ability to go out and play endlessly and learn to express yourself naturally is limited, unlike in Africa or South America. This means that we have to emphasise to them: Practise, practise, practise. Keepy uppies, ball skills; tennis balls, size one balls, size five balls.

We must also encourage participation in other sports, in gymnastics, swimming and basketball. Anything that involves co-ordination. This can actually be better than playing too much football. We want athletes first, footballers second. I'm not talking about strength here, I'm talking about athleticism. We need to nurture the right habits, sleep, diet, nutrition, stretching, deportment. All these are important. And they obviously have long-term benefits way beyond football.

We also need to develop speed. Skill without pace in the modern game is not acceptable. But speed with the ball; you have to remember to take the ball with you! It is true that we should build upper- as well as lower-body strength, but having said that, there should always be far more emphasis on skill than on sheer strength. With boys aged 13 to 15, aggression and strength will usually prevail over skill. This is where we might lose the smaller but more skilful boys, so we must guard against that.

Also, if you want to make it as a footballer, it is better to be born in the early months of the year, because of the way teams are selected. So to counteract this, I think we might have to start selecting on the basis of weight rather than age. We certainly cannot afford to reject as much as two-thirds of our potential talent at the age of 13.

CHAPTER 7

The Historian(1)
BOB CRAMPSEY

Bob Crampsey is Scottish football's most eminent and scrupulous historian. Among his many books are the official histories of Queen's Park FC and the Scottish Football League. He was the BBC's 'Brain of Britain' in 1965 and for thirteen years he was rector of St Ambrose High School, Coatbridge. He lives in Myrtle Park, Govanhill, only a few hundred yards from Cathkin Park, and like many Glasgow Southsiders, he is unashamedly sentimental about the demise of Third Lanark.

I've thought long and hard about the Old Firm leaving Scottish football and I am certain that what would be left would be infinitely more competitive. There would definitely be five or six clubs with a chance of winning the league, more than in England at the moment. Football is a business now and business is based on competition. The greatest weakness in Scottish football these days is that we don't have enough competition.

My prescription for revival would be as follows: First, reorganise the league structure. If you had a 16-club top division without the Old Firm it would be far more competitive than it is now. I wouldn't want to close any clubs down – what does that achieve? – but I'd organise the two lower divisions on a regional basis. The travelling is excessive at present.

Then I'd limit each club to a squad of 25. At present there are far too many players who have hardly any chance of getting into the first team. Two or three years ago Hibs had a squad of 54 players. Why on earth did they need 54? The only answer I can think of is to stop other clubs getting them. I'm afraid there are some players around now who take the money, sit in the stand and are quite happy.

Thirdly, we simply must stop these meaningless friendly internationals. Club managers are selfish, understandably so. Let's have a trade-off: No waste-of-time friendlies, but the national manager must get the players he needs for the competitive games in the Euro championships and the World Cup, and there the nonsense call-offs must stop.

Finally, the difficult one. We must somehow seek to re-create the supply of gifted young players, though I'm not sure how to do this. Boys don't play the game automatically any more. I'm not convinced that it is to do with facilities. You look at the recreation grounds up the road from here [his home in Myrtle Park] and at any time of the week you used to see eight games being played on the eight pitches with other teams standing by and indicating forcefully it was time for them to get on. Now all you see is a small handful of Pakistani boys playing. It all faded away through the 1960s and 1970s.

Mind you, Glasgow never produced the best players. It was the world capital of football for a long time, yet the best Scottish players came from Lanarkshire, Ayrshire, Fife, even Aberdeen. And the Scottish footballer came from a background of deprivation. For him football was the only form of artistic expression to which he could aspire. The Scottish footballer could improvise, could express himself, and could be the embodiment of his country – this was given to few others. Now men, and women, watch the game and lionise the players – though the watchers may well be eminent in their own field, maybe even rather better in their own field than the footballer is at football!

And you ask about Third Lanark? Well, I admit, I still walk up the road to look round Cathkin. To this day it seems to be revered – it's the only place round here where there is no vandalism. It had this wonderful sense of being a natural amphitheatre. The new stand was built only three years before the club died. And the demise was so painful for anyone steeped in the traditions and history of our Scottish game. You see, Thirds, or to give them their full name, Third Lanark Rifle Volunteers, were founder members of the league. They had been winners of the Scottish Cup and Scottish League Champions. That day in 1967, the day they died, was a black one.

You used to have this wonderful triangle in this part of South Glasgow. Third Lanark, the recreation grounds with the constant games, and Hampden, all within a few hundred yards of each other. Now only Hampden is in regular use.

CHAPTER 8

The Former Player
ANDY LYNCH

Andy Lynch starred as a left winger with Hearts in the late 1960s and early 1970s. He was signed by Celtic in 1973, and Jock Stein wasted little time in converting him, with the minimum of fuss, to left back. Andy was one of Celtic's most consistent players, and club captain, in the latter part of Stein's glorious reign at Parkhead. He scored the only goal in the Old Firm Scottish Cup final of 1977. He won another Cup Winners' medal, and three league championships. In 1980 he went to North America where he played for Philadelphia in the US, and then Montreal in Canada. He also became assistant coach of the Canadian national team. He now lives in the Hyndland district of Glasgow, and has property interests in Glasgow and Spain.

I don't like saying this, but the game in Scotland is at an all-time low. We've been on a pretty sharp descent for about twenty years. It wouldn't have been good enough just to stand still, because other countries like Sweden and Norway have been making real progress in this period. But we've not even stood still; we've just gone down, down, down.

I blame the SFA. They don't know what to do to take our game forward. We need more input from experienced football people, I mean people who understand the game from the inside. It was a huge mistake to allow all the foreign players in. When I went from Celtic to the North American League I learned that only four foreigners were allowed to play for any one team at any time. We should have done that here. Money used to circulate in our game. Transfers helped the feeder clubs, like St Mirren. Then all these foreign players came and the money just zoomed right out of our game. We should apologise to the younger Scottish generation whom we let down. We killed their progress by importing far too many players. So straightaway I'd say: let's have a maximum of three or four foreign players in any of our teams, including the Old Firm.

The people who are running our game, the administrators or legislators, they are not hungry. When I was in North America I played against people like Best and Cruyff and Gerd Muller. These guys all had this idea of the Scottish game; it was all about passion and skill and hunger. Well, look what's happened now.

There is a need for proper coaching, I accept that, and we've got to try to instil these qualities of passion and skill. But I think a lot of the preparation of coaches is half-hearted; it's a waste. A lot of it is tokenism. These guys get their certificates easily enough and then stagnate in some outback. They are not really helping our game at all. We need just three centres of excellence, say Glasgow, Edinburgh and Aberdeen, and we need to handpick the coaches to run these centres. If there are better coaches abroad, bring them in. You see I'm not against foreigners at all, but we just need good foreigners, preferably the best foreigners.

Football is a simple game, and should be kept simple. This applies not just to playing and coaching but to administration too. The structure should be simplified. It's far too complicated at present. And the coaching set-up should be kept simple too. Players must be encouraged to express themselves, and they must not be over-coached.

You'd be very surprised at what Jock Stein said in his team talks. He always simplified the game for us. He'd say to each player: Your job is to do this. You: Win the ball and give it to him. You: Run at the defence, open it up. We knew exactly what we had to do. Jock signed me as a winger, and converted me to full back, where I played almost all of my games for him. There was nothing complicated about the conversion. I was told before a game at Dunfermline that I was playing left back. Just like that. He simply said: You're a winger, you know what you don't like. You know how they try to handle you. So, now I'm asking you to handle them. If you're in doubt, Billy [McNeill] will keep you right. And you can still get up the wing – you can judge when it's right, and you can still get the ball across.

Yes – that was the extent of my preparation, that simple talk. Jock got so much from his players because he made the game clear and simple; he told us what we had to do and he never confused us. I think players are confused now.

The other thing is psychology, making players feel big and confident. When I was at Hearts, Jock Wallace was assistant to John Harvey. I was going through a bad patch. After training one day, Jock took me back to Tynecastle. Out on the pitch, he took me to a spot on the wing, thirty yards from the by line. He said simply: 'This is your territory. This is where you come alive. This is where you do your work. There are only two wingers who are better than you in Scotland, and if you do your work here, you can overtake them.' It was that simple. Jock gave me back my confidence in just a few sentences.

Then big Jock Wallace went off to Ibrox. John Harvey went and Bobby Seith became manager of Hearts. He made the training more and more complicated. It was hopeless, it just didn't work.

In these days, there was far more skill, and much better entertainment for the fans. Most teams had five, six, seven naturally talented players, players who could go past you with the ball at their feet. Now some teams are lucky to have one player like that. So we must work hard at instilling confidence and encouraging players to express themselves. Good coaches can do that, if they have something to work on, and if they keep it simple.

CHAPTER 9

The Fan(1)
SARAH NELSON

Sarah Nelson has, for more years than she cares to remember, been a loyal fan of Aberdeen FC. Now based in Edinburgh, she is a social researcher. Although she has some very trenchant views on the current Scottish game, she is pretty sanguine about her club's up and downs over the years. Her only real football regret is that her daughter Rowan is a Hibs supporter.

If you support a team other than Rangers or Celtic, then you inherit a long, long sense of grievance about how things are loaded against you. Many decisions, and I'm not just talking about refereeing decisions, though these are the worst, go against you over the years. And if your club dare to complain then they are treated by those in authority just like the heidie in some ghastly old-fashioned authoritarian Scottish school would treat his pupils. Criticism of referees should be welcomed, not discouraged. The game needs more transparency, more openness.

There are not nearly enough exciting players around now, players whom you would want to watch as individuals. There used to be at least three or four in most of the teams. I reckon that the skills are not encouraged as they should be in schools and youth football. My daughter's friend used to play a lot of schools football and we used to watch him. I think they were over-coached, even at that relatively young age [11 and 12]. Boys were not encouraged to show their skills.

Football is very expensive now. £20 is a lot of money if you are not going to see any entertainers, any really skilful players. I'd pay £20 any day to see someone like the late Hicham Zerouali [the Moroccan international who played for Aberdeen between 1999 and 2001]. That was money well spent. The fans of today just don't see enough of the breathtaking skills that used to make it all worthwhile.

I feel that the fans who pay the money and put up with so much are often marginalised. Football is an industry now but the club boards don't throw out incompetent directors like they do in private industry. It's easy for a board to get rid of players and managers – what about themselves? Now at last we have supporters' trusts and and fans' representatives on the boards, like Chris Gavin at Pittodrie.

I don't think it matters in the slightest if football is no longer working class. But it does matter very much if football clubs lose touch with their communities. And clubs should have far more flexible pricing policies for admission. The unemployed, mothers with children, and so on – there should be more special offers for the likes of them. The clubs are too shortsighted and too mercenary.

If you are a female supporter, you are never going to get too sentimental about the old days. Females got groped as they changed ends at half time. The conditions, the lack of women's toilets and so on, were appalling. Women still play too small a part in the running of clubs. We need people like Delia Smith at Norwich. It's all still terribly macho, and some feminine influence would help with things like fundraising opportunities and community initiatives. The comparative absence of women in the boardroom sets football apart from just about every other aspect of organised modern life.

CHAPTER 10

The Fan(2)
GRAHAM WALKER

Dr Graham Walker was once described by myself in the *Herald*, as 'the thinking man's Rangers supporter' and although he was not best pleased at the time, he is now quite happy with the designation. He is certainly the most thoughtful football fan I've ever come across. His love of Rangers is real, but he can be quite dispassionate when he believes the club deserves criticism.

Graham is 48. He was brought up on the south side of Glasgow, and played in a Boys' Brigade team, and then for Weir's of Cathcart. He has held academic posts in Glasgow, Brighton and London and he is currently Reader in Politics at Queen's University, Belfast.

Sport is by far the best alternative to alienation that we have in our society and in that context I think it is impossible to over state the significance of football. This is true of boys' football and youth football, but it's also true of the clubs. My father used to watch junior football each week and the junior clubs are even now an important part of the Scottish mix, as are the smaller league clubs, the Alloas and Brechins and Stranraers. People are still prepared to support them and make sacrifices to keep them going by helping in all sorts of ways.

As for Rangers and Celtic, in the past I'd definitely have said that they were absolutely essential to Scottish football, but now I'm ambivalent. There is among their fans an unhealthy contempt for the rest of Scottish football that wasn't there before. The culture is one of success and the anticipation of success, to the extent that there is a superiority complex. And now that the commercial base of the two clubs is based on vast numbers of season-ticket holders I believe that there has developed what I'd call a season-ticket culture.

Many of these season-ticket holders are quite young men and they are no longer playing the game, as many of them would have a generation or so ago. The actual game that they watch is just one component in a complex and protracted match-day experience. So it's an extended recreational routine and the game is only part of it. And the marketing is very slick now. It is aimed at the very young. I've taken my lad, who is seven, over to Glasgow twice, to see games at Ibrox. On both occasions, he's not really wanted to leave the superstore to see the game!

Looking at the wider picture, we still talk about professional players with university degrees as if they are some kind of oddballs. This is wrong, and totally out of date. We have to look at the US. They have organised sports studies and sports scholarships, and well-developed links between professional sport and higher education. We have to ask ourselves in Scotland whether or not we are losing a whole generation of aspiring professional footballers, at a time when coming on for half the school-leaving population is going to university. That is an area where I believe we could make fast and specific progress.

On a sadder note, I have to say that for me Hampden has lost its lustre. It's no longer a shrine. We need to keep alive the memories of the glory days. They are still vitally important. Somehow, we need to get Scottish youngsters acquainted with these marvellous past times, when Scotland did punch beyond her weight so often. We need to get the history of our game taken more seriously by our young people. One small contribution might be to take the Scottish Football Museum, which is permanently based at Hampden, round the country. If you could have a peripatetic exhibition based on the museum, that would be a start. We cannot afford to lose touch with the glory days of the past, if we are to have any more glory days in the future.

CHAPTER 11

The Former Manager
ALEX SMITH

Alex ['Faither'] Smith, MBE, probably knows more about Scottish professional football than anyone else alive. His nickname 'Faither' does not apply just to his age (he is 65 and 'grandfaither' might be more appropriate in that sense) but to the fact that he is the nearest thing that the Scottish game has to a father figure.

Alex was born in Cowie, a few miles east of Stirling. He is from mining stock, though his dad was a distinguished piper with the Argylls. He captained Stirlingshire Schools and played for the juvenile team Gowanhill United alongside Billy Bremner (Alex was best man at Billy's wedding). He was an honest, hard-working professional with Kilmarnock, Stenhousemuir, Stirling Albion and Albion Rovers. He has been a manager and coach since 1969. The clubs he has managed are Stenhousemuir, Stirling Albion (where he presided over the 20–0 defeat of Selkirk in the Scottish Cup in December 1984: the biggest win by any British senior club in the twentieth century), St Mirren, Aberdeen, Clyde, Raith Rovers, Dundee United and Ross County, where the combination of a visionary chairman, Roy McGregor, and support from Highland Council, created an excellent academy for young players.

At St Mirren Alex led the club to victory over Dundee United in the Scottish Cup final of 1988. At Aberdeen he won both the League Cup (against Rangers) and the Scottish Cup (against Celtic). Highly regarded by the SFA, Alex has also managed the Scottish Under-19 and Under-21 teams. He is the present chairman of the Scottish Managers' and Coaches' Association.

Alex, more than most, has experienced the game's ups and downs. A few weeks after he parted company with Aberdeen, he was standing on a public pitch in Strathclyde Park as the newly appointed manager of Clyde. It was 6.30 p.m., and he was waiting for his players to turn up, straight from their jobs and still in their work gear, for their first training session with their new boss.

In the summer of 2005 he parted company with Ross County, the eighth club he had managed. A few months earlier I spent several hours in his company at Victoria Park, Dingwall. It was a pleasure and a privilege to do so. In a game that has more than its fair share of egotists, boors and loud-mouths, Alex Smith is a notably patient, reflective and courteous man.

I have a different slant from most people on the consequences of the Old Firm leaving, to go to England or a new league somewhere else. I think it would give short-term encouragement to quite a few teams, but once it settled down, it would start all over again; you'd just have a new Old Firm. Aberdeen and Hearts would be the two teams, I reckon.

You can't play down the changes there have been in society, and how they have affected football. In 1957, my mate Billy Bremner went to Leeds. He was 15. When Denis Law went to Huddersfield in 1955, he was 15. That extra year in the full-time professional environment was crucial for them both. I'm not saying you should change the school leaving age back down from 16 to 15, but I'm in no doubt that most of our best potential players are wasting their last year at school and, yes, maybe learning bad habits.

Of course the main difference at that time, fifty or so years ago, was that far more teenagers played the game. Every secondary school had several teams. You'll get some Scottish secondary schools now, with only 12 or 15 kids who can play the game. Most of the teachers aren't interested any more, and I know there are reasons for that, I'm not blaming them, but we've simply got to engage them again. Then there was the Boys' Brigade who put out so many teams. And every village, even the wee ones, had a village team.

And there were the informal, rough, impromptu games. Football was easy enough to play. All you needed was a ball of some kind. You could play anywhere. You'd be playing two-a-side and before you knew it, the game had become fourteen–a-side. If you had the ball you wanted to hold on to it, and that improved your ball skills.

When I was brought up in Cowie there must have been seven, maybe more, families in the village who had at least one family member who was playing, or had played, professionally. It was the same just down the road at Fallin, and the same a wee bit further down at Bannockburn. Well, that's all gone now. You'll never get that back. That's what makes the creation of our new national coaching structure so important. Things are beginning to happen in youth development, significant things, but we're still talking about things that were talked about twenty or thirty years ago.

We need several big training centres in Scotland, maybe as many as six. I'd want the coaches to be connected with both the senior clubs and the communities. And the schools too. I'd want the coaches to be going into the schools. What we need to do is align the best coaches with the best kids. That's the way forward. It sounds simple, but it's not so easy to implement..

It's much easier for kids to be put off now. There's not the hunger there used to be. So we must never put them off with aggressive or negative coaching. But if we could get the coaching properly organised we'd be talking about something almost akin to a social revolution. We'd be helping to sort out many of our social problems – for example drug abuse, alcohol abuse – and the kids would have to discipline themselves and apply themselves. So many of them don't; we're wasting a generation.

Getting the right coaches is undoubtedly a key part in all this. I think the club managers have a job to do here. If you manage players, you soon get to know the clever ones. I'm not talking about the great ones, who are few and far between. They don't need to think about the game. I'm talking about clever players but not in the sense that they are dandy on the ball, they can do the dinky backheels and all that; I'm talking about the players who think their way through the game. That's the crucial thing, thinking your way through each game.

All the mangers know who these players are. Because they are not the best players, they have to think more about the game, and work harder at it. They learn to read the game. Many, maybe most of this type of player have so much to offer the game later on. We must encourage them, head-hunt them and recruit them, long before they have finished playing. I'm talking about when they are as young as 24 or 25 or 26. Davie Moyes was only 24 when he first came to my coaching group at Largs.

They could get a good living from the game, and see it as a long-term career. We have a wonderful opportunity to get this right. There needs to be a new culture. You want to ask them: 'What are you going to be giving back to the game?' And I'm not talking about sitting in a TV studio; though don't get me wrong, I've nothing against the pundits.

All this needs money and I cannot see the SFA and the clubs managing it on their own. But I cannot see the Scottish Executive being too generous to us, when they look at the profligacy of the bigger clubs, the way they have wasted money on so many second-rate foreign players.

I was talking earlier about 14, 15 being a crucial age. But you've got to remember too that some players are late developers. They can be 18, 19, even 20 before they take off. It's so important to help them both physically and mentally. Many of the clubs are doing their best, and they get 2 years' 'skill seeking' funding, but then the lads can be thrown onto the scrapheap, so all the effort has been wasted. We don't have that many good players, so it's criminal to waste any of them.

As for the league structure, well, it is suprising that we used to have just 36 senior clubs, and now we have 42! But I don't think the overall number of clubs is too much of an issue, though the main division, whatever it's called, should definitely have 16 clubs. Money and fear drive our game, and the fear – fear of relegation in particular – is destroying our top league.

I'm not against supporters, but the fans do demand winning at all costs. So many supporters think they have a divine right to have a good feeling on a Monday morning. There's great pressure on the club boards; don't underestimate that, and there are huge pressures against the more relaxed style of play that is so good for the development of young talent.

Looking ahead, and looking at the game in Britain as a whole, not just Scotland, I think that the clubs are going to have to stop buying so many foreign players. In England the academies are just not producing the players they were supposed to. Then at the top of the game, the Man Us, the Arsenals and the Chelseas, they are just not bringing through good young English players any more. The good English kids are hitting a ceiling and then can't get to the next stage. There are lessons for our game in Scotland. We must develop our young players so that they can progress; they can play and enjoy the game and be encouraged and well coached at every stage.

Alex and I chatted for several hours over a succession of cups of tea in a room under the main stand at Victoria Park. I thought I'd overstayed my welcome, but he insisted that we move over to what he called the 'technical' side of the ground, as opposed to the 'corporate' side where we'd been talking. I sensed that he was much more relaxed in this environment. He wanted to show me the academy, partly funded by Highland Council. Although it was now dark, we walked round four full-size grass pitches, and an Astroturf pitch. Then we went inside, and the place was buzzing. A large group of youngsters, aged ten and eleven, was assembling for training. Alex showed me the indoor Astroturf facility, complete with its viewing gallery. He showed me the learning centre, the changing rooms, the laundry, the canteen, the offices, and the boot room.

The laundry lady was still hard at work, though it was nearly seven o'clock. I reflected that it's funny how managers always seem to want you to see the boot room, and to meet the laundry lady.

When we were in the boot room, Alex looked with frank disgust at the rows of gaudy boots, golden, purple, puce, some with bright red and yellow flashing. He scrabbled round and eventually smiled in triumph as he held up an old-fashioned plain black boot. 'That's more like it,' he laughed.

Then he took me to the coaches' room, where we had toast and more tea. As we prepared to say goodbye he said: 'These facilities: all Scottish clubs –

well most of them – should have had a set-up like this 25 years ago. It's not too late. It's just that all this – it will take quite a time to bear fruit. We must not be impatient.'

CHAPTER 12

The Pundit
ALAN HANSEN

Alan Hansen excels as an outstanding football pundit with BBC television. His comments are invariably concise, clear and forceful. The consummate pundit was in his day a consummate defender with Liverpool, for whom he played 621 times, winning 8 league championships, 3 European Cups and 2 FA Cups. He captained the Anfield club to their league and cup double in 1986.

Born in Alloa in 1955, he played for Partick Thistle for 4 years before moving south in 1977. He won 26 caps for Scotland in the Jock Stein era. Had he not been a professional footballer, he could easily have been a professional golfer, and his boyhood dream was to play in the Open.

Here, with his customary concision, he gives his view on the revival of the Scottish game.

> There is one thing that is absolutely essential if we are to revive Scottish football, and it will be very, very difficult to achieve. It is simply to get the kids playing again. When I was at school in the 1960s everyone played; you played at school, you played after school, you played anywhere and everywhere. It was jackets down and you were away. Everyone played, even if you weren't all that interested. In fact you just had to play – if you didn't people thought there was something wrong with you.
>
> That all changed, very rapidly. It was in 1982, when I was back in Sauchie for a break, that I suddenly realised there were no kids playing anywhere. Not in the parks, not anywhere. When I was a kid we'd roam far and wide. We'd play football into the dark. Now parents are scared to let their kids out. And the playing culture has been replaced. Kids have their video games and their computer games now. It's ironical, because there has never been a better time to be a professional footballer. How you redress the situation I don't really know, but I think the solution has got to come from the very top, from the Scottish Executive. We have got to get the kids playing again, both at school and away from school.

As for coaching, the best advice I can give, both to the kids and to their coaches, is: 'Don't be one-footed.' I know very well how much harder it is to defend against a two-footed player. So many modern kids, even the talented ones, are one-sided. Make sure you're two-footed: that is the absolutely fundamental thing that has to be addressed from the coaching point of view.

CHAPTER 13

The Chairman
LORD FOULKES

Lord Foulkes has been involved in Labour politics for most of his life. He was an Edinburgh city and a Lothian regional councillor from 1970 to 1979 and then an MP for 26 years, representing first Cumnock and Doon Valley, and latterly South Ayrshire. He was Minister of State for Scotland in 2001 and 2002.

George Foulkes had been a loyal Hearts supporter and season-ticket holder for many years, but even so it was a considerable surprise to him when he was invited to become the club's chairman early in 2004; he was not even a member of the board, and he was in Mexico at the time.

His first priority on becoming chairman was to keep the option of remaining at Tynecastle open; many supporters were furious at the club's apparent intention to sell the venerable old ground and move either to Murrayfield or to a new greenfield location. The immediate future of Hearts is now more secure, with the tenure of Tynecastle established and a new majority shareholder in the shape of the megarich Lithuanian businessman, Vladimir Obramov.

I admit, I thought I'd seen it all. Politics can be a dirty business but football is much, much worse. The backbiting, the intrigue – Scottish football is world class when it comes to these. And money is a much bigger factor than I'd realised. I'd been at some stormy meetings in politics – you yourself have covered some of them in the past – but I'd never been at anything like the Hearts EGM in September 2004. The shareholders thought the meeting was going to push through the sale of Tynecastle, which was of course deeply unpopular. But I'd inserted a safety clause, so that defused the tensions a little. Even so, I've never seen passions running so high at a public meeting. There were thirty police present, but it took them all their time to prevent Chris Robinson [the reviled chief executive of Hearts] being assaulted. That meeting was an eye-opener. And I'm not talking about yobs or hooligans; I'm talking about ordinary, decent, committed, passionate supporters.

Yes, I was in Mexico with a Council of Europe delegation when the call came, asking me to be chairman. I'd be been a fan for over twenty-five years, and I was flattered, but I had my doubts. I knew there had been constant violent protests about the proposed move to Murrayfield. I knew the club was £19 million in debt because of all the mistakes that had been made in the past. I canvassed the views of a few people I trusted, and most of them said 'No, never, don't touch it!' But I decided to say yes, on condition that I could argue the case for staying at Tynecastle. I thought that was the crucial point. The main aim is to become established as the third force in Scottish football. From there, we can try to break the Old Firm duopoly.

I'd no idea what I was going to be catapulted into. The sheer power and sweep of football, it's amazing. A huge – and I do mean huge – number of strangers came up to me, in the street – on the train, on the plane, in the airport, at the station – everybody from window cleaners to top lawyers. And they are all so articulate, all of them with their vehement opinions about the game.

At the time when there was a campaign for season-ticket holders not to renew their tickets, I said publicly that this was utterly futile; all you are doing is harming the club. Well, here I am standing at Haymarket Station in Edinburgh when a Fife train comes slowly along the platform. The driver sees me, stops, winds down his window, and says: 'It's OK George, I've renewed my ticket!' That incident was typical. As I say, I'd been in politics for more years than I care to remember, but I'd never encountered so much animation, engagement and involvement. It's impossible to underestimate the importance of football in so many people's lives.

I have to admit that as chairman, I don't enjoy the games nearly so much. Before I'd sit in my usual seat, alongside my son, among the fans, right opposite the directors' box. I'd be dressed down, I could be irresponsible in the sense that I'd no responsibility for the consequences of what was happening on the field. And I could shout and yell and let off steam.

Now I have to behave myself. I can't scream at the ref. And there are too many worries. You worry about injuries, red cards, the size of the gate – you name it. And you have this front-of-house role. You're the host, for the visiting club, for your guests, for all sorts of dignitaries and officials. You've a lot of people and a lot of matters to look after. So I can't say I really enjoy match-days that much. We've got to get away from this notion that the stadium is some-where that is in full use just once a fortnight, and not at all in the summer. We must start to incorporate other facilities: shops, brasseries, a hotel, an old folk's home, whatever. We've simply got to use the site to integrate football more into the life of the community. And we need more people involved; we need more women, more children, more families coming to games. Take Feyenoord's stadium in Rotterdam. It has this massive brasserie, not a place for pre-arranged

THE FORUM

corporate eating, but a place where you can turn up casually, enjoy yourself, have good food and a drink – and it's totally informal, and the money goes back into the club.

The Old Firm? Well I have to say a lot of those who go to Celtic and Rangers don't see it as any kind of family-friendly, social event. They want to beat the opposition and that's it. But having said that, there's still this tribal loathing all over the country. It's not a problem that is confined to the Old Firm. In Scottish football one of our main challenges is to retain the passion, but expunge the unacceptable tribal hatred. We need to make the football experience much more benign. We need a wider spread of people on the boards, and we definitely need fans' representatives on every board. Fans are the lifeblood of the game.

The assumption is that you need business people on the board, but I have to say that some of these business people in Scottish football made an awful lot of mistakes in the past. I do think we've got to have the local authorities involved more. I've got ideas about how this might work, but I don't want to divulge them yet. I've a lot more thinking to do on this, but it's something I'm very keen on.

173

CHAPTER 14

The Fan(3)
IAN SCOTT

Ian Scott is 'addicted' to Falkirk, the town as well as the football club. He has
written a highly praised study of the town, which has had a central role in
the life of Scotland, both geographically and historically. He is an enthusiastic
folk musician. He is the former assistant principal of Falkirk College, where
he taught history for many years. Now, in retirement, he devotes much of
his time to the Saltire Society, of which he is national chairman.

I believe that football is very much part of Scotland's soul and that it plays a
most important part in the lives of many Scots. You must of course bear in mind
that it is just as important in the lives of people in many other European
countries – for example Italy, Spain and indeed England. But here in Scotland,
with our current lack of civic confidence and our problems with industrial
decline, football probably has a particular role to play in the revival of some of
our communities.

I have a picture of a Scottish football crowd in 1949 – it's a great swathe of
middle-aged and elderly working men wearing caps, not a woman in sight, just
a few boys and one or two younger men. But now football, perhaps more than
anything else that's organised in Scotland, spans class, age and, increasingly,
gender.

When I was a boy you'd come home from school and then go straight to the
park. There would be as many as fifteen or twenty games going on. We'd play
till the light was failing, sometimes on into the darkness. There's no-one in these
parks now; I don't know where the kids are or what they are doing – maybe I
don't want to know!

Then when I was teaching in a junior secondary at Bannockburn I'd take the
twelve-year-olds to play in league games on a Saturday morning. Occasionally
I was asked to referee. Everywhere you went on a Saturday morning in these
days, you met other teachers, young and old, looking after their teams. It was
the PE staff who did the coaching. The other teachers, like myself, confined our
coaching to a half-time talk. Nothing very scientific or subtle. Just: 'Get stuck
in, watch yon big guy coming through the middle', stuff like that. There was
never that much coaching, even from the PE teachers, and the tanner ba players

174

just emerged from playing constantly, day and night, night and day, on the greens, in the back streets, in the parks – all these wee pasty-faced terrier-like players. Some of them were touched with genius, and I'm afraid we're not producing players like that any more.

Nonetheless I'm convinced that we are still producing some good players and I think we talk ourselves down far too much. We over-emphasise the decline in quality, which has been gradual rather than sudden. If you look at our national set-up, the Vogts teams were poorly organised; that was the problem. Berti just could not get the best out of the players he had.

I've been a Falkirk loyalist since I was 10, though I no longer have a season-ticket. Falkirk have specialised in breaking the hearts of their supporters for well over a century, but we forgive them, again and again. I even used to go to reserve games. You'd spot the good players coming through, and these games were competitive.

One of our problems now is that too many of the good 17- and 18-year-olds are with Celtic and Rangers, and they never get a game in the big team – then, later in their careers, they get regular football with lesser teams, but by then they have missed out on the crucial development years.

Falkirk, like just about everywhere else in Scotland these days, has supporters' buses going off to the Old Firm games each week. It was not always thus. One of our local historians, Dr James Young, says that when the Irish came to Falkirk in the 1920s and 1930s, to work in the ironworks, they supported Falkirk, not ✗ Celtic – but now their sons and grandsons all support Celtic.

I reckon that a lot of the smaller teams, down the leagues, are concerned with survival first and last. Their hard-core supporters are not particularly concerned about winning trophies, though that would be nice; they are satisfied if things just keep ticking over. Maybe that explains part of what's wrong with our game; yet I do believe that these clubs are very important to their communities. In fact I think they should be helped, in terms of educational development for their young players, as well as youth football development. There should be public investment, via the local authorities.

> JIM YOUNG TENDS TO PAINT ROSY
> PICTURES – THIS IS NOT MY IMPRESSION
> OF THE FALKIRK IRISH IN THE 20/30S
> FROM FAMILY HISTORY

CHAPTER 15

The Students

Here are the views of four Stirling University students, three men and one woman. All four participate in sport, though only Adrian is involved in organised football; all support Scottish football clubs and have strong views on the game.

Adrian Dempster from Tayport is 21 and supports Dundee United:

Scottish football is in a terrible state partly because of Scottish youth culture. It is common practice in this country to start drinking alcohol at about 13 – I did, and all my friends did too. Drinking at this young age has a detrimental effect on fitness and this lowers the overall standard of youth football. Drinking can become habitual and then football becomes just a social event, nothing more. Only a select few have the talent and the mental strength to resist temptation. Even if a talented young player is scouted by a senior club, he rarely sticks at the game because the social side of life is so appealing during adolescence.

I had a friend who trained with a senior team but he would rather hang about on the streets than play football. He did enjoy playing with his friends, he played for a local club and when he was too old for that he just played for the pub team. This sort of thing happens all too often.

In other countries, like the Scandinavian ones, for example, they have a lot more good footballers because they don't start drinking till a later age and by that time they can make their own decisions without the constant pressure from their peers who are so influential in an adolescent boy's life.

To improve the situation I'd want a national focus on decreasing the amount of underage drinking – and smoking – and I'd also try to get parents to become more supportive in involving children in sport.

Alan Bruce from Dunoon is 20 and supports Greenock Morton:

The main problem with the senior game has been the influx of substandard foreigners over the past 15 years. A few top quality players from other countries have improved the quality of our game, but the fact is that too many young Scottish players are being kept on the bench to accommodate other foreign players who do not have superior ability. This stifles the progress of our homegrown players and this in turn holds back the progress of our national team.

So there should be a cap on the number of foreign players in a starting eleven. Clubs should also show more responsibility and learn to work within their budgets. For example, Motherwell have learned the hard way and have achieved some success with a young Scottish team.

Lindsay McFarlane from Glasgow is 20 and supports Partick Thistle:

The sectarianism associated with certain clubs tends to spill over into the behaviour of a minority of supporters and spoils the atmosphere. Sportsmanship should be central to our Scottish game. We need to find a way of fostering more competition in the SPL among teams outside the Old Firm. We must place more emphasis on youth development from a young age, to give our national team a chance in the international competitions.

Mark Beverley from Aboyne in Aberdeenshire is 20 and supports Aberdeen FC:

There has been an influx of second-rate foreigners and the clubs that have chosen these players over homegrown talent have caused both themselves and the national team severe problems. Young Scottish players are not being given the opportunities that past players enjoyed. Good foreign players should be welcomed to our game – it's a pleasure to watch the flair and also the passion that these players bring. It's the second-rate foreign players who have caused the problems.

All the senior clubs need to become more involved in their surrounding areas. For example, Aberdeen FC run training programmes to encourage youth development in Aberdeenshire, and this is commendable. There is an amazing amount of potential talent around, yet many youngsters slip through the net. Senior clubs must do much more to nurture young talent. The clubs should combine with the schools to run coaching schemes to encourage the development of our indigenous talent.

CHAPTER 16

The Referee
KEVIN TONER

Kevin Toner has been a senior referee for fifteen years. He is the son of Willie Toner, the Kilmarnock centre half and captain who played eighteen years as a professional player without once being booked. Born in Glasgow, Kevin now lives near Perth. He works as a marketing manager in Fife. He has a fascinating perspective on the senior Scottish game, in that, unlike most people, he is conversant with football in the various divisions. This allows him to make authoritative comparisons between the SPL and Division One of the SFL.

When I first joined the senior list we were pretty well left to our own devices. Over the years there have been huge changes, all of them for the good, I believe. George Cumming, who was in charge of referee development at the SFA, introduced development coaching and specialised fitness training. The fruits of these changes are there to be seen now. Many more good young refs are coming through.

The finances of the game have obviously changed, and the clubs are once again having to bring through young Scottish players. The current Hibs team is a good example. A few years ago, the influx of foreigners reached farcical proportions. I remember refereeing a game at Fir Park, Motherwell, when there was a professional interpreter in one of the dug-outs. Instructions were being bawled out to the players in three different languages, four if you count Scottish.

When I started refereeing senior games there were not that many foreign players in Scottish football. Then the glut came in. No doubt the game got a little better in terms of individual skill, but were the teams better as teams; was the end-product better? I doubt it.

Most Scottish referees I know are passionate about the game, but on the pitch we just want to be unnoticed and we want to avoid controversy if at all possible. If any referee showed bias he'd be found out very quickly. You simply cannot go into a game knowing you are going to call a decision this way or that. I accept that there are different levels of pressure in games involving the Old Firm but I don't believe that any referee is influenced by the heightened pressure. The ref wants to enjoy the game, just like everyone else. Having said that, I don't think many of the games in the SPL are all that enjoyable. There is still too much fear, fear of losing. There is not so much entertainment as there used to be.

The football may not be so good technically in the first division of the SFL but it may well be better to watch. The atmosphere at these grounds is often more conducive to a good experience for the spectator. I think standards are improving at this level, definitely. Most of the teams in the first division have more or less the same budget, and there are not big disparities across the division. You can have as many as four or five teams pushing for promotion, though obviously not in this season (2004–05) and I think it's much more competitive in that sense.

So I greatly enjoy refereeing first division games. Some good younger players are breaking through, and it may be that the notion of feeder clubs could be revived. There are definitely more talented young Scottish players around now than there were a few years ago. It is significant that the attendances in the first division have been rising.

There have been quite a few improvements in the SFL, as opposed to the SPL. I've been pleased to see all the new clubs coming in recent years, the likes of Inverness, Ross County, Elgin, Peterhead and so on. And it is very encouraging to see the remarkable progress of Gretna. You've got a greater geographic spread, and all these 'new' teams are developing and progressing.

I have just one more season to go and I must say that I am far more optimistic about the future of the Scottish game than I was a few years ago.

CHAPTER 17

The Player(1)
SIMON LYNCH

Simon Lynch is a 22-year-old centre forward. He is the son of the former Celtic captain Andy Lynch, featured earlier in this section. He played with the Celtic Under-15s and Under-16s and in the reserves under Danny McGrain. He was breaking into the first team at a time of great turmoil at the club, when John Barnes was fired.

When Martin O'Neill arrived at Parkhead, Simon was transferred to Preston North End, then managed by Craig Brown. He is now with Dundee having also had two loan spells, first with Stockport and then with Colin Hendry's Blackpool. Simon was successful with the Scottish Under-21 team, scoring seven goals in ten games. He has also made two appearances in the Scotland futures team.

When I was breaking through at Celtic we'd often be driven out in a minibus to train at Cambuslang. There were not sufficient facilities at the Barrowfield training ground. Then when I went to Preston I was surprised to find that the training facilities were much better than Celtic's. And the training set-ups at some of the bigger Premiership clubs in England are quite unbelievable, particularly in terms of their indoor facilities. There's a lot of attention to detail when it comes to training in England. This is an area where I think most Scottish clubs are away behind.

I think it's the same across Europe – the training facilities are generally much better. And abroad there's much more effort made to get players to learn good habits. I'd say there is still something of the drinking culture about the Scottish game.

The more you get to know about English football, the more you realise that Scottish coaches and mangers are everywhere. Not just at the top clubs, but down through all the leagues. The list is endless. Most of them are doing very well and it's sad that so many of them have left Scotland. But we seem to be much better at developing good coaches than developing good players, and you'd have thought that the one would lead to the other.

The base is not there, because there just aren't enough youngsters playing the game now. I started playing with a local club at the age of five. There is always a danger of putting too much pressure on young kids, of burning them out, but we've got to try to get more of them playing the game at a very young age, and enjoying it. That's important. It's good to get them playing some kind of organised football in the holidays. I think much more could be done in the way of football holiday camps – that sort of thing. I know some of this is going on, but there should be far more footballing opportunities in the long summer holidays in particular.

Having said all that, I'm quite optimistic about the future of the Scottish game. My experience of the Under-21s was that there were some very good players coming through, players like James McFadden, Darren Fletcher and John Kennedy. And I do think some of the clubs in Scotland are building teams of quality young players. If you pressed me, I'd mention Hibs and Motherwell.

CHAPTER 18

The Head of Youth
TOMMY BURNS

Brought up in the East End of Glasgow, Tommy Burns was eighteen years with Celtic as a player. A combative midfielder, who combined silky play with a feisty approach to the game, he won eight Scotland caps in the Jock Stein era, between 1981 and 1983. From Celtic Tommy moved to Kilmarnock where he became player-manager. In this role he led the Ayrshire club to the Premier League in 1993. He returned to Celtic as manager, and remained for nearly three years. Under him they played notably attractive, attacking football but he guided his old team to just one success; they won the Scottish Cup in 1995. He left Parkhead to work at Newcastle under Kenny Dalglish, and then spent fourteen months managing Reading, before going back to Celtic a third time, as first-team coach. When Martin O'Neill took over he made Tommy Head of Youth, giving him overall charge of all youth development.

I spoke with Tommy shortly after the Celtic Under-19 team won the 2005 Scottish Youth Cup at Hampden, beating St Mirren 2–0.

Tommy was also the principal assistant to Berti Vogts during the German's ill-fated reign as Scotland coach. He was notably loyal to Vogts, although many observers, including myself, think that Scotland would have done better in those years had Tommy rather than Berti been in charge of the national team. When Walter Smith took over the Scotland job, he retained Tommy as his deputy.

> The trend is completely against us in terms of young people's culture. Probably most kids now would rather spend a few hours on their computer than spend hours kicking a ball against the wall in their back court, like I did when I had spare time as a kid.
>
> Then when you are a wee bit older all sorts of temptations are there to lead you astray. This was always the case. When I was growing up in Glasgow there were many guys who were far more talented than I was, but they succumbed to peer pressure and they didn't come through as footballers. As coaches we can facilitate a great deal but the basic drive and determination must always come from within.

The only thing I ever wanted to be was a footballer. I'd simply no conception of being anything else. That sort of mentality isn't there so much nowadays. And when a youth joins a pro club, he does not always appreciate that he still has to work very hard. Some of them think they've already made it at this stage. We can get them to work, but they have to show responsibility.

For many years the facilities at even our top clubs were a joke. During my entire eighteen-year career as a player with Celtic, we had just the one grass pitch at our Barrowfield training ground. We grew as players despite, not because of, the facilities. It has improved now; there are three or four pitches and an Astroturf floodlit pitch as well, but it still needs to be much, much better, I admit that. I think it will be before too long.

Yet the players kept coming through. I played many games against Aberdeen in the early eighties. These games were often epic struggles, and just look at the players Aberdeen brought through, with no facilities at all – the likes of Neil Simpson, Eric Black, Neale Cooper.

It was about this time, twenty-five years ago, and maybe even earlier, that clubs in Germany and Holland were investing heavily in first-class training complexes. And excellent communal facilities were being developed at the same time. But the people running our game lacked foresight. We suffer from a shocking lack of facilities in Scotland though we've had more than enough time to get the message.

Fans can be very shortsighted, and this has got much worse in the last decade. There was a period when Scottish clubs just went stark raving mad. They brought in foreigners they literally could not afford. Chairmen were on ego trips and there was no long-term thinking. But the fans went along with this. They even encouraged it.

Just after Berti took over as Scotland coach the two of us spent an afternoon going though a long list of everyone who might possibly play for Scotland. There were very few genuine international-class players. That's the honest truth: there were plenty of good club players, but very few capable of stepping up to a higher level. We no longer had players appearing for the likes of Man U, Liverpool, Arsenal. No disrespect, but we were having to look at the likes of Plymouth and Wolves.

Now, I'm much, much more optimistic. Clubs like Hearts and Hibs and Motherwell have invested in youth, as have Rangers, and of course at Celtic we have too. At last, there's a lot of promise back in the game. There's a future to believe in. There are five or six in our Under-19 team at Celtic who are players of outstanding promise. Another two years of hard work, and they'll be ready.

At Celtic we have a full-time education and welfare officer, and we take this aspect of youth development very seriously. Their education must always be taken care of, not least because of the percentage who won't make it.

I'm convinced that the main problem with our younger players is that they just don't spend enough time on the ball. They spend an enormous amount of time in traffic, being ferried backwards and forwards. I'm talking about twelve- or thirteen-year-olds. We'll take them for training two or three times a week, two hours a time. Then they'll play a game at the weekend. That's seven or eight hours a week, and it's not anything like enough. It only adds up to about an hour a day per week. That's a joke. When I was a kid that age, I'd be practising at the local school every evening, from about 6.30 to 9.30. That doesn't happen now; the schools are not opened up in the evenings, there's no supervision.

Forty years ago the youngsters would play and practise all evening, then at the weekends you'd play and practise some more. We must somehow get our youngsters to spend much more time with the ball. I reckon that on the Continent kids of the same age spend three or four times as many hours on the ball each week.

CHAPTER 19

The Player(2)
CHRISTOPHE BERRA

Christophe Berra, despite his name, is Scottish, though his father is French. A 20-year-old centre back, he is just breaking into the Hearts first team. He has played for the Scotland Futures team and for Scotland's Under-21s. Christophe joined Hearts Under-16s from Edina Hibs and spent two years on the ground staff.

If you've got football in you, that is, if you've talent for the game and you apply yourself, it should keep you well behaved and you should certainly look after yourself better, in terms of fitness, diet and so on. But it's so much easier to learn the right habits if you have good facilities.

When I was first with Hearts we'd train all over the place, sometimes quite a bit away from Tynecastle, at places like Musselburgh or Prestonpans. You couldn't stay behind after training to practise more because we all had to jump into the van and get back to the ground. Now that we've got our training base here at Riccarton, we have far more time and that is so important.

You can stay behind after a training session, because it's here that you'll be changing. You can work on anything, on free kicks, or passing, absolutely anything, by yourself or with the coaches and the sports scientists. The support we get here is terrific. I'm sure the technical quality of our game has improved enormously in the year we've been based here.

The Old Firm are always going to be big but I look at them as a challenge, an incentive for teams like us to do much better. We'll never have their money, but we can raise our game and I believe the gap is beginning to close. You'll definitely see more and more clubs taking points off them regularly. We are certainly catching up in terms of our technical standards.

We have a lot to learn from foreign countries. Although our technical skills are improving, most of the continental countries are still well ahead. We need far more indoor centres for Scottish kids, because of the bad weather and because constant practice is needed at a young age. We must put more money into youth football. I think this is beginning to happen because the senior clubs are realising that they are having to develop their own players. This must be all to the good for our Scottish game.

CHAPTER 20

The Historian(2)
PROFESSOR TOM DEVINE

Tom Devine, FBA, OBE, is Scotland's pre-eminent academic historian. He is associate director of the Research Institute of Irish and Scottish Studies at Aberdeen University, and he is also the Sir William Fraser Professor of Scottish History at Edinburgh University. He is a consultant on anti-sectarian policy to the Scottish Executive's justice department, and he has edited a series of essays on bigotry and sectarianism in modern Scotland.

He has written many books including *The Tobacco Lords* and *The Great Highland Famine*. His two latest works, both best-sellers, are *The Scottish Nation 1700–2000* and *Scotland's Empire 1600–1815*. In 2001 Professor Devine was awarded the Royal Gold Medal, Scotland's highest academic accolade.

In the late nineteenth century it was the introduction of the Saturday half-holiday that was the vital factor in football becoming the sport of the masses. Rugby, golf, even cricket – people tried to promote and encourage these also, but football just took off. The only other non-sporting options were the pub, the Italian-style café and, eventually, the cinema. If we fast forward many years to 2005, football now has to compete, in terms of leisure activity, with a huge number of other options, and many of these are very comfortable options.

Rangers and Celtic remain big for reasons that are nothing to do with any love for the beautiful game. I'm not talking religion here; their rivalry is a result of Scotland's social history – from Irish immigration, through Irish nationalism, through Orangeism, through to the revival of the Northern Ireland problems in the late 1960s. These are the components in the Old Firm's continuing potency.

So I'd see it as essentially racial rather than religious. Sectarianism in Scottish football is not just about religion – look at how Rangers supporters don't mind in the slightest that they have Catholics playing in the team. The horrors of the 1920s and 1930s in Scotland were racist rather than religious. And the racial element is still potent to this day, partly because of the Northern Ireland situation. The split is there in Scottish civic society and we cannot deny that it's what gives the Old Firm their continuing power. Yet if you look just about everywhere else in Europe, this racial baggage is relegated to the past. And even if the Old Firm left Scottish football and went off to England or wherever, the residue would remain because they would still be based in Glasgow and play their home games there.

I think the 'safety valve' argument had merit when there was structural sectarianism: there were few mixed marriages and so on. But now structural sectarianism is almost dead. On the other hand attitudinal sectarianism is actually growing. I emphasise: the religious passion simply isn't there. Most Old Firm supporters never go near a kirk or a chapel. At the same time I know intelligent, educated, prosperous people who can hardly cope with the result if it goes against them; the tensions seem more powerful than ever now. Old Firm supporters live through the games with even greater intensity than they did before.

If you look at our football in a wider context then you see two things that are similar to many other countries. First, our national team are not potent; secondly, the non-Old Firm teams are not potent. The Old Firm are the one factor that really differentiates us from other countries. But if the Scottish national team could become seriously successful, that would unleash much hope and great waves of national pride that are much needed, in my opinion. And that would help us greatly in making our mark on the world stage.

CHAPTER 21

The Superfan
DREW ALLAN

I have known Drew Allan for fifteen years and he is simply the best and most wholehearted football fan I have ever met. He is forty-seven and lives in Portobello, though he works in Glasgow. He has seen his beloved Hibs win just two trophies: the League Cup in 1972 and again in 1991. He grew up in a tenement in Leith, among Hibs fans, but his family moved when he was nine and he did not see his first game at Easter Road till he was thirteen. He has been making up for lost time ever since and his greatest footballing ambition is to see Hibs win the Scottish Cup.

My partner Jan's daughter lives in New Zealand, and we decided to go over for the birth of her first baby – Jan's first grandchild – in February 2004. The flights had been booked and the arrangements made when Hibs beat Rangers in the League Cup semi-final. So I was going to be in New Zealand at the time of the final against Livingstson, and I had to accept that I was going to miss it. But I tried to discover if there was any chance of seeing the final live on television in New Zealand.

Eventually I learned that though Setanta were not showing the game in the southern hemisphere, they had been persuaded to put on special screenings in Sydney, Perth and Melbourne. I said to Jan: 'We'll fly over to Australia for the weekend.' It was a 4000-mile round trip, and it cost £800 for the flights from Auckland to Melbourne.

And so I found myself at the Melbourne Celtic Club at 5 a.m. in the morning with about forty Hibs fans – including one who had driven more or less non-stop across Australia for two days – and one Livvy fan. We lost 2–0. After the game we just sat in silence for a while.

I find it impossible to imagine not being a Hibs fan. I've experienced the lows, as in Melbourne, but football has also given me some of the highest moments I've ever had. Hibs have not won the Scottish Cup since 1902, and I live in hope. My father is seventy-eight now and he's had three heart attacks watching Hibs. It would mean even more to him than it would to me.

Each year I make sure I have booked a holiday for the week after the Cup final. If we won, I would want to be able to celebrate properly. I have it all worked out. Apart from the game itself on the Saturday, I'd join the crowds cheering the triumphant team touring on the open-top bus on the Sunday. On the Monday I'd have plenty of champagne, to clear my head in style. Then I'd spend the next few days winding up every Hearts fan I know. I accept that this is perhaps not completely rational, but who says football has to be rational?

I've been to support Scotland in the final stages of three World Cups and, yes, Scotland means a lot to me; but if I had to make a choice I'd rather see Hibs win the Scottish Cup than Scotland win the World Cup.

I've seen football in Spain, Italy and Germany and their fans seem just as passionate as we are, though maybe a bit more sober. I don't think the intensity with which you support a team has anything to do with how much money you have. You can be just as passionate about it with nothing in your wallet, or £50, or £500.

I've enjoyed this season, 2004–05, much more than the last four or five. I haven't seen many bad games. If you take the Old Firm out, the other teams are all pretty well matched now.

I think we should go back to clubs sharing the home gate. This would help the non-Old Firm clubs greatly. I also would like to see further improvements in the grounds. It can still be an embarrassment to take a woman with you to watch a football match in Scotland. There are still not enough facilities for women.

The general atmosphere is less friendly than it used to be. And with all-seater stadia you can find yourself, as a season-ticket holder, sitting next to an arsehole for a whole season! Many fans would like to stand rather than sit, and I think most of them would like each ground to have a big standing section.

I know that some people in the game deprecate the growth of the Internet and its use by supporters but I think it's a great way for fans to communicate with each other and I believe that in a way it has helped to democratise the game.

CHAPTER 22

The Union Man
FRASER WISHART

Fraser Wishart was a hard-working right back with Motherwell, Rangers, St Mirren, Falkirk and Hearts, and then player-coach at Clydebank and Airdrie. He was brought up in a family with what he describes as strong, old-fashioned socialist views and he has always believed in political engagement. He was the Motherwell club rep for the Scottish Professional Players' Association when he was only twenty, and now, twenty years later, he serves as the secretary of the Scottish Professional Footballers' Association, which is a branch of the GMB, Britain's general union. Based in Glasgow, he is deeply committed to the welfare of his members and he is passionate about reviving the Scottish game. He represents football on SportScotland, the body that was formerly the Sports Council for Scotland.

There has been chronic mismanagement in the Scottish club boardrooms, and I think one of the problems was that too many directors refused to take any kind of responsibility. OK, there is usually just one majority shareholder, but a lot of directors just sat on their hands and said nothing when bad decisions were being made. The profligacy at some clubs almost defied belief. At the time when I was ending my playing career, players' salaries rocketed up to unbelievable levels. At some of the clubs they went up tenfold, and that is no exaggeration.

When the SPL was formed, there was a good TV deal. But that money was not necessarily going to continue forever and the people running the clubs should surely have foreseen that. Instead they spent as if there was no tomorrow. And then the transfer market collapsed, so that clubs who'd brought in expensive foreign players could not sell them on. There was no financial discipline, huge debts were run up and clubs had bought players they simply could not afford. And there was no regulation, no control. There was no penalty for this recklessness.

Not enough has been made of the knock-on effect. Football clubs should be rooted in their communities, but a lot of small, local businesses now don't like or trust the local football club. This is corrosive. These local businesses are struggling because debts have not been paid by the football clubs. Local businesses were left massively out of pocket when clubs went into administration, although some of the clubs continued to spend big money on players. There was no proper system of punishment. In England, if you went into administration, you lost ten points in the league. Nothing like that happened here. So we have a situation where many people don't respect their local clubs any more, and that is very bad for our game.

We need more responsibility and realism in the boardrooms. We need to develop more of our own young players. I want to see all the Scottish teams with a Scottish backbone. This would help the national team and if you have a successful national team that in turn helps you develop more young players. But it is not easy. People's lifestyles have changed so much. Life is better for most people now, and aspirations are higher. The expectations are that there will be good facilities. Parents demand a proper coaching structure and proper facilities. When I was a kid during the holidays I'd be given a packed lunch and I'd be out the house all day. I'd just be told to be back at six. You weren't necessarily playing football, but you might well have been. It's not like that any more. Parents worry much more now.

I sometimes wonder, where do people play on the south side of Glasgow? We played at Toryglen, where there's now a supermarket. We played at Cardonald; they called it 'the fifty pitches' though there were nothing like fifty. But there aren't any at all now.

Work is beginning, at all levels, on the long task of improving facilities. Local authority money and Scottish Executive money is coming into football for the building of new facilities. SportScotland is often criticised, but it's an enabler, it can't fund everything. I believe that it's the local authorities that have the biggest pot of money to put into football.

When we're developing young players with the clubs, there must be an educational element. They must work hard at their education, because there's a big dropout rate. It's easy to forget this. In football, you don't often get a second chance. In England, they track what happens to the apprentices. Only fifteen per cent make it through to the senior game. We don't have the figures for the Scottish game, but I suspect it's about the same. As clubs and as a nation we have a duty to develop our young players, and coach them well. But we must be realistic, and prepare them for failure as well as success. Obviously a lot of them are not going to make it, but it can shatter young lives if they are discarded at eighteen or nineteen, and they are three years behind in the job market.

I believe the key to progress is to involve more professional players in the game, and in decision-making, even when they're still playing. Some of them do think a lot about the game and they have considered views. If you can marry the right professionals to people with genuine business and administrative acumen, that is the best way forward.

CHAPTER 23

The Legislator
DAVID WILL

David Will is one of the most important men in world football. He is vice president of FIFA, the game's world governing body. An Angus solicitor, he is chairman of FIFA's legal committee and a member of the executive committee and the World Cup organising committee. He travels the world on football matters and his commitment to the game is exemplary. Unsurprisingly, he resents any suggestion that the international legislator's life is one of constant junketing.

He was asked to become chairman of his local club, Brechin City, when he was just twenty-seven. He served for twenty-five years. He is now the club's honorary president. He was president of the SFA in 1984, the year he joined UEFA. He became vice president of UEFA in 1986. In 1990 he moved across to FIFA. He intends to resign his posts (voluntarily) after the World Cup Finals in Germany in 2006, when he will be seventy.

I am in no doubt that two great blows have been delivered to Scottish football in the past twenty years or so. The teachers' strikes in the1970s and 1980s had a devastating effect on schools football, and the effect of the Bosman ruling was very bad for our bigger clubs in the 1990s. After Bosman, a kind of desperation set in. Our clubs kidded themselves that anyone from overseas must be good. They paid enormous sums, money that they could often not afford, for overseas players who were often worse than the home-grown players who could have been developed locally for next to nothing. I have to admit that I never foresaw this happening. Scotland suffered more than most countries from the Bosman ruling because some really bad decisions were made here in its aftermath.

Now, I'd love to see a rule whereby at least six of the players on the park at any time must be from the country they are playing in. This would help many Scottish clubs and would have an equalising effect. More importantly, it would help the national team. The trouble is that such a rule would contravene European Law. UEFA are keen to move forward in this direction but obviously we cannot break European Law. If all the clubs agreed, if they decided to do this voluntarily, then you could get it through. But I'm sure one or two clubs would break ranks, pleading an injury crisis or whatever.

As for youth development, we were clearly far too slow in putting in place a national policy, but at last that is now happening. Better late than never!

The most important development in European football is the new licensing system that UEFA are introducing. This will bear on all clubs taking part in European competition and it covers stadia safety and security, the introduction of structured youth training systems and financial discipline. The last point is important, for it would stop clubs using administration as a means of getting round the system. I believe that this licensing system will eventually have a dramatic influence for the good in smaller countries, such as Scotland.

As for the general structure of Scottish football, I don't think there is anything seriously wrong with it. The SFA is the supreme body and it is well run. The SPL and the SFL are subordinates. I do regret the SPL being separate from the SFL, but that is not a major issue. The SPL does sometimes have difficulty in accepting that the SFA is the governing body, but then the SFA looks after disciplinary matters, and that quite suits the SPL.

I'd like to make two points about Scotland in the context of world football. The first is that our referees are exceptional. Please don't underestimate how good our refereeing standards are. We should appreciate our referees more. They are fit, they are competent, they are well trained and they are very highly respected internationally.

Secondly, despite our very poor current national ranking, our overall reputation remains remarkably high. Partly this is a question of tradition and history, but it is also to do with the high standard of coaches and managers that we consistently produce. Our current lack of quality players is a big concern, and this is reflected in the low standing of our national team. This has been the case for ten years and more, so it can't just be blamed on the post-Bosman scenario. And I must say too that Craig Brown, when he was national coach, did an unbelievable job in organising the players he had available.

When I joined the SFA I was maybe at first looked down on a little because I came from a small club in an obscure part of the country, though I personally felt it was perhaps an advantage not to have ties with a big club. But with both UEFA and FIFA I've been respected right from the start, and I think that was because Scottish football is very much respected internationally. That respect gives us something to build on.

CHAPTER 24

The Club Executive
ALEX TOTTEN

Alex Totten's experience of senior Scottish football, as player and manager, is probably second only to Alex ['Faither'] Smith's. At present he is working as income generation manager at Falkirk, the club he supported as a boy and has been associated with for much of his career. When I spoke with him in April 2005 he was euphoric, because the second stand at the new Brockville had just been completed, bringing the ground's capacity to over 6,000. More importantly, the club had at last been officially promoted to the SPL, having been denied rightful promotion twice previously on somewhat spurious technicalities regarding ground capacity.

Alex played with Liverpool, Dundee, Dunfermline, Queen of the South and Alloa. He then managed Alloa, and his beloved Falkirk, before Jock Wallace engaged him as his assistant at Ibrox. After his spell at Rangers he went on to manage Dumbarton, St Johnstone, East Fife and, once again, Falkirk.

> I feel sorry for the fans now. I really do. I wouldn't exactly say they are short-changed, but there's no doubt that the entertainment factor is much less in evidence. There is an excitement missing in our game, and I put that down to the absence of wingers. I'm an enormous, passionate believer in the importance of wing play. The best of all the Scottish entertainers were the great wingers – the Alex Scotts, the Willie Hendersons, the Jimmy Johnstones, the Davie Coopers. They were the ones the fans loved to watch.
>
> I'd go so far as to say that there is too much emphasis on passing now, and not enough emphasis on developing players who can take their opponents on. And it's not necessarily old-fashioned to say this. Just look at the success of Chelsea, a very sophisticated and well-organised team under Jose Mourinho: the success is partly based on outstanding wingers like Arjen Robben and Damien Duff. Chelsea are not the same team without them.
>
> When I was a manager I'd always be looking for first-class wide players. I'd say to the scouts, 'Get me good wide men.' And I'd always emphasise that I was there not just as manager but as a fan. I always wanted entertainment and excitement. Of course, twenty or thirty years ago managers had so many more

players to choose from. You could go to the Junior game and pick up good players, just like that. I'm afraid there are nothing like so many good young players in the Juniors now – there are far more has-beens.

If I was coaching again I'd keep stressing the importance of getting wide and taking people on. That's how you develop exciting players. But that raises the question of training facilities, and this is one of the worst things about our Scottish game. Scottish managers have always had to beg and borrow their training facilities. When I signed for Liverpool in 1961 I was amazed at the training set-up Bill Shankly had. There were five training pitches at the Mellwood complex. Even today, more than forty years on, only four or five of the Senior Scottish clubs have their own permanent training facilities. You do wonder where all the money went all these years ago; why it wasn't properly invested. When I was a kid supporting Falkirk, there were often crowds of 20,000 at Brockville. I ask you: Where did all that money go?

CHAPTER 25

The Politician(2)
BRIAN MONTEITH

Brian Monteith, Tory MSP for Mid Scotland and Fife, is an ebullient and enthusiastically controversial politician. Formerly his party's parliamentary spokesman on sport, culture and education, he retains a particular interest in football, not just because he is a long-standing Hibs fan but also because his twin sons, Callum and Duncan, are very promising players. At the time of writing they were in the Under-17s at Livingston and were shortly to learn whether they would be offered full-time contracts with the club. Brian is a qualified Under-12s coach.

Thanks to Callum and Duncan I've been involved right through from the first organised football at seven and eight, via the boys' clubs and the schools network and onto the Senior club. Much still has to be done in youth football, but of one thing I am certain, and that is that the boys' clubs picked up what was largely lost by the schools, and kept the game going at this level, through an enormous amount of voluntary effort.

There were, however, far too many games for the better players, mainly because there were too many cup tournaments. The best players in the best teams tended to get to the finals of all the competitions, which meant a huge number of games, and so there was always the danger of burn-out.

Many boys – and girls – want to play the game at an organised level, though the overall number has declined, mainly because of the demographic shift. When I was a pupil at Portobello High School there were well over 2,500 on the roll, now it's less than 1,500.

I agree with Walter Smith, our new national coach, when he says that we need more informal games for the youngsters – we have to ask how we get the kids playing in the parks again. We all accept that they cannot play in the streets any more. This is a huge challenge and it's by definition not something you can organise.

I'd be nervous about the Executive getting involved in the running of football in any way apart from in two specific areas. First, the provision of new facilities. Nothing like enough has been done to provide indoor training facilities. We should never forget how awful the weather can be in Scotland. We should never forget how difficult it is to coach youngsters outdoors when it's wet, windy and cold. Far more big indoor halls are needed.

The Executive should also help with getting the schools opened up after hours and in the holidays. While I'm dubious about getting the teachers involved again, I think the schools could open up their facilities more. I don't think schools football as such is all that impressive and the refereeing can be very poor and biased.

I think the Senior clubs should establish links with the colleges rather than the schools. This is more beneficial than linkage with schools when you are getting to the age of 14 or 15. There is a case for removing really talented players from school at this age and getting them to go to college in partnership with a club. I envisage schemes where you train every morning and work at the college every afternoon. Local colleges are much more flexible than the schools, both in terms of time and in terms of the educational development offered. The very worst situation is when a talented youngster fails at school and also fails at football. Not every club will be able to set up links with a college, but many of them would be well placed to do so.

The key aim must be to combine football development with continuing education. So if that does mean taking the best young players out of the schools, I'd welcome it. I've seen some really good footballers at the age of 13 or 14 who have discovered fags, booze, girls and goodness knows what else, and they just drop out of the game. Teaching kids good habits is something sport can do and these kids do respect the clubs, if little else. So the clubs must use their influence, and act together with the local colleges.

CHAPTER 26

The Player(3)
STEVEN PRESSLEY

Steven Pressley, 31, is captain of Hearts. A thoughtful man, a natural leader and a fine centre back, he was born in Elgin and brought up in Fife. He was with Rangers till he was 20, then he played briefly for Coventry before returning to Scotland, where he starred for Dundee United. He signed for Hearts in 1998. He has won 22 Scotland caps.

I talked with Steven immediately after he had finished training at the Hearts Academy at Riccarton, just west of Edinburgh. The academy is an integral part of the Heriot Watt University sports complex. The facilities are impressive and Steven is very appreciative of them.

A few days after we spoke, Steven was promoted to first-team player-coach.

I think most senior clubs coach their young players in the right fashion: Touch, passing, awareness, all the right ingredients. Funnily enough, the problems can arise when you break into the first team because you are not always asked to play in the manner you've been taught to. In particular, the passing aspect of the game can be overlooked. There is so much pressure to win, and there's maybe some pressure to forget what you've been taught. Results become all-important. It need not be like this. At Ajax in Holland they are taught how to play the right way from the age of 8 or 9. At 18 or 19, when they are breaking through, they are encouraged to keep playing the same way. The pressure may be greater, but the playing methods and style are the same.

Managers are changed far too often in Scotland. Continuity always helps in football. Every club should be structured to provide a continuous process, so that there is one style of play that is played at all levels.

International football is completely different from club football. The international game is more like chess. You need to be very disciplined and exceptionally well organised. There is more thinking required, and more of an emphasis on passing.

I believe that good times are ahead for Scottish football. I'm very hopeful. We've got some fantastic young players here at Hearts. The Senior clubs have gone back to the grass roots and are investing in youth. What went wrong before? Well, too many Scottish clubs looked at the English premiership and thought we could be the same – but we can't, with the possible exception of the Old Firm. There was a terrible short-sightedness and far too much money was spent on foreign imports. Now there is a new financial discipline and the clubs are bringing though their own players again.

The facilities here at Riccarton are fantastic. Many of the boys now choose to stay behind after training and carry on practising. Before we had these facilities we had to move around, transporting makeshift goals all over the place, in the back of a van. During winter, the conditions could be terrible. There are excellent indoor facilities here at Riccarton and we have the benefits of a first-class gymnasium and we can work with professional sport scientists. The phsyio has his own rehab set-up here. Everything is far better organised and more efficient. The players have benefited and I think we have responded well.

It is difficult for boys of 14 or 15. Some come from good environments, others don't. You have to hope that youngsters can be mentally strong – you need to be to make it as a footballer. The clubs can definitely help. There's a case for regular drink and drug tests for players at this age. A lot of players do fall away because of outside pressure, from their mates and so on, when they are aged between 13 and 16. And many of the best players are very volatile characters. They, maybe more than most, need guidance and support.

CHAPTER 27

The Fan(4)
JOHN LOUGHTON

John is 17. When I interviewed him he had left school, and was working as a community activist in North Edinburgh, before becoming a full-time politics student. Although he lives in the Pilton area of the capital, he is a Rangers supporter. John is a passionate and combative defender of Scotland's young people, and his belief, in his own splendid phrase, is that 'Young people are not the adults of tomorrow but the citizens of today.'

Yes, I'm a fan of Rangers, and proud of it, although I live in Edinburgh. Why? I suppose it's a family thing. My granddad was a Rangers man. Most of my mates support Hearts and I do sometimes get stick about glory seeking.

I think there's a failure of communication as far as football is concerned. Plenty of young people are playing football and kicking balls about, in the streets and all over the place. It's not true that this just isn't happening any more, as many older people will tell you. In fact some young lads are obsessed with playing football. Probably a smaller number than there used to be, OK, but the youngsters now make this deliberate decision; they either endorse the game or they refuse it. They make a choice. There are so many other cool things to do than just play football. So those who do choose football are committed, and enthusiastic. They love kicking a ball around. They've made a definite choice and they stick with it.

I think these young people, who love football, have got to push for more schools football. The schools aren't interested any more. The Scottish Executive should step in. The Executive should work with the schools, and the clubs, to get the best out of the kids who have chosen football. When I say there's a failure of communication I mean that our youngsters are not shown that if they are given the chance to work at the game and learn to play properly then there's this pathway to the next stage.

Young people are more strong-minded than older people give them credit for, and they have their ambitions. The trouble is that they are just not shown the route to the next stage.

As for the Old Firm, I think Rangers and Celtic should stay in Scottish football. It is ridiculous that they should be excluded from Scotland because of their achievements. There is sectarianism, yes, but I believe that it's being dealt with. Put it this way: it would be harder to get rid of sectarianism if Rangers and Celtic weren't there. And I wouldn't support a team that ran away from Scotland. I think both Rangers and Celtic would lose fans, not gain them, if they played in some other league.

As for the national team, they are not as good as they could or should be. The managerial standard has been poor. Rangers and Celtic are clearly better teams than the Scotland team. But I believe, and most of my mates share this view, that the Scotland team can and will be revived.

PART THREE
THE GOAL THAT WON IT

*The only thing that has never changed in the
history of football is the shape of the ball.*

– The words of Denis 'The King' Law,
probably Scotland's greatest-ever player,
though he never played for a
Scottish league club.

CHAPTER 1

OCTOBER

On a Saturday evening in October 2004, a month or so before I started work on this book, I was sitting with my wife in a bar in Calvi on the island of Corsica. It was the end of the tourist season and the people in the bar were clearly not tourists, but locals.

The television in the corner was showing the France–Ireland World Cup qualifier, a dreary 0–0 draw, but no one in the bar, apart from myself, was paying the slightest attention. I said to Julie that this would be unimaginable back home: the national team playing in a key World Cup game, and not a soul watching. She pointed out that many Corsicans, though technically French, have an intense dislike of the mainland French. She reckoned this explained the indifference to the football. She had a point, but I thought in that case the Corsicans should have been cheering on the Irish. I found the utter lack of interest in the game astonishing.

I already knew that earlier in the day Scotland had lost 1–0 to Norway in another crucial World Cup-qualifying game at Hampden. Later I learned that the 48,000 Scots fans had been – as usual – magnificent, the players less so. The tactics and organisation had been, as so often under Berti Vogts, woeful.

It was obvious by this time that Berti was on borrowed time. His appointment had been nothing short of a national disaster. (The SFA must take the blame for that; but to be fair, they had made three good appointments in the previous twenty-seven years – Jock Stein, Andy Roxburgh and Craig Brown – and their last mistake had been the appointment of Ally MacLeod in 1977. In this area, anyway, the track record of the country's governing body had been more than reasonable.)

A week or so after we returned from Corsica, Celtic played Aberdeen in a midweek league game at Parkhead, before 58,000 fans, 10,000 more than had watched Scotland in the key World Cup qualifier a fortnight earlier. What was particularly significant that night was that a 'home' game was taking place at exactly the same time at Pittodrie, Aberdeen's ground. Inverness Caley Thistle were playing Dundee in a SPL game – in front of a derisory crowd of 1,254 people. This conundrum, which typifies the muddle and disparities of Scottish league football, is explained by the fact that ICT were having to play their so-called home games at Aberdeen, almost a hundred miles from Inverness, because their stadium was not deemed big enough for a Premier League team.

Surely no sane league anywhere in the world could tolerate a disparity on such a scale as that; two games involving four clubs in the same twelve-team league playing at the same time with one crowd *well over forty* times bigger than the other. Scottish football was always posited on the wee guys beating the big boys, but this was ridiculous.

Of course the circumstances were exceptional. However, another game was being played that night, between two well-established SPL clubs, Motherwell and Kilmarnock. The crowd was 4,520. This was not in midwinter, but in October, when the competition was still in its early phase. Disillusion, tedium, predictability, apathy – had all these already set in?

The crowd at Parkhead was thirteen times larger than the crowd at Motherwell. That figure gives a stark indication of the inequalities in the lopsided SPL.

But the saga of ICT having to play at Aberdeen rather than at their own stadium in Inverness was indicative of something far worse than a lopsided league. It spoke of serious incompetence. The Scottish football authorities had not been able to manage that most basic of league functions, promotion and relegation. In the summer of 2004 the SPL reaffirmed that member clubs would need a stadium with a capacity of at least 10,000. ICT's ground could accommodate only 6,000. Thus the 'groundsharing' arrangement with Aberdeen. (Later the stadium capacity criterion was reduced to a minimum of 6,000 seats.)

ICT were not the only club to suffer. In 2003 Falkirk should have gained promotion to the SPL but were denied their place because they did not satisfy the stadium criterion. As the MSP for Falkirk East, the redoubtable Dennis Canavan pointed out, all three of the SPL clubs in administration (because of their incompetence and mismanagement) voted against the promotion of the financially solvent and well-run Falkirk FC.

To conclude this series of vignettes from October 2004, at the end of the month one of the brighter young Scottish managers, Craig Levein, an-nounced that he was leaving Hearts, a club that was undoubtedly one of the top five in Scotland, to join Leicester, a club drifting in the lower reaches of the Coca Cola Championship – in other words, the old English second division. On the measure of the league positions at the time he left, he was actually swapping a top five club in Scotland for the thirty-sixth club in England. He said laconically: 'People will ask if Leicester City are a bigger club than Hearts.' He was right: they did. And certainly in terms of attendances Leicester were the bigger club, averaging almost 30,000 to Hearts' 12,000.

These various episodes reflected several aspects of the sickness in Scottish football: the dire decline of the national team, partly because of a paucity of truly international-class players, but mainly because of a disastrous managerial appointment. The preposterous disparities in our top 'showcase' league, as exemplified by the farcical inequalities in attendances; the chronic administrative incompetence, evinced by clubs in administration and a failure to be consistent and fair on the basic issue of promotion and relegation; and finally, the inability to retain our brightest young talent, as typified by the departure south of the impressive Craig Levein.

It was a sorry picture; yet, a few months later, having looked as openly as I could at various aspects of our national game, I surprised myself by becoming persuaded that the doom was being overdone. For a start, Berti was away, having been replaced by the wise choice, Walter Smith – a man who could at the very least organise a team and motivate his players. Meanwhile, Falkirk, with their new stadium, had at last been officially promoted.

But the resurrection of the Scottish game will obviously require much more than a competent manager in charge of the national team, and the belated righting of an administrative injustice that prevented a well-run team gaining deserved promotion. More importantly, my researches had led me to believe that meaningful work was at long last under way to deal with the two bigger problems: the paucity of good young Scottish players, and the disparities in the league set-up.

It pains me to write this, but a club that epitomises the failure of the 1990s is Aberdeen FC. Pittodrie Stadium, in all its flawed and skewed absurdity, physically exemplifies the lopsided nature of Scottish football's ambitions, the stark disparity between reality and aspiration. Behind the beach-end goal, the colossal Dick Donald Stand looms, towering over the other three stands. The Dick Donald Stand was built in 1992–93, at a time of spurious optimism in the Scottish game. It was to be the first stage in a spectacular redevelopment which never transpired. So it remains, dwarfing the rest of the ground, a testament to unfulfilled and unrealistic ambition.

But far worse, where are the club's training facilities? Where is the coaching complex? Through all the fat years of the late 1970s and early 1980s, through the less rewarding but still rich years of the late 1980s and early 1990s, there was no investment in training facilities. I wrote in Part One, with admiration, about the vision of the late Chris Anderson. But even Chris and his chairman, Dick Donald, the man whose memorial is the huge beach-end stand, spent no money on the real future, on a training complex with indoor facilities.

At the beginning of 2005 I had a chat with the legendary Willie Miller in his office in Pittodrie. Willie, Aberdeen's greatest ever player, had spearheaded the club's glory years in the 1980s. He had been appointed club manager in 1992, but wasn't given anything like long enough to guide the club back to former glories. He then developed a dual career as both a respected media pundit and a successful businessman in the hospitality industry. When he was appointed the club's director of football early in 2004, it was on the understanding that he would not give up these two roles; in other words, he now has a very busy diary.

I asked Willie about the club's training facilities, or rather the lack of them. He said simply: 'Yes, it's an embarrassment. You could say – the beach.' Then he smiled, and added: 'When the tide's out.'

He continued: 'We are committed to the provision of proper facilities, but this costs serious money. The expense for our club will be massive. There are all sorts of other requirements too. We need a sports science programme, we need to do much more to look after the education and welfare of our young players, we need more specialised coaching, we need to develop our scouting set-up.'

All these requirements reflect criteria set out in the SFA's ambitious Youth Initiative, which is being developed, among others, by Campbell Ogilvie – and Willie Miller himself.

Willie is excited about the initiative and its implications for the future of the game and he convinced me that it will lead to a much brighter future. But the amount of work, as well as money, that all this requires is formidable. Let me now quote Willie once more, this time from his letter to shareholders of Aberdeen FC, sent out early in 2005:

> Our élite youth programme covers eight centres throughout Scotland and underpins our core strategy of developing our own stars for the future. It has proved successful in the past, and of the 17 players involved in the 3–2 victory

at Celtic Park this season, 13 were developed though our youth programme.

Another area of responsibility is my involvement on committees within the SFA and SPL. I am a member of three committees, namely the Football Working Group which is a strategic group looking at areas of improvement within the game, the SFA Youth Initiative Committee, which is responsible for the development of the Youth Initiative at Senior level throughout Scotland with the objective of developing a greater wealth of Scottish talent and ultimately for the benefit of the Scottish National Team. The last committee is the SPL Heads of Youth which covers all the SPL clubs' managers for Elite Youth and tries to ensure that the focus of developing the quickest pathway for young players is achieved.

I have also taken the first step in reviewing our Community Department headed by Neil Simpson. The programme delivers, along with other SFC community and SFA objectives, the football community plans for Aberdeen and Shire councils. It is my plan to review and restructure our community plan to deliver a focused AFC plan in the community and consult with the SFA and Councils to totally re-evaluate our relationship with their bodies.

This amounts to serious commitment to the development of young talent, not just for Willie's club, Aberdeen FC, but for the whole of Scotland. It is genuinely far-sighted and indicates that the future of the Scottish game is being tackled energetically and wholeheartedly. The worrying points are however, that the overall structure remains complex and very bureaucratic, and there must be always be a danger in having so many separate committees, initiatives, working groups and so on. There is bound to be at least some overlap and confusion.

There is also always going be an inevitable tension between the needs of a club and the needs of the wider game, although if all the people involved are men of vision and integrity like Willie Miller that should never be too much of a problem. Indeed, on the most basic need of all – the development of international-class players for the future – club and country clearly both stand to gain. Overall I think it is tremendously encouraging that someone like Willie Miller, a football man through and through, a consummate professional who excelled as a club and international player and knows the game inside out and who has also made his mark in the wider Scotland as a successful businessman, should be so deeply involved in the crucial work of progressing our national game.

Perhaps the most crucial priority is for the Senior clubs to develop their facilities. This is a key component of the crucial SFA Youth Initiative. There is a lot elsewhere in this book about Scottish managers and coaches having to scrape around town, and well beyond, for even half-adequate training facilities. Some experts reckon this has been the single biggest failure in Scottish football over the past 50 years. When I reviewed the post-war history of the Scottish game with Sir Alex Ferguson, this was the first issue he raised.

I enjoyed a chat of unashamed reminiscence with George Smith, who was a speedy and skilful right winger and then centre forward in the Partick Thistle teams of the late 1950s and early '60s. I asked him about training. He said: 'A wee bit of organisation did come into our pre-season training, but apart from that the training was laughable. We often trained on our own, completely without supervision. We were never properly coached. The manager's job was basically to pick the team, give a team talk before the game and another one at half time. That was it. The man who revolutionised it all was Jock Stein, who was the ultimate professional. At Dunfermline, Hibs and Celtic, Stein brought in a new spirit of organisation and professionalism.'

I asked George about training facilities and he chuckled. 'Well, we had the pitch.' The pitch at Firhill? 'Yes that was it. And the groundsman was king in those days – quite often the players weren't allowed onto the pitch, so we had to improvise our training on a small area behind the goal.'

After many years of wholehearted service for Thistle, George moved on to Dundee United and then was briefly manager of Ballymena United, before he left football for a career in education. Looking back on his playing days, he reckons that we produced so many world-class players in that period simply because of the enormous pool of talent. 'In every community, every village, every town, kids were literally playing non-stop. Some of them were bound to be exceptional. They came through despite the clubs' efforts at training and coaching, not because of them.'

You would have thought that the lesson would have been learned well before now; but at long last there are signs of significant progress. Rangers have built a £14 million state-of-the-art complex at Milngavie. This will almost certainly be the most significant legacy of the David Murray era at Rangers. Hearts have come to an arrangement with Heriot Watt University to use the sports science facilities at the Riccarton campus just west of Edinburgh, where the university's sports facilities incorporate the impressive Hearts academy. Hearts players speak almost with awe when they describe the difference these facilities have made to their training programmes and to their desire to practise more.

In the far north, at Victoria Park, Dingwall, Ross County have a superb facility that has been developed jointly with Highland Council, and has been warmly praised, among other organisations, by the SPFA. These are three examples of what has been achieved in the last year or so. But other clubs must follow suit. Celtic have improved their set-up at Barrowfield, but the facilities there are a long way behind those of their great rivals at Milngavie, though as I write this there are whispers that they will shortly announce plans for a similar complex. Hibs are another club who have neglected to invest in adequate facilities. They sometimes train publicly, before a scatter of interested onlookers, and maybe one or two spies, at Edinburgh Academy's playing fields in the Inverleith area of Edinburgh. And as I say, it grieves me as an Aberdeen supporter when I reflect on the club's need to use Aberdeen beach.

Politicians will argue about almost anything but I suspect that most of our MSPs at the Scottish Parliament have more or less reached a consensus that the Executive must take a lead in providing better playing and training facilities for youngsters throughout Scotland. The clubs can and must develop facilities, on their own or in conjunction with other bodies like universities or local authorities, but the country as a whole requires far more facilities than the clubs can provide, particularly because, as everyone admits, kids are no longer playing in the streets or even in the parks. Even a football-minded Tory like Brian Monteith, a man who is naturally suspicious of big government, believes that the Executive must help to develop facilities.

The tireless Scottish Nationalist MSP Kenny MacAskill is determined to keep up pressure on the Executive to provide more pitches. He constantly cites the example of Norway, a smaller country than Scotland, and yet 51 places ahead of us in FIFA's world rankings, at the last count. In Norway football is enthusiastically played by literally hundreds of thousands of boys, and girls, and there they build about 70 new full-sized all-weather pitches each year.

The Norwegians are also constructing a series of indoor halls with full-sized artificial grass pitches. Early in 2005 Kenny asked the Scottish Executive where similar artificial pitches were being developed in Scotland. He was told that under the Building for Sport programme just one award had been made across Scotland, for a synthetic pitch at Oban High School. That did not sound, to Kenny or indeed to me, like spectacular progress.

Kenny MacAskill has also exposed flaws in the arrangements for funding the ambitious Action Plan for Youth Football, which was launched by Frank

McAveety, then Scotland's sports minister, in March 2004. This decade-long scheme was to cost a total of £31 million year. Later the Executive admitted that they could not identify where as much as a third of their proposed £12 million contribution to the action plan was to come from. And other parts of the budget, for which the SFA was responsible, were also in doubt.

These are recondite and complex matters, involving various action plans and initiatives and several different agencies. There is a danger of administrative and bureaucratic confusion. But the great goal remains, and it is not at all recondite. It is about more than just sport. It is a commonplace that many of our kids are picking up bad habits all too early in their lives. They are becoming obese, they are not undertaking nearly enough organised physical activity, and are getting sucked into a booze (and drugs, but drink is the bigger problem) and fags culture in their early teens or even younger. The ease with which Scottish 12 and 13 year-olds get access to alcohol is a national scandal. In this wider context, the paucity of sports facilities is shameful. New facilities simply must be provided. They would have great benefit for the nation's long-term health. It is necessary, as I shall explain later, for football to become a kind of counter-culture in opposition to this degradation.

What else can the Executive do? First, they should work with the local authorities to make sure that there is access to school sports facilities beyond normal school hours and during the holidays. When I was a kid my primary school playground was kept open long after school finished. Tommy Burns reminisces elewshere in the book about how his school was opened up for several hours every night.

And, again working with the local authorities, the Executive should find money to get teachers involved in school sport again. This would cost money, but as Donald Gorrie, MSP, so rightly says, 'Put £10 million into the health budget and it just disappears.' On the other hand, put £10 million into sport, and you reap vast benefits, not just in sporting development, but in health and education as well. There needs to be an understanding that sport spending will be inextricably linked to improvements in both health and education as well.

At the same time, the governance of sport must be independent of national or local politicians. Scottish football is beginning, at long, long last to reform itself. A thriving football culture at all levels – Schools, Youth, Junior and Senior – would do wonders to the nation's sense of identity, for our well being, pride, respect and health. A thriving football culture could not but help to eliminate the scourges of teenage alienation, premature physical wreckage and anti-social behaviour. It would also help dying communities to revive. I shall develop this notion of football becoming a beneficial counter-culture, but meanwhile I must emphasise: This is not pie in the sky; it's just common sense. So the Executive should and must help and support where appropriate, and mainly in the provision of facilities.

Some would argue forcefully that the Executive must do much more. Take Professor Grant Jarvie. He is a man who is passionate about sport, and in particular its ability to help both individuals and communities. His enthusiasm is based on academic objectivity. He is head of sports studies at Stirling University and an international authority on sport history and sociology. He heads the only sports department in the UK that combines academic research, teaching programmes, applied practice and a vast complex of state-of-the-art sports facilities. Grant told me:

> I am certain that the revival of football in Scotland could help people to escape from deprivation, could help to counter much low grade anti-social behaviour, and could help greatly to revive the notion of civic communities. I am well aware that various agencies are working hard on several projects but we need to connect all this work so that there is administrative, financial and structural clarity. To put it crudely, the Scottish Executive must take football more seriously, and must knock heads together.
>
> The Executive must signal that it understands how important sport, and football in particular, is to Scotland. It would be logical, for a start, to have a ful-time, committed and well-advised Minister of Sport. Football would be a major component in this portfolio. [At present sport is lumped in with tourism and culture; we do not have a dedicated minister of sport]. And the Executive should play its part in producing a clear and effective national football strategy. In Scotland we have tried to be good at everything. Football is one of four sports [the others being bowls, shinty and golf] which have a clear Scottish identity.
>
> In essence there must be a clear pathway through school, and the local community, with the school facilities being used more, through to the club, then the professional club, and on to the pinnacle, the country, which takes you right onto the world stage.

Traditionally, funding for sport has been administered largely through education budgets, but Grant told me this was beginning to change: 'The United Nations, no less, has picked up on this. Now the UN is talking about funding sport directly on a worldwide basis, and not just through education programmes. The thinking is not that sport alone can solve the problems of the world, of course not, but it can make a much greater contribution than has been realised till very recently.'

Another passionate exponent of greater Executive leadership is the legendary Scottish rugby international John Beattie, now a distinguished broadcaster and sports journalist as well as a property developer based in Glasgow. John told me:

> The Executive simply must get things moving, and soon. The First Minister cannot much longer tolerate the situation where he sits with other politicians watching the supposed cream of Scottish manhood being stuffed, time and time and time again in the international arena, whether it's football or rugby. He'll have to do something, if only because of the sheer embarrassment of these constant national humiliations.
>
> We don't try hard enough as a country. We don't say: 'Here is a potential winner, let's develop him.' If you find a really good youngster, you must place him in a culture where sport is the be all and the end all. The studies would continue: education is important, but at the same time you would coach him and develop him in a way that is simply not happening at the moment. This implies a national centre of excellence, and I'd suggest Stirling as that centre.
>
> You have to concentrate on the nuggets; you develop and polish them, and eventually they can be farmed out to the professional clubs. At present kids with huge potential are wasting their time, and other people's, sitting in traffic for hours at a time as they are ferried round to training facilities once, at best twice, a week, where they get two-, or, if they are lucky, three-hour sessions. That's nothing like enough. You've got to stop that nonsense now and put the national cream into one centre where they'd be permanently based and thus have far, far more time to develop.
>
> In this national centre, sport would be everything. You don't neglect the brain, of course you don't; you keep the educational sides of things ticking over, but what you're really saying is: 'You are a potential winner, you have it in you to be a world-class footballer, and we're going to make you one if you will work at it.'

In summary: I am convinced that the various SFA initiatives, and particularly the Youth Initiative, in which Campbell Ogilive and Willie Miller, among others, are heavily involved, will bear fruit. I am convinced that a significant number of our Parliamentarians are disposed to put serious pressure on the Executive to help with the provision of desperately needed facilities.

I am convinced in particular that as our top clubs develop the detailed youth programmes required by the Youth Initiative, and meet all the detailed criteria, these clubs will start producing significant numbers of really talented young players.

If this is concurrent with a radical reshaping of the league structure, to help to revive the old 'feeder' clubs of the first division of the SFL, to encourage ambitious up-and-coming clubs like Gretna, and most of all to assist leading SPL clubs like Hearts, Hibs and Aberdeen to mount a regular and sustained challenge to the Old Firm, then, in say five or six years' time, things will be beginning to look very much brighter. Only a fool could expect instant results.

The much smaller sized clubs like the two Edinburgh teams, the two Dundee teams, and Aberdeen need not always be at a disadvantage vis-a-vis the Old Firm. There are actually benefits in being relatively small. I shall explore this theme later.

Already there are signs that the long and all too easy supremacy of the Old Firm is being threatened as it was for a time in the 1980s. Exciting young Scottish players are being introduced by clubs like Hibs, Motherwell and Aberdeen. In turn, attendances are moving up. Hearts are benefiting from a new influx of money and from the use of a magnificent training complex. Provisional figures for the season 2004–05 indicate that Aberdeen had an average home gate of just over 13,000; Hibs and Hearts both averaged just over 12,000; while Dundee United had about 7,500 and Dundee 6,750. Next came Motherwell with about 6,500 and Kilmarnock with 6,000.

These attendances are nothing like good enough, although Hearts and Hibs are showing signs of progress. I reckon that Aberdeen, Hibs and Hearts should aim, at the very least, to have average home gates of 15,000. Dundee United, Motherwell and Kilmarnock should all aim at 10,000, as should Dundee, once they get over their current travails. These are not unrealistic targets.

Aided by an imaginative and progressive new league structure, these clubs would need to concentrate on four areas: the development of their own young players, which Hibs in particular are already doing; the playing of entertaining and intelligent football; the aggressive promotion of the clubs in their own catchment area; and the encouragement of attendance at the less glamorous games through imaginative pricing packages and special offers. Work is under way in all these areas already, but it is sporadic and at times ill-focused.

Above all, the fans need to be given a dual, interlinked sense of community and continuity, which encourages them to have a sense of ownership. Not ownership in the literal sense of shareholding, nor being involved in the running of the club, though there is a place for that through Supporters' Trusts. Rather a feeling that they are part of something that is developing and moving forward. Committed fans used to attend reserve games, in considerable numbers, to spot the stars of the future. When these players duly broke into the first team, the fans had a sense of vicarious achievement and enhanced identification with the team.

Nowadays far too many fans content themselves with baying for the quick, extravagant solution. They eschew the mid-term or long-term view. This is the sort of support that must be revived. Clubs don't pay enough attention to the psychology of their fans. We are forever hearing about sports psychologists working with players; maybe the fans could do with a little psychology too.

So I have a word of warning. I'm not a very good fan these days, but most fans, good and bad, have tended in recent years to put too much pressure on their clubs for short-term fixes. It was mainly the boards who were guilty in the post-Bosman spending frenzy that did so much damage to Scottish football. But the fans have been guilty too, of craving big celebrity buys rather than their own homegrown stars.

This is shortsighted, not just from the point of view of the health of Scottish football, but from their own more parochial interests. There is no point in praising the new realism in the boardrooms if the fans are doing their best to undermine it. A club tends to be more settled and to have a better rapport with the supporters in the long term if there is a sense of continuity, a palpable sense of organic growth. This may not apply quite so much to the Old Firm, but it certainly should apply to all the other Senior Clubs.

I asked above what else the Scottish Executive could do to help football. One thing they must not do is make things worse, but that was probably the net result of their botched attempt to host the Euro Championships in 2008. This was a joint bid with Ireland, and it was expected by most pundits to come second or third, with an outside chance of gaining the prize. As it happened, when the results were announced at UEFA headquarters in Switzerland in December 2002, the Scottish-Irish bid came a poor fourth.

It had been estimated that a successful bid would have benefited the Scottish economy by as much as £500 million. Even more importantly, in the context of this book, a successful bid would have been very good for all levels of Scottish football.

When the bid failed there was the predictable recrimination. After that died down, some bravehearts said we should regroup and bid hard, on our own, for the 2012 championships. Sadly, I have been persuaded by various experts that such a bid would not be feasible, and anyway that this time the championships are due, on the small–big rotating principle, to go to a 'big' country.

The essential point is that far from benefiting Scottish football, the failed bid probably did it harm. What the Executive must do for football in the meantime is concentrate not on big grandstand projects, but on supporting the game in a sensible pragmatic manner throughout Scotland. Get the basics right, and the time will come when we can effectively showcase Scotland to Europe, and indeed the world.

CHAPTER 2

THE OLD FIRM

I wrote this book with an open mind, but I admit that I was pretty certain that I'd end up advocating the exit of Celtic and Rangers from Scottish football. Having thought about it hard, I'm now convinced that they should stay. I think it is in the overall interests of the Scottish game that they should remain part of it.

Is it in their interests? Possibly not, in the longer term, but I'd be wary about breaking away at this stage. They are not yet members of the G14 group, the unofficial grouping of Europe's most powerful clubs which was set up in 2000. They are not yet ready to join Europe's super élite. They would not be welcomed with open arms into the English Premiership, and Europe's leading clubs would be cautious about receiving them into some new midweek super league. They are not regarded as being in the top ten or twelve clubs in Europe. This is more a matter of playing pedigree than size or wealth, for in terms of the latter they are very big indeed. A more likely new home for them might be the UEFA-sanctioned Scandinavian Royal League, for the élite clubs of Denmark, Norway and Sweden, but most of these clubs are much smaller than Celtic and Rangers.

The Old Firm are an integral part of our Scottish game, for both good and bad, and the imbalance of our most prestigious league should not be blamed on them. To put it crudely, it is not their fault that they are much bigger than everyone else in this small country. Of course they could behave more responsibly, for example in being a bit more careful about signing up promising young Scottish footballers whom they then leave languishing in the reserves and on the bench during the crucial development years.

Our imbalance is, however, also a result of a poverty of ambition on the part of other Scottish clubs with serious potential, such as Hearts, Hibs, Aberdeen, Dundee and Dundee United. I have been castigating Scottish clubs for extravagant and unrealistic spending on foreign imports in the post-Bosman era, but that was frivolous and downright stupid ambition. Realistic, responsible ambition is much harder to fulfil and it requires foresight and planning and hard work in the boardrooms, and patience and responsibility on the part of the fans. These are not easy qualities to nurture in an era of instant gratification, where everything is done at speed and it is difficult to persuade people of the virtues of patience and long-term investing.

In Part One I rehearsed the golden era of the New Firm in the 1980s when Aberdeen, and to a lesser extent Dundee United, dominated Scottish football. In the decade 1980–90 Celtic won the premier division four times, Aberdeen won it three times, Rangers won it twice and Dundee United once. Aberdeen won the Scottish Cup four times, Celtic won it four times, Rangers won it once and St Mirren won it once. Even more significantly, Aberdeen and Dundee United both reached European finals, and Aberdeen even won the European Super Cup. Dundee United, as well as reaching the UEFA cup final, were desperately unlucky to lose 3–2 on aggregate to Roma in the semi-final of the European Cup.

But it is salutary to recall that in that golden decade attendances then were nothing like as good as they should have been. Even when they were playing exceptionally exciting football, and sweeping through Europe, the New Firm often played before crowds at Pittodrie and Tannadice that were scandalously meagre. I see no reason to believe that if Rangers and Celtic disappeared, and the Scottish game became more competitive, attendances would rocket up as a consequence. Further, I see no reason whatsoever to believe that the television companies would be desperate to pour money into a new Old Firm-free league.

But what if the Old Firm stay? Could we ever see a repeat of the 1980s? Many people believe such a gloriously 'democratic' decade cannot be repeated. They say that the work of the likes of Graeme Souness and David Murray at Ibrox and Fergus McCann at Parkhead has allowed the Old Firm to exploit their almost unlimited potential as genuinely global brands. The Old Firm have an international dimension that much smaller teams like Hearts or Aberdeen can never aspire to.

Both Old Firm clubs now have huge stadia to accommodate around 50,000 season-ticket holders attending home games; Aberdeen and Hearts, the next biggest clubs in Scotland, have been in such a rut that they think their attendances are reasonable if they average around 12,000. Rangers have a £14 million state-of-the-art training complex; while Aberdeen's lack of training facilities is, as the club's director of football admits, embarrassing. And so on. I could spend a whole chapter pointing out the various measures by which Rangers and Celtic are away ahead of their nearest Scottish rivals.

Further, it is generally agreed that the game's paymaster is increasingly television, and that television is interested only in the big clubs and in the Champions' League in particular. And that league is blamed for creating an élite across most of Europe, where in the élite countries only two, or three or at most four clubs, have a meaningful chance of winning their domestic leagues. Again, if Rangers and Celtic departed from Scottish football, could any kind of lucrative television deal be negotiated on behalf of the rump that was left? On the other hand, if Rangers and Celtic stay, they would no doubt regard themselves as being denied a huge media income. English Premiership clubs are more or less guaranteed upwards of £12 million media income a year. The Old Firm struggle to get much more than £1 million a year.

How on earth can I be optimistic about a revival of democracy in the Scottish game? Well, the first point must be that the relative smallness of clubs like Hearts and Hibs and Aberdeen should be an advantage in attracting the best young talent. These three clubs have done very well in the past in developing young players who went on to give them good service, despite the fact that many, perhaps most, of these young players were avowed Rangers or Celtic supporters. It is psychologically important to a young player of real promise to believe that he will have the chance of meaningful first team competitive football at a relatively early age. That is the offer which the likes of Hearts and Hibs and Aberdeen can provide, in a way that's much less easy for Rangers and Celtic.

In many parts of Scotland, and in many family homes, there is a desire to see the Old Firm brought down a peg or two. Many Scots long for their comeuppance. Some fans, including very intelligent ones, who support either Rangers or Celtic, cannot understand how non-Old Firm fans take the attitude 'a plague on both your houses'. They are so obsessed with their own embittered and intensive Old Firm rivalry that they find it hard to understand how many of the rest of us lump the two of them together, and take the view that one is as bad as the other. But that is the mindset of many Scots, possibly even the majority.

Indeed, the very size of the Old Firm clubs could militate against them. Influential figures such as parents, teachers and coaches might well wish a promising youngster to sign for a genuinely ambitious mid-size club rather than a huge one where he might be swallowed into oblivion.

Secondly, Rangers and Celtic come complete with baggage which gives them their potency but which also makes many decent people resent them, not out of jealousy or envy but out of sincere high-mindedness. I am utterly certain that the majority of Old Firm supporters – and players and directors and support staff – are decent people, but collectively the Old Firm message can be one of arrogance and paranoia, a rather unpleasant combination.

The generalised dislike of the Old Firm can be made use of by other clubs, in a responsible and judicious kind of way. Add to that the fact that the Rangers and Celtic have embraced the big-time corporate ethic, and have become huge businesses, and you have something else that many people instinctively dislike and are suspicious of for perfectly proper motives.

When Aberdeen won the European Cup Winners' Cup in 1983, the legendary Alfredo di Stefano famously (and generously) commented: 'Aberdeen have what money cannot buy: A soul, a team spirit, built in a family tradition.' That quality is exactly what the non-Old Firm clubs in the SPL must rediscover and build on. Some will regard this as naïve and senti-mental tosh, but I'm not so sure, and that's why I'm punting it. Even in football, money can't buy everything. And if you are a big international business with a global outreach then you are unlikely to have the soul that Alfredo di Stefano talked of: something that, as he noted, money can't buy.

If you have developed a multi-million-pound brand, with superstores and strings of other merchandising outlets, then you are bound to exploit your fans, particularly the younger ones. You are growing turnover away from the pitch, away from the actual game, the playing and the watching. The word 'club' is important. When the club becomes a megabusiness, it is essentially no longer a club, in the best sense of the word. If it is to remain a club, it has to work incredibly hard at being a community, with communal facilities and so on. The bigger Rangers and Celtic become, the more they are businesses a rich first, football clubs a poor second. They lose contact with the soul factor.

I was born in Glasgow and I come from long line of Protestant West of Scotland stock. In many ways, it is a fluke that I am not a Rangers supporter. No doubt the main reason is that my family moved to Aberdeen when I was four, and when I eventually and belatedly became seriously interested in football, in my early teens, Aberdeen were the club that caught my imagi-nation.

My father, who was not in the slightest interested in football – he preferred to spend his Saturday afternoons on the golf course – did put in the odd appearance at Pittodrie during the twenty years or so he was based in Aberdeen. As far as I can recall, every time Rangers were the visitors. But he was essentially indifferent to the fact that my brother and I became staunch Aberdeen supporters. In other words, I inherited absolutely no atavistic loyalties. Nobody ever tried to influence me to support this club or that.

I think this gives me at least some objectivity, and some insight into the way in which Rangers and Celtic are both disliked, and sometimes loathed, across much of Scotland. I've written about the visits of their supporters to Aberdeen in the 1950s, when even people who could not care less about football were delighted if they were sent back to Glasgow defeated. This was mainly because of the arrogant and unpleasant way their fans strutted around town, full of menace and insolence. One of the more miserable aspects of the Old Firm is that some of their more aggressive supporters actually seem to glory in the fact that they are disliked by so many people.

There is a poison that cannot be ignored. A minority of their fans nurse a hatred, obviously for the other part of the Old Firm, but I sometimes reckon, for the rest of Scotland also. And Old Firm games can literally generate mayhem, not only in the vicinity of the grounds, but many miles away. When Rangers and Celtic play each other, hospital accident and emergency units, pubs and public transport (even ferries crossing the Irish Sea) can all be affected by anti-social behaviour which frequently spills into hooliganism and at times, sustained and vicious violence. Even worse, this violence can also take place within the privacy of the home.

Early in 2005 a senior police officer, based not in Glasgow but in West Lothian, said that alcohol-fuelled aggression built up in Old Firm supporters when the two teams clashed, and was often expressed in brutal domestic beatings. He said that incidents of domestic violence could rise by 75 per cent after Rangers–Celtic clashes.

It is impossible to discuss the Old Firm in this context without discussing sectarianism. On the whole I agree with Professor Tom Devine, quoted in Part Two, when he says that contemporary Scottish sectarianism is attitudinal rather than structural. Ominously, he added that attitudinal sectarianism was possibly getting worse. I also agree with him that the problem is essentially racial rather than religious.

When I was researching a previous book on the Church of Scotland I was both amazed and appalled to find just how mired in racism the Kirk had been in the 1920s and '30s. The most prominent figure in the Kirk at this time was a man called John White, minister of the Barony Church in Glasgow from 1911 to 1934. He was moderator of the General Assembly of the Kirk after the Union (of the Church of Scotland and the United Free Church) in 1929 – a union he had worked tirelessly to achieve.

White led visceral and wicked racist campaigns against Irish immigration to Scotland. He asserted that a superior race was being supplanted by an inferior race. He called for the deportation of Irish-Scottish Catholics deemed as undesirable. He held many public meetings, raised petitions and used the Kirk's new Church and Nation Committee as a vehicle for his repellent agenda. He asserted that the issue was being pursued 'entirely as a racial and not as a religious question'.

To be fair to the Kirk, it eventually cleansed itself of this racism, mainly through the leadership of a fine and saintly man called John Baillie. But the nastiness had been there for two decades, and in these matters folk memories are kept alive, sustaining the bitterness. The revival of the Troubles in Northern Ireland from the late 1960s clearly did not help.

It may seem pathetic that such matters infest a significant part of our national game, but they do, and we cannot run away from this fact. I reckon that some people want the Old Firm out of Scottish football not because they are too big, and win too often, but because of the racist prejudice and bile which are so closely connected with them.

And while the racist element predominates, it would be foolish to ignore the religious dimension that still exists. It would also be very foolish to pretend that this is a problem that is confined to the Old Firm. When Hearts played Celtic in a Scottish Cup semi-final tie at Hampden in April 2005, the minute's silence for Pope John Paul II was disgracefully interrupted by a significant minority of Hearts fans, who made such a sickening mockery of the 'silence' that the minute had to be cut short by forty seconds.

The religious element was compounded over the years by the refusal of Rangers to sign Catholic players. To be fair to Celtic, the signing of Protestants was not a problem for them. When they won the European Cup so stylishly in 1967, their manager was a Protestant; so were almost half the team. One of these Lisbon Lions, Tommy Gemmell, was brought up as a Protestant in Motherwell. He has recalled that he knew that Celtic had many Protestants playing for them before he joined, and that he never encountered any problem regarding his denomination when he was at the club. His contemporary, Alex Ferguson did, alas, encounter problems regarding religion when he was playing for Rangers. Not because he was a Catholic – he wasn't; but because his wife was a Catholic.

WHO SAYS KEEP RELIGION OUT OF FOOTBALL – WHAT HAD THE POPE TO DO WITH THIS GAME?

To be fair, over the past few years both clubs have made serious attempts to address their residual sectarian problems. But the cancer remains.

It is worth asking if the Old Firm are genuinely Scottish institutions. Celtic have a dual identity, both Irish and Scottish, bridging two separate cultures. Brother Walfrid, the founder of the club, aimed for social integration; Celtic were to be a club that both Irishmen and Scots could support. Some observers reckon that they see far, far more Irish flags in the Celtic stands than Scottish saltires.

As for Rangers, they are a Scottish club, but they are linked strongly with Unionism. In their case, the Union flag is more prevalent than the Scottish saltire. Maybe it is naïve to look for saltires in the Old Firm stands on European nights, but the point remains: why should fans of Scottish clubs brandish Irish tricolours or Union Jacks?

The Union Jacks are explained by the fact that there was at one time a strong link between Unionism, Orangeism and the Tory party. This has largely dissolved, but in the 1920s and '30s it was very potent, at the very time when there was much bitter labour agitation in Scotland. On Clydeside, and in the coalfields of Ayrshire, Lanarkshire and Fife, many of the Catholic Scottish-Irish moved almost *en masse* into the Labour Party. Rangers were more associated with the Conservative and Unionist Party, as it was then known in Scotland.

I personally regard both Celtic and Rangers as Scottish teams. I am pleased when they do well in European competitions. But there is undoubtedly a case to be made that their Scottishness is far more diluted than that of other senior Scottish clubs.

There is a further point regarding their Scottishness. Partly because of their exploitation of their world fan base, and their vast cohorts of season-ticket holders, they are now wealthy clubs. They are in debt, but they are still wealthy. In the Deloitte Football Money League, for 2003–04, Celtic were 13th, with a turnover of £69 million. Rangers were 19th, with a turnover of £57.1 million. (The top three clubs were Manchester United, with £171.5 million, Real Madrid, with £156.3 million and AC Milan, with £147.2 million.)

Because of this wealth, and their automatic assumption of participation in Europe each year, Celtic and Rangers are perceived in the European game as big players, despite the relative smallness of our domestic league. This allows them, far more than other Scottish clubs, to invest in foreign players of genuine class. These players, in the nature of things, come and go, and not many of them stay for as long as the real greats, such as Laudrup with Rangers, or Larsson and Petrov with Celtic.

When I talked with Barry Divers, a young advocate who is the son of the fine Celtic forward, John Divers, he asked me a very good question: If Celtic had won the UEFA cup in Seville in 2003 (which of course they lost un-luckily to Jose Mourinho's Porto, 2–3) would that have been in any meaningful way a success for Scottish football? A Celtic team brilliantly managed by a man from Northern Ireland, and with only a couple of Scots playing, hardly represented something quintessentially Scottish. Of course similar questions could be asked of many top clubs appearing in European finals, but I took Barry's point.

I had been delighted during Celtic's exceptional run to that final, when they beat leading English clubs like Blackburn and Liverpool. I regarded these as straightforward Scotland–England clashes. But were they?

In a sense it was easier for non-Celtic supporters to take a simple Scottish pride in the achievements of the Celtic team in the 1960s, when I first became interested in football. The Lisbon Lions, the never-to-be-forgotten team that won the European Cup in 1967, not only played superb attacking football of a fluency, majesty and invention that we will probably never see again, but the team was made up of Scots born in or around Glasgow.

Again, in the 1960s, when I watched Celtic or Rangers at Pittodrie, I obviously wanted Aberdeen to win, but I could respect the Glasgow teams more readily because of the many great Scottish internationalists they had in their ranks. I've written about watching the inimitable Slim Jim Baxter sweeping perfect passes out to those wonderful Rangers wingers, Davie Wilson on the left and Willie Henderson on the right. If Rangers were disliked, and they were, they were also admired because of the superb Scottish players they had playing for them.

Of all those I spoke to who felt that the Old Firm should detach from Scottish football, the most quietly vehement was the academic Steve Morrow, who is deputy to Grant Jarvie at the Department of Sports Studies in Stirling University. When I met Steve he was about to go off on secondment to the University of Bologna in Italy for six months, but he kindly gave me a couple of hours of his time and also various papers on aspects of Scottish football which he had prepared over the years. Steve told me:

> I believe that the Old Firm must go – simply because the sporting and the financial imbalance has just become too great to sustain. The current situation is bad for the Old Firm, and bad for the rest of Scottish football. I'd like to believe the SFA and the SPL could jointly liaise with UEFA, admit frankly that

we have a problem and then see if we cannot work out a solution which would allow them to play elsewhere. After all, there are precedents.

(In an aside here I should point out that there are indeed precedents – Welsh teams play in the English league, a New Zealand team play in the Australian league, and so on – but what would concern UEFA would be the creation of a new and powerful precedent. For example, if the Old Firm could play in a league outwith Scotland, why shouldn't the leading Portuguese clubs, Porto, Benfica and Sporting Lisbon, play in the Spanish League?)

The final point that needs to be made about the Old Firm is that if they did find some way of departing from Scottish football and playing in the English Premiership or some other existing league, or even some new European league, they would still presumably be based in Glasgow. Their home games would still be played at Ibrox and Parkhead. Some of those who dislike the baggage that they bring to our game seem to assume that this baggage would be neatly transported beyond our borders if they were no longer playing in Scottish competitions. But that is not the case.

There is also, sadly, no reason whatsoever to hope that their departure into some other league or competition would lead to a revival of other Glasgow clubs: Partick Thistle in particular, and to a lesser extent the amateurs of Queen's Park. Over the years, the non-Old Firm Glasgow grounds have been very poorly attended, despite the apparent multitudes who will insist to you that they are lifelong Partick Thistle supporters.

When I first became interested in Scottish football Partick Thistle had a fine team. Not outstanding, but a good, solid league side. In season 1962–63, for example, they finished third in the league, behind Rangers and Kilmarnock and ahead of Celtic. At that time Glasgow was a huge city with over a million inhabitants, and the average attendances for the season were: Rangers 30,685, Partick 10,590 and Celtic 24,643.

Third Lanark, incidentally, were fourteenth in the league, three places above the relegation slot. Their average attendance was 5,148. There has been quite a lot about the demise of Third Lanark in this book. They had finished third in the league in 1961, and they scored 100 goals that season. Their average crowd then was 11,088, and thereafter the decline was inexorable. Their very last game, played against Dumbarton at Boghead, was watched by only 581 spectators.

I mentioned in Part One that Aberdeen played Partick in Glasgow when they clinched the league title in May 1980, breaking fifteen years of Old Firm dominance. I remember that game well. The attendance at Partick's ground, Firhill, that Wednesday night was under 7,000, and at least two-thirds of the crowd were Aberdeen supporters. That only about two thousand Partick supporters, or other Glasgow neutrals, could be bothered to turn up on that historic night speaks volumes about the real nature of the Glasgow football supporter. The unfortunate truth is that there has never been a credible alternative to the Old Firm in Glasgow, and I very much doubt if there ever will be.

Significant numbers of Glaswegians never supported Partick Thistle, or even Third Lanark, in a sustained, loyal and serious way. Again, there is a frivolity about the way that the people of Glasgow have allowed clubs like Linthouse and Cowlairs, and more recently Third Lanark, to wither and die.

If Partick Thistle became mired in desperate trouble, and the club's continued existence was in serious doubt, there would be a lot of emotive and sentimental concern, but much of it would be so much hot air. I do not write that out of spite. Partick Thistle are a particularly decent club, and the good people who keep the club going are among the most pleasant in football. The people I am indicting are not the small band of dedicated and real Thistle enthusiasts. One of them, Lindsay McFarlane, who regularly goes to games with her father, is quoted in Part Two. I am criticising the much larger number of supposed Thistle fans who haven't been near Firhill in years.

Commentators on the Scottish game frequently bemoan the national pulling power of the Old Firm; buses leave for Old Firm games from places as far from Glasgow as Dumfries and Peterhead. But the other side of this is the situation in Glasgow itself. It is a city that has done little to sustain non-Old Firm football. The likes of Clyde, Partick Thistle, and Third Lanark have had flurries of success over the years, but they have never been supported in serious numbers and they have never mounted a meaningful or sustained challenge to the Old Firm.

On the other hand, there must surely be many, many thousands of football-minded Glaswegians who don't want to support the Old Firm. Where have they been, and where are they now? This is one of the great mysteries of Scottish football. A very few of them support teams like Aberdeen and Hearts. But for whatever reason, the city of Glasgow cannot provide a meaningful alternative to the Old Firm.

It might seem perverse to finish a chapter about the Old Firm by writing about Partick Thistle; but in a way the sad plight of that club exemplifies the problem.

CHAPTER 3

FITBA MONEY

This is a small chapter about a big subject: Money.

That well-known Raith Rovers supporter, Gordon Brown, is much given, when he reviews his handling of the nation's finances, to vaunting his prudence. Whatever qualities have been manifest in Scottish football's wood-panelled boardrooms over the years, prudence is not one of them.

Indeed, the recent record is so woeful that we are asked to take the fact that the SPL's debt burden is now understood to be less than £100 million as some kind of triumph for a new-found financial responsibility. I suppose in a way it is, if you consider that two years ago the accumulated debt peaked at almost £200 million.

On the other hand, the picture remains bleak. At the time of writing, the last full official figures available were for the year that ended in the summer of 2004. For this period Rangers had a net debt of £74 million, Hearts of almost £20 million, Celtic of almost £16 million, Kilmarnock of almost £12 million, Hibs of £10 million and Aberdeen of almost £9 million.

Despite extensive cost cutting and the much trumpeted new realism, there is little mid-term likelihood of any of our big clubs managing a sustained period of profitability.

Some of the figures are staggering; Rangers have lost nearly £150 million over the past decade or so, while three years ago three senior clubs had wages to turnover ratios well in excess of one hundred per cent (Dundee at 154 per cent, Dunfermline at 132 per cent and St Johnstone at 112 per cent.)

Another problem is that there were far too many players. In season 1999–2000, for example, Celtic used 37 players in their league matches. Aberdeen used 35, as did Kilmarnock and Rangers. Dundee United used 33. Many of these players were only putting in occasional 'cameo' appearances and yet many of these 'occasionals' were on big wages, earning more in a week than most supporters earn in a month. To put these absurd figures into perspective, Jose Mourinho, the wonder boy of the English Premiership, runs Chelsea with a squad of 24 first-team players. OK, several of them are world-class players; but the point remains: far too many Scottish managers have not been encouraged to run tight squads.

The mismanagement was such that various clubs had to go into administration. The effect of this on the local communities – in particular on small businesses providing services for the clubs – was dire. And where clubs were showing some determination to mend their ways (notably Celtic and Aberdeen) the fans seemed for the most part unimpressed. Indeed, fan pressure cannot be discounted as a factor in driving directors down the pocked road of financial irresponsibility.

Mind you, I would never wish to castigate the Scottish fan overmuch. He or she has to pay a great deal for his or her football. You typically pay £20 to watch a SPL game, and at that price you have to ask: are you getting anything like value for money? Probably not, particularly when you look at how cheap – yes, cheap – football is on the Continent. In Germany you can watch Bundesliga football for as little as £7 a game. In Italy, you can watch Serie A football for just a little more: £9 a game. Nobody could possibly deny that the standard of football in the Bundesliga and Serie A – two of Europe's top three leagues – is significantly better than what is on offer in Scotland.

One problem is that our clubs have been too unimaginative and inflexible in their pricing policy for admission. Although some clubs have done their best with special offers, there is a need, as Sarah Nelson suggested in Part Two, for clubs to bring in more fans with imaginative deals and one-off promotions.

Meanwhile, as our two giant clubs build their brands across continents, they seem, superficially, to be secure in their massive season-ticket fan base. Yet the danger signs are there. The Celtic supporter Barry Divers told me that many Celtic season-ticket holders were becoming bored to the point of disillusion with some of the more predictable fare, and were simply not prepared to turn up to watch, say, an anticipated 2–0 win over Livingston, even though they had already paid for the game through their season ticket. A similar point was made to me by Campbell Ogilvie, the Rangers director-secretary.

I detest the word, but I suppose it comes down to the product – and its marketability. The academic Steve Morrow often uses the phrase 'uncertainty of outcome'. He is not talking about how the latest big purchase from overseas is going to perform – will he be a Larsson or a Scheidt? – but rather what in the economics of football is the crucial factor for encouraging purchase of the product. In other words, you are not likely to pay to see a game if the outcome is pretty certain.

I am not convinced about that when it comes to the Old Firm supporters, who until recently anyway, seem to have had an unlimited appetite for watching much smaller teams being duly defeated, and it certainly does not apply to the hard-core supporters of the smaller clubs who will follow their team regardless of the near certainty of regular defeat. But in terms of attracting new customers, this clearly is an important consideration. And as I noted, there are growing signs that the huge army of Old Firm season-ticket holders are indeed beginning to fret at the 'certainty of outcome.' This is what makes it so important that teams like Hearts, Hibs and Aberdeen raise their game and present meaningful and sustained challenges. At long last, there are signs that this is beginning to happen.

Underpinning this discussion is the attitude of the customer, the fan. It surprises me that there has not been any seriously sophisticated research done into the attitudes and aspirations of Scottish fans. One answer to many of our game's problems would be for fans, particularly of the bigger clubs, to temper their intense desire for success with an understanding that the most important thing of all is for their club to be financially secure. I know that this sounds dull, and implies that supporters must be prepared to achieve success gradually. Is this collective mindset feasible? Possibly not.

Fans are not always rational, but neither are they greedy. And it is also remarkable that for all the mismanagement and extravagance in the board-room, most club directors are not in the game for what they can get out of it. They have made terrible mistakes, but usually with the best of intentions and the genuine aim of gaining success for their clubs. And Fergus McCann managed to pull off a wonderful feat: he saved Celtic, no less, and made money at the same time.

Several prominent businessmen and entrepreneurs have put very significant amounts of money into Scottish clubs over the last couple of decades. But because these men tend to be unusually wealthy any gratitude for them tends to be superficial and even grudging.

It must be said that there has been more greed in the dressing room than in the boardroom. But if footballers are offered crazy money, you cannot really blame them for taking it. You can certainly blame them for taking it and not giving a hundred per cent, or putting something back into the game. Many fans seem remarkably reluctant to vent their anger on high-earning but under-achieving players and instead turn their ire on the players' agents, although this is a sort of generalised wrath, because they often don't know who these people are.

There has certainly not been enough transparency when it comes to the work of clubs and agents, but my understanding that is that the industry average for an agent's commission is about five per cent of what the player will earn, and that seems if anything slightly on the low side. Sometimes the details of specific deals leak out in a way that annoys fans. For example, when the defender Jean Alain Boumsong left Rangers after just a few months to sign for Graeme Souness's Newcastle, his agent, Willie McKay, apparently made £500,000 out of the £8 million transfer. But the Boumsong deal was by any standards an excellent one for Rangers Football Club.

I am in fact quite relaxed about agents, even if few other people seem to be. It is wrong to imagine that they are a new phenomenon; they have been around for a long, long time, with varied degrees of prominence. Obviously the post-Bosman situation made life richer for them.

If celebrities like best-selling novelists and high profile actors and actresses and singers can have agents then I don't see why footballers can't. And when the players are not superstars or particularly marketable, I suspect that their agents often don't make very much.

I have certainly heard of negotiations at Aberdeen FC where the agents involved did not take any money at all from either the players or the club. To say that agents are 'nasty, evil and pointless scum' as an English Premiership chairman did, is to miss the point. Agents are an easy target and they are not responsible for the financial travails of Scottish football. I have a hunch that in the future a lot of the criticism of agents will focus not on their actions on behalf of players, but on their actions on behalf of managers, and indeed entire management teams.

As for the managers, there is, quite reasonably, a colossal disparity in what the SPL bosses earn. In recent times the top earner has been Celtic's Martin O'Neill. Given his excellent record at Parkhead prior to his retirement for personal reasons in the summer of 2005, and looking at industry comparisons, his salary of circa £1.2 million a season did not seem at all excessive. He was the only SPL manager earning more than £1 million. To put his salary into perspective, Graeme Souness at Newcastle and Davie Moyes at Everton are both understood to earn around £1.5 million per year. At the other end of the scale, though not the league, Craig Brewster of Inverness CT is understood to earn less than £40,000. (These figures are per annum, and exclude bonuses.)

So far I have managed to write about money without mentioning the dreaded word 'television'. Scottish football has managed, thus far, to avoid a disaster quite as cataclysmic as the collapse of the English Nationwide League's deal with ITV Digital in 2001, which cost the clubs about £80 million a season over four seasons. In 2001 the SPL did not manage to renew its deal with Sky, and a two-year deal with the BBC, worth about £8.5 million a season, was negotiated. Then in 2004 a four-year pay-per-view deal was negotiated with the Irish broadcaster Setanta. Thirty-eight live matches were to be broadcast each season, and obviously by far the majority of these would feature the Old Firm. The company's target was 80,000 subscribers in the first year, but they have not yet revealed whether this target was reached.

The institution which has probably done more practical good than any other for Scottish football in recent years is the Bank of Scotland.

The bank's exposure to SPL club debt (they are the bankers to ten of the twelve SPL clubs) is about £120 million. When I put this figure to a senior spokesman for HBOS, the bank's parent company, he cautiously agreed that it was pretty accurate. But he did not particularly like the word 'exposure', nor did he like the alternative word I offered, 'underwriting'. 'I'd much prefer if you put it this way,' he said. 'The absolute credit limit, on the basis of the business plans the clubs have submitted to us, is approximately £120 million.'

Given its enormous service to Scottish football, the bank seem curiously coy about accepting any credit – appropriate word – for their contribution to keeping Senior Scottish football going. Maybe this is because of an understandable desire, for a bank, not to be regarded as some kind of sports charity.

'Yes, it has been somewhat challenging,' the spokesman told me in his careful way. 'But we remain happy to be so closely involved with SPL clubs.' Was this a signal of intent for the future? 'Yes,' came the response. 'We have had corporate bankers working with the clubs for many years now, and we look forward to a time when they are much more commercially successful.'

I spoke with Sir Peter Burt, who was senior chief executive of the Bank of Scotland from 1996 to 2001 and thereafter deputy chairman of HBOS from 2001 to 2003. He said simply but eloquently: 'Football is such an important part of Scotland's life, the country's leisure and cultural activity, that we were very happy to support the SPL clubs at a most difficult time.'

Neither Sir Peter nor the HBOS spokesman would tell me if the 'new realism' in the boardrooms owed much to firmly applied pressure from the bank, but I suspect that it did. Anyway, it is rare – particularly in sporting books – to praise banks, but as Jamie Moffat, the former chairman of Kilmarnock, told me: 'The Bank of Scotland have been incredibly supportive to most of the clubs in the SPL. Without this one bank, our football would be in much deeper trouble.'

Of course a cynic might aver that the bank are trapped. They would not want to be known as the bank that pulled the plug on some much-loved clubs, or even as the bank that killed Scottish football.

A man who can take an authoritative and objective view of the finances of Scottish football is David Glen, partner with PriceWaterhouseCooper. He loves the game and he also understands its finances better than many of those deeply involved in the clubs. As he says wryly, he was not good at playing the game, but he was always good with a calculator. For fifteen years he has been carefully scrutinising the books and producing the much respected annual financial review of Scottish football. He told me:

> I've a hesitant optimism. The clubs have cut back on their costs. The debt mountain has been tackled, albeit with varying degrees of urgency. But I'm still very worried about what happens to SPL teams that are relegated. There is not an automatic bounce-back.
>
> There also remains a lot of pressure from the fans, who want the clubs to spend and spend. I do quite a lot of talks with groups like Supporters Direct, trying to explain the financial realities. Fans will need to show both patience and understanding, and I know it is difficult to ask for this. I reckon the clubs themselves could communicate rather better. They need to explain the financial situation in detail, and be frank with the supporters. They need to spell out the message: *We simply cannot afford what you are demanding.*
>
> And if youth development is the future, which it is, you are going to need a great deal of patience.
>
> I still think the clubs are spending too much on wages. I advocate that no more than 55 per cent of turnover should be spent on wages. Then, when you start to generate surpluses, you re-invest: in youth development, training facilities and so on.

That is a dose of necessary financial realism. But David's final words to me were: 'Even if every club in the land went bust, Scottish football could never die'.

CHAPTER 4

AS ITHERS SEE US, AND LOST LOYALTY

It is salutary to get a perspective on our Scottish game from detached observers elsewhere. I turned to two highly respected sportswriters based in the south of England, Brian Viner of the *Independent* and Denis Campbell of the *Observer*, for an outside view of our football. I asked them to outline not only their own opinions, but also to describe what they thought the wider English perception was. Brian Viner told me:

> While my own personal view is sympathetic, I think the prevalent English view of Scottish football is that it has become a joke. This derives entirely from the duopoly of Rangers and Celtic. It's a good time to talk about this, because for the first time people in England are just starting to realise that we too are getting into a Scottish situation, as it were.
>
> Here in England there is a trio of clubs that can win our top league. So we have three out of twenty. That compares with your two out of twelve. And if you look at the current gap in England between first and fourth, it's enormous. So in that sense there is in England a misconceived sense of superiority. Intelligent fans in England are increasingly coming to realise that only a tiny minority of our teams is capable of winning our title and that has never been the case in the past.
>
> There has been a bewildering loss of Scottish players in England. There are still many good Scottish managers and coaches around, but where are the players? Wonderful, wonderful Scottish footballers used to grace our game. Our top clubs would look to our lower divisions and to Scotland as their feeders. But they look abroad for their talent now.
>
> And that applies to English fans. They also look abroad. Many of them take a keen interest in Spanish and Italian football. I'm sorry to say that there is hardly any interest in Scottish football now. It is just sneered at, or completely disregarded. That's a shame, but it's the reality.

Denis Campbell said:

> I think there is a generalised and probably correct perception in England that over the past ten or fifteen years, the rest of Europe have been getting better while Scotland have been going backwards – both in terms of the national team and the clubs. So the decline in Scottish football is seen to have occurred at exactly the wrong time.

I personally believe, and I think a lot of other journalists do too, that the style of football is all wrong north of the Border.

I've been to most of the top grounds in Scotland and the Scottish fans seem to demand this instant thrill – it's still a case of baying wildly at the players to get stuck in, get the ball up the park. In some of the grounds, like Tynecastle, the fans are right on top of the players and this kind of attitude puts pressure on them to play totally the wrong type of football. This kind of up and at 'em style of play simply doesn't work any more.

Football is so much more technical now. So I'd say that the Scottish kids must start learning the modern way of playing the game. And if they want to be professional footballers they must understand that the deal is that they live properly and better themselves. I'm not suggesting that anyone has to live the monastic life, but I think that the clubs have to do far more to make the home-grown players, and this applies in England too, respect the great chance they are being given, and not waste it.

There's a lot of lifestyle adjustment needed. I think we need to understand the difference between the culture of young people abroad and at home, in both Scotland and here in England. I think the clubs have to educate their young players in all sorts of ways.

I stress that both of these perceptive commentators are essentially sympathetic to the Scottish game. I could, easily enough, have gathered some quotes from other respected journalists that bordered on the contemptuous. On the other hand, implicit in Brian's remarks is the understanding that the English can no longer be too cocky. The danger signals are certainly there in England. The English Premiership is becoming the plaything of three megaclubs, whose domination is such that they now start a league campaign expecting to lose, at the worst, one or two games. Arsenal won the premiership in 2003–04 without losing a single game; Chelsea won it in 2004–05 and lost only once. These facts put the Old Firm's domination of Scottish league football into perspective.

And as I write this Manchester United fans are consumed with fury about the Glazer takeover and other fans in England are mercilessly mocking their discomfiture. There is also widespread disgust at the way Chelsea have apparently bought their way to success by trawling the Continent for hyper-expensive imports. And, alarmingly, attendances, after several boom years, are beginning to drop. As we look south of the Border, we can point to various worrying trends and a growing malaise. We cannot be complacent, but we can point to our new realism, and wonder how long it is going to take to arrive in England.

These matters are important not least because football is about identity and national pride and self-confidence. I've written elsewhere in this book about how I see no contradiction between my strong admiration for the English and my pronounced distaste for their egregious national team. I get almost as much pleasure from the English national team being beaten as I do from the Scottish team winning. At the same time I'm delighted when a team like Liverpool or Manchester United does well in Europe (not so much the likes of Chelsea or Arsenal: I have an aversion, these days, to London clubs. Given the fact that under-achieving but bombastic London has not yet managed to produce a European Cup/Champions League winner, when Glasgow, Liverpool, Manchester, Nottingham and Birmingham all have, the arrogance and conceit of London's self-regarding football establishment is a wonder to behold).

There is also much comment in this book about second-rate foreigners flooding into the Scottish game. There is nothing racist in an objection to poor foreign imports stifling the development of Scottish talent, but it is still necessary to stress that you can object strongly to the post-Bosman influx without being in the slightest xenophobic.

When I had a conversation with Jack Davidson, sometime journalist and distinguished advocate, he told me that his main concern about the Scottish game focused on what he called the many transient mercenaries who took their money and moved on. He said:

A few of these players have indubitably brought colour and variety and excitement to our domestic game, but too many of them have just taken the money and vanished. There's been no continuity, and the careers of promising young Scottish players have been thwarted before they were properly started. So I'd reduce the number of foreign players that any team can field. I don't want to suggest a specific quota – that could be agreed by the clubs and the SFA. That would be my main prescription for improving Scottish football.

Then Jack, an urbane and civilised man, obviously without an iota of racial prejudice, added: 'I'm not xenophobic, don't get me wrong.' Of course he isn't. The difficulty is that given football's common association with tribalism, bigotry and insular prejudice, if you make perfectly reasonable points about too many foreigners being in our game, and choking the development of homegrown talent, or indeed about disliking the English national team, then you can all too easily be presented as some kind of backstreet bigot. This is absurd. We must not be cowed into a loss of national pride, a failure of identity, because of any need to be politically correct.

I was struck, when I was talking with another journalist, Kevin McKenna of the *Scottish Daily Mail*, when he suggested that football should be a vehicle for national aspiration, but Scotland appeared to have lost this aspiration:

> It is not as if God in His wisdom despises Scotland and has decided that we should suddenly produce only dud players. We have a lot going for us: We are an affluent country. We have quality.
>
> Where the quality is lacking is in the coaching. Our kids are being destroyed at grass-roots level, at 11 or 12 or 13, before they have had a real chance. The talent has not disappeared, it's just that there is no science in the coaching. Look at Davie Moyes, a classic example of a Scottish coach who thinks. When he was 22 or 23 he was already thinking about being a coach. We need a lot more like him.
>
> My view is that our great natural resource, good players, is still there – I'm certain there are still very talented players being born to Scottish mothers, but there's no vision, no intellectual desire, no burning urge, to sort out this talent and develop it. This suggests complacency as well as a loss of confidence, and we can slide into a belief that we're just no good. Well, we're no good at developing the talent. But the talent hasn't disappeared.

As well as national pride, there is the issue of continuity, raised by Jack Davidson. I mentioned in the first chapter of this book that the doughty Dons stalwart of the 1960s, Ally Shewan, played 313 consecutive games for the club. Back then, the teams used to be the same, week after week. There was maybe not enough variety, but now things have swung far too far in the opposite direction.

I suspect that many fans are divided over this issue. On the one hand they like to see their club developing players through the youth system, and they have a kind of cerebral understanding that this organic growth is the way it should be, and the most sensible path forward. On the other hand they want the instant fix, and despite past unhappy experiences, they put pressure on their managers and directors to spend too much and keep bringing in new foreign players. There is clearly a contradiction here. I'm amazed, personally, that after the post-Bosman frenzy there is still so much faith in the efficacy of bringing in big money buys from abroad.

The two Scottish footballers I have respected most flourished in the New Firm era. First, Willie Miller – and that's maybe not a surprise. Willie played with exemplary consistency for Aberdeen FC from 1973 till 1990, and for Scotland from 1975 till 1990. Sir Alex Ferguson described him as the best penalty box defender in the world. This being the case, he obviously had chances to leave Aberdeen for bigger clubs – but he stayed at Pittodrie and said, when his playing career was over, that he never once regretted doing so.

The other player would be Maurice Malpas, every bit as much a model professional as Willie. A Fifer, Maurice began training with Dundee United when he was 14. He became a part-time professional with the Tannadice club when he was 17. His father insisted that he should continue his education, and he gained an honours degree at Abertay University.

He went on to play 55 times for Scotland, between 1984 and 1993, including two World Cup final rounds, in Mexico in 1986 and Italy in 1990. Still with United when they were relegated in 1995, he stuck with them, and eventually he hung up his boots when he was 38. Altogether he played more than 800 games for the club.

If I were asked to characterise the playing careers of Willie and Maurice, I'd cite one simple word: Loyalty. I'd love to see this kind of magnificent loyalty becoming commonplace in our game again. Perhaps that is very naïve, in this over-commerical era, but loyalty would lead to continuity and our game is crying out for that quality.

One of the greatest, if under-reported, achievements of Sir Alex Ferguson during his long stewardship at Manchester United was the way he nurtured a group of marvellous youngsters: the Neville Brothers, Butt, Beckham and, in my opinion, the best two, Giggs and Scholes. With the exception of Beckham, they were all local lads. He developed them simultaneously, so that they broke into the first team within a year or so of each other, and they grew as footballers together and stayed with the club as success bred success.

Eventually, after six or seven seasons, Beckham and Butt left, but it was quite remarkable to have a nucleus of home-grown players playing together for so long at a club that was actually a megabusiness, perhaps the biggest international football brand of them all. Only Sir Alex could have created in the midst of this hugeness a family atmosphere. I am convinced that at least some of United's enormous success under Sir Alex derived from this continuity factor.

When I talked with Barry Divers, the son of that exciting Celtic player Johnny Divers, he reminisced about growing up in an environment where other players who were team-mates of his dad were constantly in the house. Even now they still keep together socially. Again, we are talking about continuity and the idea of a 'family' club. But the bigger the club, the less easy this is to achieve, and the current Celtic team is very different from the team of Johnny Divers. Here is an opportunity for the Aberdeens, the Hearts and Hibs, the Dundees and Dundee Uniteds. Ignore the short term temptations, build from the grass roots, take your fans with you, and you may yet have a strength and integrity at the heart of the club that bigger clubs can only dream of.

More reminiscence: Perhaps the best story about loyalty in Scottish football I heard during my researches was from that great Partick Thistle favourite of the 1950s, George Smith.

George was brought up in Bathgate. His family were Rangers fanatics. The man George's father admired more than anyone was Bill Struth, the legendary Rangers manager. With his speed and his penchant for scoring spectacular goals, George made quite an impact in schools football. The first Senior club that came for him were Partick Thistle, and George signed provisionally for the Glasgow club when he was 14.

Two years later Bill Struth, no less, contacted his father. Rangers wanted to sign George! 'As far as my father was concerned, Bill Struth was God,' recalls George. 'Now here he was, the great man himself, wanting me to report to Ibrox. But my Dad said to me: 'Son, you signed for Thistle when you were 14. They've been looking after you since then. You'd better stay with them.'

That story says a lot about the values that used to be commonplace in the Scottish game. Can we rediscover them? I hope so.

That wise English manager Sir Bobby Robson, said not so long ago: 'Nobody can understand losing any more. The game's about losing as well as winning, but they can't take losing.' He was talking about the English game, but his words apply with equal force to Scotland. These words maybe explain why there is so little continuity in Scottish football management. I mentioned that after the departure of Alex Ferguson Aberdeen went through nine managers in eighteen years.

As I write this, in the past calendar year there have been eight changes of manager in the SPL. A lot of this frantic sacking and hiring, coming and going, is driven by the fear of losing. Yet all the evidence is that the more time a manager is given, the less likely he is to be a loser. In part this is because, obviously enough, a successful manager is less likely to be fired; but if you look at the outstanding career of Alex Ferguson, he was far, far more successful in his second four years at Aberdeen than in the first four; and at

Manchester United it took him three and a half years before he won his first trophy.

I am a great believer in constant competition, and the elimination, as far as possible, of meaningless games. Yet it has to be admitted that if you create a league structure which produces a ferment of excitement, and a multiplicity of games in which the stakes are high, then this is going to militate severely against the magic quality of continuity. There will be even more pressure on managers and coaches to deliver. There is a problem here, and I cannot quite see my way through it.

There has been a lot in this book about Celtic and Rangers, about Aberdeen (of course), about Hibs and Hearts. There has been less about the smaller clubs. I recalled that when the *Scotsman* undertook an investigation into the ills of Scottish football in 1971, the main conclusion that a number of the smaller clubs should be expunged from the league. I'd certainly not argue that case now. These clubs represent continuity, in their own way, more perfectly than anything else in the Scottish game.

Here are the views of a loyal Dumbarton supporter, a man called Gregor McSkimming. Gregor teaches physics in Edinburgh, but he returns to Dumbarton to watch 'the Sons' and to keep in touch with his mates, as often as he can.

Football is a game, not a business, and you still see that truth in the smaller clubs. The game cannot be allowed to be just about Sky TV and about the Old Firm paying megabucks for big name celebrity players. At the smaller clubs like Dumbarton, football is very important socially. The club helps to hold the community together. My main contact with my former schoolmates is through the club. I cannot, in all fairness, regard the Old Firm clubs as being part of any community.

Every Saturday, yes, people leave Dumbarton to follow Rangers or Celtic. More than follow Dumbarton, far more. But well, that gives us real Dumbarton supporters a kind of sense of righteousness. And we have things that the Old Firm's fans don't have, like the Scottish Cup draw which means little to them. The Scottish Cup still means so much to us; we dream of a cup run.

Or the Tartan Army. It's supporters of clubs like Dumbarton, Cowdenbeath, Queen of the South and so on who are the foot soldiers in the Tartan Army. You won't find that many Old Firm fans in the Army.

I was four or five when my dad took me to my first game at Boghead. When I go now to the Strathclyde Homes Stadium, I'm continuing something that started when I was a very wee boy. I'll always be a Dumbarton supporter. It keeps me in touch with the things that matter.

The academic Steve Morrow says that the 'existing ownership model' has failed most Scottish clubs. He wants stakeholder groups, such as supporters, community representatives, even the local council, to become directly involved in the ownership, management and governance of Senior clubs. He commends the organisation Supporters Direct for their drive to get Supporters' Trusts to become stakeholders in the clubs. (Already there are trusts at 30 of the 42 senior clubs.)

When the Cross Party Sport Group at the Scottish Parliament, convened by Dennis Canavan, presented their submission to the Enterprise and Culture Committee's Inquiry into Scottish Football, one of their key points was that the Scottish Executive should continue assisting Supporters Direct. This was so that ordinary fans would have a stake in both the ownership and the running of their clubs.

Even more important than the issues of ownership and stakeholding is the involvement of the club in the wider community. I have been hard, elsewhere in this book, on Aberdeen FC for their lack of investment in training facilities. So it is only fair to redress the balance by looking at the impressive array of youth activities that the club organises throughout its vast catchment area.

These include an annual soccer academy at the Balgownie fields by the Bridge of Don; after-school coaching through the Shell Donslink scheme, which is organised round fifteen different venues in the Aberdeen area; the running of North East Soccer Sevens involving small-sided games at a variety of venues in Aberdeen on Saturday mornings; school holiday coaching programmes, which reach out to over 6,000 children in the North-East; and specialised goalkeeping clinics at various locations. This is a commendable range of involvement, yet the club's director of football, Willie Miller, told me, 'We can and should be doing much more.'

There is direct spin off for the club in many of these activities, apart from possibly finding the next Denis Law. Aberdeen currently have more than 1,500 season-ticket holders under the age of 12. But the spin offs are not just for the club. The Soccer Sevens project, for example, is not only about developing football skills; it is also about 'encouraging co-operation, respect for others, acceptance of rules and decisions, self-discipline and the need for teamwork'. All of this cannot but be good for civic Scottish society as a whole. Indeed I can envisage football, despite its bad press, becoming a kind of counter-culture for a better Scotland, and I shall develop this theme in the next chapter.

CHAPTER 5

COUNTER CULTURE

I'd like to conclude with three short chapters: two in which I make various proposals for the improvement of our game, and a final chapter where I explore briefly a huge subject, the way that football has colonised the Scottish psyche.

One of the reasons why we are finding it difficult in Scotland to develop international-class players is to be found in the pervasive youth culture that prompts so many promising young footballers to go astray.

This culture comprises many components: in our post-modern society, there is an emphasis on individualism, and team sports are less 'cool' than they used to be. The rise of the computer cannot be discounted; many young people choose to spend many hours isolated in their rooms playing computer games. There is also a relatively new and somewhat insidious sense that betterment, if it involves discipline and hard work, is not 'cool' either. And even basic educational attainment is sometimes sneered at.

When I was an education specialist in the 1970s, a phrase that was often used to describe secondary schools in parts of Glasgow was 'Fort Apache'. I first heard it used by an inspector of schools, but it became quite common currency. The point was that if a youngster came from a difficult or even a dysfunctional background, the school offered a place of security and support. Sadly, I suspect that this is no longer so.

Indeed, the saddest theme that emerged as I researched this book was that many people in the world of professional football felt, privately, that the secondary school was becoming a hindrance rather than an asset in fostering a good young player's development. This was more than just a reflection of the sad decline of schools football; it was also the expression of a belief that the school could be a place where young people learned bad habits.

Just about everybody I spoke to in the football world stressed the need for educational development in parallel with football development. There was a realisation that too often in the past Scottish football had been perceived as being anti-education. Those who were seriously worried about what they regarded as the negative influence of the secondary school were also embarrassed, and felt it was not something they were prepared to discuss on the record.

I heard quite a lot of anecdotal evidence about very talented young players who round about the age of 13 or 14 had succumbed to peer pressure and given up on a potential football career. To put it crudely, they'd decided to hang around the streets, drinking with their mates, rather than work at developing their football skills. To make it as a footballer requires a lot of practice; ideally, a minimum of 20 hours a week, at the very time in a young life when the temptation not to bother is at its most powerful.

It requires much mental strength and discipline to resist peer pressure and follow the stony path of self-discipline and hard work. Indeed, you could say that resistance to temptation has never been more difficult. So: our good young footballers need all the support we can give them.

Alex McLeish, the Rangers manager, spoke out about the perils of drinking in the summer of 2005. He said that alcohol was the root cause of the declining number of home-grown players progressing in the Scottish professional game. Further, he intimated that he intended to take a hard-line approach to ensure that everyone at his club was well aware of the dangers of drinking, and binge drinking in particular.

I thought his comments were wise, timeous and salutary. Although the SFA was actually founded in a temperance hotel in Glasgow, for as long as anyone can remember, Scottish football has been soaked in an irresponsible boozing culture. The fans have been worse than the players, but not by much. I have played my own insignificant yet reprehensible part in this; I have recalled that I was so drunk at the England–Scotland debacle at Wembley in 1975 that I was removed from the stadium.

Scottish football is awash with sodden stories of heroic and not-so-heroic drinking. At every level, people have been guilty: directors, managers, coaches, supporters, players. The manufacturers of alcoholic beverages have used both clubs and actual competitions as an effective means of sponsorship. Some managers have used heavy drinking sessions to build up team spirit, and no pun intended. The fact that our game existed in a drink-fuelled haze was almost regarded as a matter of national pride. Yet some of the finest players we have produced would have had longer careers and would have been even more effective players had they not succumbed to the booze.

There were also many personal tragedies. Hughie Gallacher, one of the greatest Scottish forwards, was actually once sent off for being drunk and disorderly in a match in Budapest. Hughie had an inventive way with words as well as the ball and his excuse was that it was such a hot day that he'd been washing his mouth out with whisky and water. Later in his career, when he was playing for Chelsea, he was often found legless outside King's Road pubs just hours before he dazzled at Stamford Bridge. Later, Hughie took his own life. In 1957 he stepped in front of an express train on the main Edinburgh to London rail line.

Another magnificent player who was sometimes drunk literally an hour so so before a game was the sublimely talented Willie Hamilton, whom Jock Stein described as the most talented player he ever worked with. Willie sometimes had to be placed under a cold shower to sober up just minutes before kick off. There are plenty of other examples, not least that of the great Jim Baxter. Sometimes it almost seemed as if the greater the talent, the more likely the player was to forfeit that talent to the demon drink.

I have recalled visiting the Scottish squad at Largs in the early 1970s. I did not personally see any evidence of excessive drinking, but I heard plenty of stories. No doubt the serious boozing came later, before they went out boating.

So all of us, whether we were at the epicentre of the national game, or far out on its furthest fringes, were complicit in a kind of sodden glorification of drinking. The fact that there was a funny, gallus, even crazy side to it all merely made it all the more insidious.

The legislation that was introduced in 1980 by the late Frank McElhone, MP – a fine man and a fine sports minister – did much to reduce drunkenness inside Scottish football grounds, but it actually did very little to rid football of the pervasive booze culture.

All this is to say that it is going to be doubly difficult to use football as an antidote to the abuse of drink, for the simple reason that for far too long our game has been synonymous with boozing – and has often been celebrated for that very reason. The links between alcohol and Scottish football seem well-nigh indissoluble.

The provision of good all-weather training facilities is vitally important for the future of our national game. But more than that is needed: the managers, the coaches, the journalists, the teachers, all who have any influence, have got to become almost evangelical in a much-needed crusade against the abuse of alcohol. Who knows: if they succeed, alcohol could yet go the way of tobacco. Attitudes to smoking have changed enormously in the last thirty years.

I'm not so naïve as to advocate an ascetic lifestyle for young male athletes, nor am I suggesting that promising professional footballers should be required to join the Band of Hope. I just want to create a greater awareness of the ravages that alcohol is producing in our society, and I'd hope that football could be used not to encourage this abuse, but to combat it.

It is certainly arguable that our greatest single social problem in Scotland is the pervasive drinking culture. Alcohol abuse costs the NHS in Scotland well over £100 million a year, and more and more young people are literally dying as a result of this abuse. Access to alcohol is shamefully easy for young Scots, and a heavy drinking culture often develops as early as the age of 12 or 13. This isn't only deleterious physically; it also rots the will to train and to learn. In that depressing context, I began to think of football almost as a counter-culture.

If we could get more decent facilities and more young people playing the game on an organised basis, there would be widespread benefits for our society as a whole, in terms of both health and education. As for talented footballers, they probably need to be placed in a special environment.

I would advocate very forcefully that there is a case for really good young players being removed from school as early as 12 or 13, and given dispensation to continue their education under the auspices of a professional club. Ideally, they would train and work at the club for half the day, and continue their education at a local authority college the other half. Brian Monteith, MSP, is a politician who has thought this issue through and he emphasises that colleges are much more flexible than schools. They do not shut down for long holidays and they could provide specifically developed educational programmes.

This idea is radical and would require the endorsement of the Scottish Executive. The obvious problem would be the setting of a precedent. If young footballers could be removed from the school system well before the school-leaving age, why should similar schemes not be developed for promising individuals in other specialisms?

The benefits of this proposed scheme would be twofold: clubs would be able to work with the players intensively, and their education would probably flourish also. As I suggested, for too long there has been an insidious undercurrent of anti-educationalism in Scottish football. Fraser Wishart of the SPFA touched on this briefly when we were talking, but his remarks stayed with me. I was also told by the Rangers fan Graham Walker that we should have far more graduate footballers. (The French eleven that won the World Cup in 1998 was an all-graduate team.) We have got to create a climate where educational development and football development are seen as two sides of the same coin. For example, working for a degree need not inhibit the progress of a talented young player. As noted in the previous chapter, that superb servant of Dundee United and Scotland, Maurice Malpas, gained an honours degree for which he studied when he was a part-time player, between the ages of 17 and 21.

One of the difficulties in preparing young men for careers in professional football is of course preparation for failure. Obviously not everyone is going to make it. But if the education has been looked after, and specifically geared to the needs of the individual concerned, then he will be better equipped for a life outside football than is the case at present.

Most professional clubs in Scotland are not too far from a suitable local-authority college. Young footballers selected for these twin-track approach schemes – football education with a club, academic education with a college – would not be isolated: I would envisage at least three or four or five taking part with each club. This would instil a sense of joint motivation and team spirit.

The alternative to this twin-track approach – the clubs attending to the football, the colleges to the education – would be to create a national academy (probably at Stirling) where élite youth from all over Scotland could gather for intensive football development and educational study. The problem with this would be the relationship between the professional clubs and the national academy.

In any event, I believe that we must as a nation think very seriously about the waste of young talent that is currently occurring. It is not as if we have so many good youngsters, as in the 1950s and 1960s, that a lot of the cream will come through anyhow.

The schemes proposed above would obviously cater for only a very small minority of potentially excellent footballers: those who had already been identified, at the age of 11 or 12 as the likely greats of tomorrow. The wider Scotland could, however, benefit from a much greater level of participation in football. The loss of schools football has never really been replaced, despite the sterling efforts of those involved in youth coaching and in the boys' clubs.

The Scottish Executive surely has a role to play in providing many more facilities, particularly all-weather and indoor facilities, in opening up the schools, and in encouraging the teaching profession to resume their involvement in organised schools football. All this would cost money, of course it would; but it is not fanciful to suggest that the social dividend, in a much fitter and healthier generation of youngsters, in a decline of anti-social behaviour, and in a renewed spirit of co-operation and teamwork, might be immensely ameliorative for our wider Scottish society.

Meanwhile: I reiterate – alcohol is not just sapping our national sport; it is in danger of wasting an entire generation.

CHAPTER 6

LABORATORY

Scottish football has a long and proud history. When I was in Brazil in 2004 I learned about how Scottish loco engineers helped to introduce the great game to the country that produced, in 1970, the finest team we have ever seen. Brazil have won the World Cup a remarkable five times, and are *the* footballing nation, followed by Argentina – a country where Scots also played a key role in developing the game.

Scotland contested the world's first international match. As early as 1893 there were more than 800 players professionally registered in Scotland. Hampden Park, Glasgow held many records for crowds, most notably in 1937 when 149,547 turned up to watch the Scotland–England match – and just a week later, 147, 365 were back at Hampden to watch a club game, Aberdeen playing Celtic in the Scottish Cup final. Then in April 1970, in a game switched to Hampden from Parkhead, 135,826 fans saw Celtic beat Leeds United in the European Cup semi-final, second leg. All three of these crowds comprise records that have not been beaten in Europe, for international, club and European games.

Then we come to the individuals. Peter Craigmyle, Jack Mowat, Tom 'Tiny' Wharton and Bobby Davidson were highly admired international referees; David Will of Brechin is a much-respected international administrator. Sir Matt Busby, Sir Alex Ferguson, Bill Shankly and Jock Stein are included in the litany of the most distinguished managers of all time; and Hughie Gallacher, Billy Liddell, Jimmy Johnstone, Denis Law and Kenny Dalglish are ranked among the finest forwards in the entire history of the game.

When Celtic became the first British club to win the European Cup, in 1967, they won the trophy with style, zest and a purity of attacking football that has probably been surpassed only by the Real Madrid side of di Stefano, Puskas, Gento and Kopa in 1960. And these greats claimed the trophy at Hampden Park, which has a good claim to be one of *the* spiritual homes of world football.

Cynics would aver that none of this signifies very much at the present time when, as I write, our world ranking is in the low 80s. But I prefer to think of the wise words of Sir Alex Ferguson, who told me: 'In Scottish football we've got pride, we've got respect, we've got tradition. We must build on these.' Obviously the most rewarding way to build on them, in more ways than one, would be for Scotland once again to produce truly great players, and hopefully also leading club teams and a fine international team that we could all be proud of.

Meanwhile, one area where I believe that we can utilise our residual high standing in the world game is by becoming a kind of laboratory for controlled and responsible experiment. As Denis Law rightly says, about the only thing that hasn't changed in football is the shape of the ball.

Football is in a perpetual ferment of change, and while people of conservative disposition deprecate what they regard as tinkering, I would argue that constructive innovation, in a sensible manner, is necessary to the continuing progress of the beautiful game. Bob Crampsey, the eminent Scottish football historian, assured me that before too long the crossbar would be raised by six inches, and the goal would be widened by a foot. He was not suggesting that this should happen in Scotland before anywhere else – that wouldn't be allowed, anyway – but he felt it was inevitable, given the larger physiques of players across the world.

I wonder if the main impediment to sensible innovation is mockery. When one J. A. Brodie of Liverpool invented the goal net, he was apparently mercilessly mocked. I'm not necessarily arguing for all the ideas to come from within Scotland. All sorts of things are happening all over the world, and I'd like to see Scotland become a forward-looking nation where intelligent ideas from elsewhere are given a fair shot. Our legislators are respected, and so are our referees. That gives us a head start.

One idea involving referees that I heard of in South America is that the ref. takes the field with a small can of spray. Not to spray in a miscreant's face if he is threatened, but rather to spray on the pitch at the exact spot where he awards a free kick, and then to spray a line after he has measured out the ten paces, a line which the 'wall' must not cross.

At present what holds games up more than anything is the endless fooling around after a free kick is awarded, particularly if it is in the vicinity of the penalty area. I've seen as many as two or three minutes lost as the ref tries to line up the wall in the correct position; while he's doing this, as often as not, some comedian is moving the ball from the spot where the kick was awarded.

The spray would not disfigure the pitch, incidentally; the marking would be temporary and disappear after a few minutes. I can think of no other innovation that would be more likely to speed up the game, and eliminate tedious passages when the ball is dead.

This is, of course, old technology; what of new technology? Electronic aids and video replays, I'm not so sure about, though a chip in the goal stick would certainly help in determining whether a ball had fully crossed the line. But some country will need to be the laboratory for the testing of technology in such matters, and I don't see why Scotland should not be that country.

It is easier to innovate in terms of structures and the awarding of points. I know that Campbell Ogilive, perhaps our most imaginative legislator here in Scotland, is an enthusiast for a 'four points for an away win' rule to encourage attacking football away from home. I've also heard of a system whereby any team that has more than three 0–0 draws loses rather than gains a point if they play out a fourth one, though I'm less certain of the efficacy of this particular innovation.

I think it would make sense to have all the SPL teams playing away from home in the third round of the Scottish Cup, and for them to be seeded so that they did not play each other. I certainly think there should be a cap on the size of club squads. I don't see the need for any club having more than twenty-five eligible players in any one season. As for encouraging home-grown players, UEFA are already planning to introduce new rules to ensure a minimum number of home-grown players in each team.

I mentioned Campbell Ogilvie. I know that he and some of his colleagues are working on exciting structural proposals which, if implemented, will help to democratise our game and bridge the gap between the SPL and SFL. Because too many directors and officials in Scottish football have let us down over the years, we shouldn't blind ourselves to the fact that there are in our administrative circles some real visionaries, enemies of insularity who are possessed of genuine farsightedness.

One 'old' rule, which should be brought back, is gate-receipt sharing.

A structural change, which is often mooted, is that we should have just the one governing body. At the moment the SFA are supreme, but there are tensions – and sometimes downright silly bickering – between the ruling body and the SPL, and to a lesser extent the SFL. It is a commonplace in our Scottish game that it is not well run, but I strongly believe that most of the failures have been in the boardrooms of individual clubs.

The SFA were not responsible for the reckless post-Bosman spending frenzy, and nor are they wholly responsible for the shameful lack of investment in decent training facilities, though, on the second matter, they could no doubt have done more to incentivise the clubs, and they could have helped to provide more communal facilities. At last this is happening, especially though the national Youth Initiative, which I predict will be, in due course, an enormous success.

I know this is not a popular point to make, but I think the SFA record on discipline has been generally fair. Non-Old Firm fans such as myself tend to believe that most of the dubious refereeing decisions go against the non-Old Firm teams. This is a subjective judgement possibly based on an inherited sense of grievance that is passed from one generation of fans to the next by some mystical osmosis. I think our referees are pretty competent, and the SFA must take the credit for that. If you watch continental or indeed English football on television, it cannot be argued that the refereeing standards on display are in any way superior to ours.

The SFA are ultimately responsible for our national team and here the most important function is the appointment of the national coach. As I pointed out earlier, the record is not too bad. Indeed, if you remove Berti Vogts and Ally Macleod from the equation, over the past thirty-five years or so it has been not bad at all. Before that, the 'blazers' were at their worst, often interfering where they had no right to interfere. Petty and parochial prejudice was often the order of the day in national team selection. Denis Law, undoubtedly one of the two or three finest forwards in the world in the 1960s, was only selected four times for Scotland in the years 1967–72, when he was aged 26–31. This snub was mainly based on the extraordinary notion that he wasn't patriotic enough; he never played for a Scottish club. (That actually said far more about the stupidity of Scottish clubs, particularly his home-town club Aberdeen, who could easily have signed him when he was a precocious schoolboy scorer.)

The SFA's principal achievement over the past forty years or so has been a notably successful series of coaching courses. The three men most closely associated with these ventures are Andy Roxburgh (who was the SFA's technical director before he became Scotland's national coach, and then moved on to be UEFA's technical director), Craig Brown and Alex ['Faither'] Smith. Several people have told me that Roxburgh is far more highly regarded abroad than he is at home in Scotland.

It is indisputable that many fine managers learned the rudiments of coaching on these courses, first held at Largs and then at various other venues. Alex Smith bridles slightly when he recalls that there was considerable scepticism in the early days, directed at the 'Largs Mafia', who were by some derided as being too technical, coaches who carried clipboards and were obsessed with charts and data.

And yet many of those who went there as fresh-faced young men later returned as instructors themselves. Among them are figures such as Alex Ferguson, Walter Smith and Tommy Burns. Others who have learned a lot of what they know as managers on these courses include Alex McLeish, Gordon Strachan and Davie Moyes. The courses were never introverted or parochial; among those whom Roxburgh brought to Largs was the greatest coach of them all, the late Rinus Michels. And those who have passed through the SFA course include household names far beyond Scotland, such as Jose Mourinho.

So the SFA can take much of the credit for the fact that Scotland continues to produce and develop fine managers. Of course, great managers tend to spawn other managers. When Alex Ferguson managed Aberdeen, his players included Alex McLeish, Gordon Strachan, Neale Cooper, Mark McGhee, Eric Black, Andy Watson and Billy Stark. All of them went on to careers as managers and coaches.

There is in all this a conundrum. If we produce so many respected managers and coaches, why do we not produce better players? I asked Alex Smith about this and he surprised me by saying that there are so many difficulties with lack of facilities, a declining pool of potential players and so on, that it was almost surprising that we had as many half-decent players as we do at present. He said we actually needed far more good coaches, who were the key to the future. He emphasised that existing managers should be trying to develop not just promising players, but promising coaches, if Scottish football was to revive. His view was that there would always be one or two potentially good coaches in any professional team – not necessarily, indeed probably not, the best players – and the managers would know exactly who these players were. More would have to be done to encourage them to start their planning, during their playing careers, of a long-term career in football.

If there is one area in which our legislators have let us down in recent years it has been in that most basic of administrative functions, promotion and relegation. It seems that just about every summer we are treated to a ridiculous squabble about who is to be promoted and who is to be relegated. You'd have thought rules are rules, but apparently not as far as some of our officials are concerned.

Meanwhile, despite its reputation for conservatism, the Scottish league game has moved forward. The arrival of four Highland clubs in the 1990s, and more recently, the exciting Gretna from the other end of the country, has helped to make our league football more genuinely national. Gretna had actually played in English football for many years before being elected to the Scottish League in 2002. Bankrolled by a remarkable entrepreneur called Brooks Mileson, their progress continues to be spectacular.

Although Inverness Caley Thistle's crowds have been disappointing, their progress through the divisions has been most refreshing. And all over Scotland, from Balmoor Stadium at Peterhead to the Strathclyde Homes Stadium at Dumbarton, there are trig new grounds. The capacities may be modest – and realistic – but at least fans are now being treated with some respect in terms of their viewing conditions.

But I'd better stop, for this is becoming almost complacent, and that would never do.

CHAPTER 7

ENVOI

Football is the beautiful game, the popular game, and the cruel game. It is probably the cruellest of all sports.

This is because the outcome of a game of football, unlike tennis, golf, rugby, cricket, or basketball, to cite a few other popular sports, is decided by very low scores. The majority of league football games across the globe finish with three or fewer goals having been scored.

The most common score in organised football is actually a draw, 1–1, with the second most frequent score being 1–0. When three or fewer goals are scored over a minimum of ninety minutes, there is obviously scope for unfairness, even for grotesque miscarriages of natural justice. There is sometimes scant correlation between the persistent trend of the outfield play and the actual scoring. Teams can totally dominate a game and still lose. Or to put it more crudely, the score often lies.

This, I am convinced, makes the game eminently suitable for that wonderful and gloomy construct, the Scottish psyche. You can be defeated, and still, with validity, claim to be the superior team. You can be defeated, and legitimately insist that you were robbed. Thus we have the syndrome of glorious failure, so beloved of so many of us Scots down the years, and its concomitant, splendid defiance in the face of bad results.

I was somewhat ponderously putting this theory to an expatriate Scottish intellectual when he cut me short and said 'Yeah, but glorious failure has recently been more like justified failure.'

And this has certainly been true of the national team, which is closely associated with our national sense of identity.

In the 1960s, when we had an abundance of world-class players, we could not qualify for the World Cup Finals. For example, the great Jim Baxter never graced the final stage of a World Cup with his extraordinary skills. Then, as the talent began to dwindle away, we suddenly discovered the knack of getting to World Cup Finals, though we could never progress to the second stage. About six years ago, the stream of even half-decent international players seemed to dry up. The dearth of talent was compounded by the inferior management of Berti Vogts. We plummeted down the world rankings, from a respectable twentieth six years ago, away down to the low eighties. There was nothing glorious about failure any more.

At the same time, the Tartan Army, Scotland's magnificently loyal supporters, had reinvented themselves. Arrogance and swagger were expunged; a new self-deprecating bonhomie became the order of the day. This was all very pleasant, but it confirmed the sense that they were no longer particularly defiant. The splendour of defiance, which used to characterise Scottish football, had faded away, to be replaced by the acceptability of humiliation. Or so it seemed.

And yet at club level there is still a passionate intensity. Attendances, particularly outside the Old Firm, are not what they should be, but no one can gainsay the passion of so many ordinary Scottish fans. Jock Stein once opined that a game without a crowd is nothing, and the Scottish crowd, at its best, is well informed, passionate and slightly mad, all at the same time. You care desperately about something unfolding before you that you have no control over. This is fate. The script has not been written. This is the glory of spectator sport in general, and football in particular. If you go to just about any other form of public entertainment or cultural event, the script has been written. The interpretation may vary, but the outcome is pre-ordained.

If low scoring makes football cruel, it can be even more cruel if a goal or goals are scored in the final few minutes. I remember this so well from my days as a football reporter for the *Scotsman*, sending over reports of Wednesday night games in takes for the next morning's paper. Just as you started your intro, at about 9.10, some bugger would score an equaliser or a winner; you'd have to rip up the fancy intro and start all over again.

Football fans have a tremendous, well-honed, lovingly nurtured sense of fate. Sometimes it is almost as if they want the worst to happen, in the dying minutes of a game, to confirm their sense of the inevitability of it all going wrong.

This is particularly true when a team is desperately clinging to a one-goal lead, which should have been more. Here is a scenario specially made for the suffering Scottish fan. It was perhaps most classically played out forty years ago, in October 1965, when Scotland played Poland at Hampden in a crucial World Cup qualifier. They had done the difficult part earlier in the year, drawing with a strong and gritty Poland team away from home. Now, resplendent with an array of talent we'd die for in contemporary Scotland, and before a Hampden crowd of over 100,000, they were, so we thought, about to take a giant step out of the World Cup wilderness.

The forward line was Willie Henderson, Billy Bremner, Alan Gilzean, Denis Law and Willie Johnston. Can I repeat these wonderful names? At least three of these players were indubitably of world class. The manager was the great Jock Stein.

After only fifteen minutes, Billy McNeill headed Scotland into the lead, from a Willie Henderson corner. Scotland dominated the rest of the half, dazzling but deceiving, as only Scottish teams can. 'We should have killed them,' said Denis Law later. 'We should have been leading by five.' Slowly but surely, as Scotland could not score the elusive second goal they undoubtedly deserved, Poland gained confidence.

Five minutes from the end, Poland equalised. Three minutes later, they went ahead. Jock Stein said after this most bitter of 2–1 defeats: 'I have nothing to say.' Raymond Jacobs wrote in the next day's *Glasgow Herald* that after a first half of pace and enthusiasm, Scotland ended up reduced to a condition of total ruin. I love that phrase: 'A condition of total ruin'.

Except that it couldn't have been total ruin, for a lot more that was really ruinous had still to happen. Total ruin? You should have seen us under Berti Vogts, Raymond. But we've got past that stage. I'm an optimist. The good times are coming back. Maybe even better times than we ever had before.

In January 2005, on a dreich Glasgow morning, I visited the Scottish Football Museum, deep inside Hampden. I found it good value for the £5. I was surprised to find that I was the only customer, and that remained the case although I was there for over an hour. I admit that I spent quite a lot of this time – well, OK, maybe seven or eight minutes – sitting in a corner where a television screen was showing constant repeats of Archie Gemmill's wonderful World Cup goal against Holland, scored far, far away in Mendoza in 1978.

There was something symbolic about the scenario; not so much the goal, glorious and defiant in its improvised brilliance as it was, but the fact that this telly was playing just the one goal, over and over and over again, with the one punter staring at the little screen, utterly mesmerised. It was like a scene from some existential Scandinavian art-house movie.

Don't get me wrong. That goal was truly great. In fact the more you watched it, the better it got. But always remember: the day after it was scored, we were on our way back home, defiant, yes, but also abject and disgraced.

My hope, my not completely irrational hope, is that one day that little screen – or maybe a larger one – will be showing something else to a big crowd of constantly ecstatic watchers. The goal that won it.

SELECT GLOSSARY

Dens Park	Home of Dundee FC.
Easter Road	Easter Road Stadium, Edinburgh, home of Hibs.
FIFA	Fédération Internationale de Football Associations, world football's governing body, founded in 1904 and based in Zurich, Switzerland.
Hampden Park	Home of Queen's Park FC and Scotland's national football stadium; the holder of many crowd records and venue for the greatest club game of all time, Real Madrid (7) v. Eintracht Frankfurt (3) in the European Cup final of 1960. Situated in the Mount Florida area of Glasgow.
Ibrox	Ibrox Stadium, Glasgow, home of Rangers FC.
MSP	Member of the Scottish Parliament.
New Firm	Aberdeen and Dundee United (briefly, in the 1980s).
Old Firm	Celtic and Rangers.
Parkhead	Celtic Park, Glasgow, home of Celtic FC.
Pittodrie	Pittodrie Stadium, home of Aberdeen FC.
Rugby Park	Home of Kilmarnock FC.
SFA	Scottish Football Association, Scotttish football's supreme governing body, founded in 1873 in Glasgow and based at Hampden Park. Has over 6,000 affiliated clubs and over 130,000 registered players.
SFL	Scottish Football League.
SPL	Scottish Premier League.
Tannadice Park	Home of Dundee United FC.
Tynecastle	Tynecastle Stadium, Edinburgh, home of Hearts.
UEFA	Union des Associations Européennes de Football, European football's governing body. Based in Nyon, Switzerland.
Wembley	England's national stadium, in North London. Currently being redeveloped.

ACKNOWLEDGEMENTS

I am most grateful to the following for their assistance:

Alex Barr; John Beattie: Christophe Berra; Mark Beverley; Graham Birse; Alan Bruce; Tommy Burns; Sir Peter Burt; Denis Campbell; Dennis Canavan MSP; Bob Crampsey; Jack Davidson; Adrian Dempster; Prof. Tom Devine FBA; Barry Divers: Mark Elliot; Laura Esslemont; Sir Alex Ferguson; Fred Forrester: Roddy Forsyth; Lord Foulkes; Alasdair Fraser; Doug Gillon; David Glen; Donald Gorrie MSP; Alan Hansen; Richard Holloway; Prof. Grant Jarvie; Russell Kyle; Lyn Laffin; John Loughton; Andy Lynch; Simon Lynch; Kenny MacAskill MSP; Ian McConnell; Colin McDiarmid; Lynsey Macdonald; Lindsay McFarlane; Jack McLean; Bruce McKain; Kevin McKenna; Louise McKenzie; Gregor McSkimming; Willie Miller; Jamie Moffat; Brian Monteith MSP; Steve Morrow; Kathleen Munro; Sarah Nelson; Campbell Ogilvie; Steven Pressley; Catherine Reid; Hugh Reid; Rob Robertson; David Ross (twice); Trevor Royle; Jan Rutherford; Ian Scott; Liz Short; Alex Smith MBE; George Smith; Angie Traynor; Alex Totten; Kevin Toner; Brian Viner; Graham Walker; Jack Webster; David Will; and Fraser Wishart.

I particularly wish to thank two people: Drew Allan, Hibs superfan and all round good guy, for far more help than I deserved, generously and unstintingly given; and to John Crawford, strategy director of Halogen Communications, for his constant interest and support.

INDEX

Names beginning 'Mac' and 'Mc' are indexed as spelt